Financing Development in Latin America

Each volume in this series is designed to make available to students important new work on key historical problems and periods that they encounter in their courses. Every volume is devoted to a central topic or theme, and the most important aspects of this are dealt with by specially commissioned essays from specialists in the period. The editorial Introduction reviews the problem or period as a whole, and each essay provides a balanced assessment of the particular aspect, pointing out the areas of development and controversy and indicating where conclusions can be drawn or where further work is necessary. An annotated bibliography serves as an up-to-date guide to further reading.

Financing Development in Latin America

EDITED BY

KEITH GRIFFIN

Macmillan
St Martin's Press

First published 1971 by
MACMILLAN AND CO LTD
London and Basingstoke
Associated companies in New York Toronto
Dublin Melbourne Johannesburg and Madras

Library of Congress Catalog Card No. 70–145587

SBN 333 09131 0 (hard cover)

Printed in Great Britain by
RICHARD CLAY (THE CHAUCER PRESS), LTD
Bungay, Suffolk

Contents

Preface

THERE is a considerable body of literature on the general aspects of economic development and on the problems of resource allocation and planning for faster growth, but there is relatively little material available in convenient form for the student interested in the financial aspects of development policy. The intention in preparing this volume was to examine the various ways in which resources could be mobilised in order to accelerate growth and diminish inequality in Latin America. We have concentrated on the problem of development, and ignored other possible objectives of public policy, in the belief that the promotion of greater material well-being for the mass of the population is, or ought to be, the primary concern of all governments in the region.

This approach has forced us to be comprehensive and to consider methods of raising finance that often are neglected in studies which concentrate on taxation. In addition to conventional fiscal instruments, we have examined the role played by nationalised enterprises, the possibilities of financing growth via inflation, the connection between income distribution and private savings, and the contribution of foreign capital. Each author has been free to develop his argument as he wished and no attempt has been made to present all sides of each issue. We have tried instead to provoke discussion and stimulate further research.

K. B. G.

Oxford
May 1970

Introduction: Monopoly Power, Material Progress and the Economic Surplus

KEITH GRIFFIN

LATIN AMERICA is a volatile region. Accounts of riot, revolt, rebellion and revolution dot the pages of our newspapers. At the same time it is a region of palace coups – which through change succeed in changing nothing – and of lengthy military or civilian dictatorships – which occasionally change a great deal. The region is a cornucopia of momentous events and ephemeral happenings. It includes the first and the most recent of the great revolutions in this century. But it is also a region of great injustice, where the right to own thousands of acres of land (with no obligation to cultivate them) is enshrined in constitutions. It is a continent where attempts by the weak and the poor to organise themselves for political action often are ruthlessly suppressed in the name of law and order. It is also a continent where the disappointments of a football match can ignite passions and lead to violent international conflict.

Despite the bewildering variety of contemporary political activity in the region, most of the Latin American republics have inherited from the past certain institutional characteristics which profoundly affect the structure and performance of the economy. The institutions are not, of course, identical in each nation, but they serve a common purpose in concentrating economic resources in a few hands. In the most general and abstract terms, the concept of monopoly power is the key to understanding Latin America.

(a) Origins of Monopoly

From the very beginning of the sixteenth century, when Latin America was first incorporated into the world economic system, monopoly has been the most prominent feature of the economy. In the early colonial period labour was the scarce resource, and institutions were created to ensure that this resource was available in large quantities and at low cost to those who held power. Scarcity was translated into abundance, for the few.

For about a hundred years mining was the most important economic activity, and the central economic problem was how to amass and organise the large labour force needed to extract and transport precious metals. At first the *conquistadores* resorted to slavery, but enslavement of the indigenous population was prohibited by Spain in 1528. (Negro slavery, however, was not prohibited. African slave labour, in fact, was introduced almost immediately on the sugar plantations of the tropical lowlands of Brazil, Venezuela and the Caribbean islands.) Next, the *encomienda* system was devised, under which the captains of conquest were granted rights and authority over the Indian population. This system enabled the Spaniards to undertake desired investment in the mining sector, supply themselves with the necessary consumption goods and channel substantial savings to Spain. One way of looking at the *encomienda* and similar institutions is as a primitive tax system in which obligations were discharged in several forms – by payment in commodities (usually foodstuffs), in specie (normally gold), and in the form of labour services (e.g. the *mita*).

The systems devised for controlling and organising labour were effective in squeezing a surplus from the indigenous population and transferring it to the European conquerors. Indeed, quite often more than the surplus was extracted, and a combination of greed, disease and warfare pushed the standard of living below the subsistence level and led to a rapid decline of the native population. An alien minority enjoyed rapid material progress, while the majority collapsed into underdevelopment.

By the middle of the seventeenth century the mining boom had passed its peak and the centre of economic activity shifted to agriculture. At first livestock production predominated, but by the eighteenth century food grains were more important in most parts of the region. This shift from mining to agriculture was accompanied by the decline of the *encomienda* system and a reduction in the direct exploitation of Indian labour. The population ceased to decline, and in fact began slowly to expand. The increased emphasis on agriculture, on the other hand, led to a sharp rise in the demand for land, and labour was replaced by land as the scarce factor of production. Once again, institutions were created to ensure that the scarce resource was monopolised by those who held political power.

Monopoly of land, of course, gave the landowners considerable command over labour, since in an agrarian economy one's livelihood depends upon access to land. A single institution, the *latifundia* system, was sufficient to enable a small class to control both land and labour and to appropriate for themselves most of the surplus income above subsistence. The precise way in which this was done varied from place to place and time to time. The *latifundia* system has not been static; on the contrary, it has been capable of adapting to changed circumstances, and particularly to changes in the land:labour ratio, in a remarkably effective way.

The *latifundium* or *hacienda* is a multi-enterprise institution composed of the *empresa patronal* (that portion of the land managed directly by the landowner or *patrón*) plus peasant holdings. In other words, the management (but not the ownership) of the *hacienda* is divided between the *patrón* and the peasants, and the proportion managed by each is influenced by the relative bargaining strength of the two protagonists. In particular, the balance of strength swings in favour of the *empresa patronal* as labour becomes less scarce relative to land, and hence the bargaining position of the landlord increases. On the other hand, the growth of employment opportunities in urban areas would tend to weaken the power of the landlord. Similarly, the *empresa patronal* would tend to pay for labour services with land when land is abundant, and in cash when labour is abundant. Thus the form of labour payment (in land or in cash) and the division of managerial responsibility (between the peasants and the *patrón*) are sensitive to the degree of control over the factors of production which the landlords exercise.

The relative strength of the landlord *vis-à-vis* the workers depends on many things: the degree of monopoly of land and of other resources, such as water, capital and technology; the size and rate of growth of the labour force; the organisational strength of the rural population and their level of education; the extent and type of investment in agriculture (e.g. tractors reduce the demand for labour whereas irrigation raises it) and the number and rate of growth of job opportunities outside agriculture. These are the forces at play, and they lead to four basic types of *latifundia*.[1]

First, when labour is very scarce relative to land, the *patrón* acts as a rentier. The *empresa patronal* is in this case quite small, most of the land being rented to peasants who undertake virtually all of the managerial responsibilities and who become, in effect, small entrepreneurs. Second, as labour becomes less scarce the *empresa patronal* expands.

The labour employed on the land managed directly by the landlord is paid with rights to use land. The rest of the land remains under the management of peasants, as in the first case. Third, the growth of the labour force leads to increasing relative scarcity of land and abundance of labour. The landlords respond to this by increasing further the size of the *empresa patronal*. The landlord hires labourers for a money wage, although some payment in land remains. Only a small part of the land is farmed by peasant entrepreneurs. Finally, as land becomes very scarce relative to labour, the *empresa patronal* expands until it occupies the entire *hacienda*. The permanent labour force is paid almost entirely in money wages and seasonal labour is provided by workers from the *minifundia* located on the fringes of the *latifundium*. Thus as the labour: land ratio rises, the bargaining strength of the landlord is increased. This, in turn, leads to an expansion of the *empresa patronal*, a decline in the number of peasant entrepreneurs, the creation of a rural proletariat of landless workers, and a shift in the means of payment from land to cash. These changes, obviously, tend to alter the distribution of income in favour of property owners and to increase their share of the economic surplus.

Of course, Latin America today is not primarily an agrarian region. Non-agricultural activities account for most of the domestic product, varying from about 70 per cent of G.D.P. in Guatemala to about 85 per cent in Uruguay. One might imagine that as urban industrial and service activities increased the monopoly power of landowners would decline and material progress would be more widely spread among the population. This has not occurred, however.

The reason for this is that urban development has been financed largely by private savings out of the surplus appropriated by the landowning class. There is no 'modern capitalist class' which is distinct from the 'traditional, feudal landowning class'. On the contrary, there is a considerable overlap of the urban industrial and professional groups and the large landlords. For example, case studies of twelve *latifundia* in Guatemala produced only one example of a landowner who lived on his farm and devoted himself exclusively to agriculture. All of the others lived in Guatemala City. Six of these were engaged in commerce, two were industrialists, one was a financier, another a doctor and the last an ex-military man.[2] Similarly, Frank reports that in Peru, 'Of the 45 family and corporate entities on the Board of Directors of that country's *Sociedad Nacional de Agricultura*, 56 per cent are important stockholders in banks and financial companies, 53 per cent own stock in insurance companies, 75 per cent are owners of companies engaged in urban construction or real estate, 56 per cent have investments in commercial firms, and 64 per cent are important stockholders in one or more petroleum companies.'[3] And again, a study of Argentina has shown that thirty-two landowning family groups 'control or influence 54 per cent of the capital of the industrial companies listed in the [Buenos Aires] stock market in 1960'.[4]

Thus we see that a monopoly structure which originated in mining was transferred first to the agricultural sector and then to industry and services. The economic system evolved in the course of time, but the basic feature of monopoly persisted. This, of course, was inevitable, since expansion in one sector could occur only by investing part of the surplus generated in another. As long as the surplus was owned and controlled by a small group monopoly was bound to be perpetuated.

(b) *Income Distribution and the Surplus*

The monopoly structure that evolved in Latin America has been a major determinant of the composition of output, the level of efficiency within each sector and the distribution of income.

First, in most Latin American countries the gross national product is small, *per capita* income is low and its distribution is unequal. As a result, the level of domestic demand for most commodities is insufficient to justify large-scale production. Given the size and structure of the economy, it is almost inevitable, particularly in the early stages, that production should be biased towards exports. Monopoly concentration restricted domestic demand, and this compelled the economies to become export-oriented. Of course, some production for the home market occurred, but apart from basic foodstuffs this consisted primarily of the production of luxury consumer goods for the upper classes. Again, the reason is that there was little demand for anything else.

Thus a distinct and typical pattern of production tended to emerge. Production for export centred on the large *haciendas* and plantations and in the mining sector (including petroleum). Relatively little labour was employed in these activities, since extensive methods of cultivation were used on the *haciendas* and capital-intensive methods were used for extracting minerals. Production of food for domestic consumption was confined largely to the *minifundia*, and it was here that most of the labour force was employed. Even today, there are only four countries in Latin America where less than a third of the labour force is employed in agriculture, viz. Venezuela, Chile, Uruguay and Argentina; in most of the others the proportion is nearer two-thirds. The industrial sector usually is quite small, employing less than 15 per cent of the population and producing mostly luxury consumer goods, although in the larger countries some capital goods industries exist.

Second, the structure of an economy affects not only the pattern of production, it also affects efficiency. Theorists have argued for a long time that a monopoly would tend to have a lower output and higher unit costs than a competitive industry. Empirical research in developed countries, however, seems to suggest that the quantitative significance of monopolistic inefficiency is low. For example, Professor Harberger's study of the U.S. economy in 1929 shows that the elimination of monopolies would raise the national income by, at most, 0·07 per cent.[5] One must not conclude from this, however, that inefficiency in Latin America is unimportant. On the contrary, there is evidence that inefficiency is widespread and of considerable importance.

A recent study by Henry Bruton of the growth experience of Argentina, Brazil, Chile, Colombia and Mexico in the period 1940–64 concludes that the growth in 'pure' productivity – i.e. productivity which cannot be attributed to changing capacity utilisation – has been approximately zero since 1955.[6] In a study of a single Latin American country, Chile, Harberger used extreme assumptions in an effort to determine what would be the maximum possible gain from increased efficiency. His guess was that an improvement in the allocation of capital and labour might raise national income by 9–15 per cent.[7] In a study of the agricultural sector of Colombia, it has been estimated that a more efficient use of resources in agriculture would raise output in that sector by 17 per cent.[8] Similarly, it has been shown that a land reform in Guatemala, by improving efficiency, would lead to a substantial increase in output and employment.[9] There are no comparable studies of industrial inefficiency in Latin America, but the fragmentary data that we do have imply that it is considerable. Leland Johnson, for instance, estimated that for each dollar of foreign exchange saved by the Chilean programme of import substitution in the automobile industry, two to four dollars of local resources were consumed.[10] Thus inefficiency is not negligible, and its cause is monopoly.

The third consequence of the monopolistic structure of the Latin American economies is a highly unequal distribution of income. In general, the richest 10 per cent of income recipients appropriate about 40 per cent of the national income, while the bottom 40 per cent of households receive only about 15 per cent. Evidence from the three largest Latin American countries, which account for approximately 63 per cent of the population of the region, is presented in the table below.

Table 1. Distribution of Income in Three Latin American Countries, *c.* 1960

Deciles	Argentina[a]	Brazil[b]	Mexico[a]
0–40	17·3	14·4	10·5
40–90	43·6	44·1	48·0
90–100	39·1	41·5	41·5

[a] Family income.
[b] Personal income.

Source: ECLA, *Estudio Sobre la Distribución del Ingreso en América Latina* (1967).

The best data on income distribution refer to Mexico, and it is instructive to see what has happened in that country in the last quarter of a century. A study by Mrs Navarrete of the period 1940–50 indicates that average real wages, measured in 1950 prices, rose by more than 30 per cent, viz. from \$266 to \$355. At the same time, the average agricultural wage declined by over 10 per cent – from \$95 to \$85 – and the average non-agricultural income fell by 6 per cent – from \$550 to \$517.[11] In other words, the rise in the average wage was a result of a transfer of labour from low income to higher income sectors, but within each sector the average wage actually declined.

In 1940, about 37 per cent of the labour force was in the higher wage sector and 63 per cent in the low wage sector. In 1950, by coincidence, the proportion was exactly the reverse. Obviously, the 37 per cent of the labour force still in the low wage sector in 1950 were worse off. Moreover, the 37 per cent of the work force who were originally in the higher wage sector also were worse off, since their real wages declined as a result of the influx of workers into their job categories. The only beneficiaries were the 26 per cent who transferred from one wage category to another – and their average income rose 445 per cent! The remaining 74 per cent of the labour force, however, experienced a decline in their standard of living.

Beginning in 1950 we have data for Mexico on the distribution of income by households.[12] Between 1950 and 1963–4 there seems to have been a sharp redistribution of income against the richest 10 per cent of households, their share falling from 49·0 to 41·5 per cent. At the same time, the share of the poorest 40 per cent of households fell relatively even more, viz. from 14·3 per cent to 10·5 per cent.[13] The beneficiaries of the redistribution were essentially those families which occupied the eighth and ninth deciles, i.e. the upper middle classes. The share of this group rose from 19·4 per cent in 1950 to 29 per cent in 1963–4. Thus even in Mexico, a country which has combined a social revolution with rapid growth, the mass of the poor have been excluded from enjoying the fruits of material progress. In most of the rest of Latin America conditions are even worse, since there has been neither a revolution nor rapid growth.

Knowledge of the distribution of income clearly is important in reaching a judgement about the well-being of a country's population. But in assessing the investment and growth potential of a country – and in evaluating the use it has made of that potential – it is the size and distribution of the economic surplus which is most important.

This point can be illustrated with a hypothetical calculation based on Brazilian data. In 1966 Brazil's *per capita* income was about $333. Let us assume that the minimum income required for subsistence in Brazil is $150. The economic surplus, hence, is about $183 per head, and the total surplus is roughly 55 per cent of the national income. This is a measure of the proportion of total resources which in principle could be used to finance economic development. We know from Table 1 that the top 10 per cent of the population receive about 41·5 per cent of total income. The surplus of this tiny minority of wealthy individuals is equal to two-thirds of the total surplus of the country, and it is the use that is made by the rich of their surplus which largely determines the fate of the nation.

In general, there are three alternative uses for the surplus. It may be dissipated on luxury consumption, it may be channelled into private savings and investment or it may be transferred to the government. In turn, the government may use the resources to finance unproductive expenditures (e.g. monuments and defence) or development (e.g. technical education and investments in infrastructure). In other words, the surplus may be squandered or used productively, and this can occur in either the private or the public sectors.

Ideally, we would like to know – for each country – the share of the surplus in national income and the proportion of the surplus that is used productively. Unfortunately, the data for such calculations do not exist. We can, however, following the conventional analysis, consider the determinants of total (and private) savings in G.N.P.

Most theories of consumption would lead one to expect that consumption as a percentage of G.N.P. would be much higher in poor countries than in rich and, conversely, the savings ratio would be much lower. In fact the relationship – if it exists at all – is very weak. This was first demonstrated by Simon Kuznets, who examined the data for a large number of countries for the post-Second World War period.

Professor Kuznets organised countries into seven groups in accordance with their income *per capita* and then estimated private consumption as a percentage of G.N.P. for each group. He found that in Group I – which includes the very rich countries such as the U.K. and U.S.A. – private consumption accounted for about 65 per cent of G.N.P. On the other hand, in Group VII – which includes extremely poor countries such as Nigeria and Burma – the percentage was only slightly higher, viz. 73·1 per cent. Kuznets said, 'it is surprising that the range of the share of private consumption expenditures for countries by *per capita* income is so narrow'.[14] Even more surprising is that within the five groups of underdeveloped countries there is no association whatever between the private consumption ratio and *per capita* income. Group III (which includes Argentina and Chile) and Group IV (which includes Colombia) both had a higher share of private consumption in G.N.P. than the poorest countries in Group VII.

In an earlier study Kuznets examined long-run trends in investment and savings in a few countries which had reliable data extending back to the nineteenth century. He concluded from this research that 'the rather simple relations assumed in much economic analysis – close associations between levels of income and the savings proportions and between capital formation proportions and the rate of growth – are not confirmed by the long-term records. The relation between capital formation and *per capita* income (as a determinant) and the rate of growth (as an effect) is too irregular and variable to warrant being given much weight in any realistic analysis. The association between national capital formation proportions or savings rates and levels of income is not close. . . .'[15]

An examination of the data from Latin America confirms the view that the association between the savings rate and the level of *per capita* income is not close. A cross-section econometric analysis of twenty Latin American economies by Luis Landau suggests that the correlation between the savings ratio (S/Y) and *per capita* income (Y/P) is positive but weak.[16] In fact, statistically the estimated equations ought to be considered unsatisfactory. Two of his many equation for the years 1956 and 1961 are presented below.

Results for 1956:
$$\log (S/Y) = -4\cdot58 + 0\cdot46 \log (Y/P); \ R^2 = 0\cdot30$$
$$(0\cdot17)$$

Results for 1961:
$$\log (S/Y) = -4\cdot92 + 0\cdot49 \log (Y/P); \ R^2 = 0\cdot21$$
$$(0\cdot23)$$

Landau also ran regressions on time series for each of the twenty countries to see if there was any association over time between *per capita* savings and *per capita* income. He concludes that 'the results are generally poor'.[17] In fact, in three cases the association is inverse (but statistically not significant); in another nine cases the standard error is more than one-third the size of the slope coefficient; of the remaining eight equations, four have an R^2 of less than 0·50. That is, of the twenty equations, only four are even moderately satisfactory.

A study of Brazil, the largest country in the region, indicates that the savings rate, at best, remained roughly constant between 1939 and 1960 – despite the rapid rate of growth of G.N.P. and increase in *per capita* income that occurred in that period.[18] The average savings rate in Brazil in the eight years of wartime hardship, 1939–46, was about 18·5 per cent, whereas in the last eight years of the period, 1953–60, it had declined to 16·1 per cent. All the evidence we have about Latin America indicates that knowledge of *per capita* income does not enable one to predict accurately the total savings ratio, the private savings ratio or the government savings ratio. For example, *per capita* income is virtually the same in Brazil and Colombia, yet the total net domestic savings rate is considerably higher in the former. Similarly, in the period 1962–4 the private net savings ratio was about 4 per cent in Venezuela and 7 per cent in Honduras, yet the *per capita* income of Venezuela is four times that of Honduras. Again in 1962–4 the government net savings ratio was about 5 per cent in Ecuador and 1 per cent in Costa Rica, despite the fact that Costa Rica is twice as prosperous as Ecuador.

Many economists believe that an unequal distribution of income is likely to be associated with a high savings rate. This is supposed to be true in part because the rich save more than the poor and in part because the rich have a larger taxable capacity. Yet if one compares the percentage of total income accruing to the top 10 per cent of income earners with the net domestic savings ratio, one finds there is no positive association between personal income inequality and national thriftiness. For example, the upper 10 per cent of income earners in Chile, Colombia, Guatemala and India receive, respectively, 47–9 per cent, 48 per cent, 44 per cent and 33–7 per cent of total income, while the savings ratios in the same countries are about 3 per cent, 6 per cent, 4 per cent and 10 per cent respectively. India, the least inegalitarian of the four countries and poorer than every Latin American country except Haiti, has the highest savings ratio.

Similarly, if one examines individual countries it is not obvious that the rich always save more than the poor. Kaldor's research on Chile suggests that 'the proportion of national resources engaged in producing goods and services for the luxury consumption of the well-to-do is at least three to four times as high in Chile as in Britain'. Moreover, 'British property owners appear to have saved 48 per cent of their post-tax income . . . whereas the Chileans saved 26 per cent . . .'[19] Professor Kaldor relied on national income data for his analysis. His results are supported, however, by microeconomic data. Marvin Sternberg, for instance, studied the consumption and savings pattern of twenty *latifundistas* in Chile's Central Valley, and his research indicates that the mean proportion of disposable income consumed was 83·6 per cent and the median was 99 per cent.[20] The poor could hardly save less. Unfortunately, we do not have detailed studies of the savings habits of the rural poor in Latin America, but fragmentary evidence suggests that it is not always insignificant. In Colombia, for example, the savings department of the Caja de Crédito Agrario accounts for 53 per cent of all the institutionalised savings in the country, yet the average deposit in this bank is only about $20. Research on rural savings in India indicates that gross cash savings range from 8 per cent upwards, and a cash savings ratio of about 12 per cent is typical. If non-cash savings are included, the savings ratio in rural areas rises to approximately 20 per cent.[21] If these figures are correct they imply that the miserably poor Indian peasant is saving a much larger fraction of his surplus than the upper classes of Latin America. Finally, a study of Mexico casts further doubt on the proposition that a high share of property income or profits leads to a high savings rate. Sturmthal's study concludes that 'for the period 1939–46, while the share of profits rose from 26·2 to 45·1 per cent of net domestic product at factor cost, the share of savings in the gross national product remained below the level of the base year, while the subsequent slight drop of the profit share (to 41·4 per cent for 1950) was accompanied by a substantial rise in the ratio of savings to gross national product'.[22] The author concludes that 'the shift to profits in the distribution of the national income was not very effective in stimulating capital formation'.[23]

In summary, monopoly power in Latin America is largely responsible for the great – and sometimes growing – inequality in the distribution of income. As a result of this inequality the surplus is concentrated in the hands of a small minority of the population, and this enables the economy in principle, despite the relatively low level of average income per head, to achieve a high rate of savings. In fact, however, the private savings rate in Latin America is quite low. Thus the obvious disadvantages of monopoly and inequality are not compensated by a high rate of accumulation of capital and a rapid rate of material progress. The evidence we have suggests that if the growth rate is to be sharply accelerated, and particularly if this is to be accompanied by reduced inequality, the government must assume greater responsibility for financing development. Whether this is possible within the existing political context is a question to which we now turn.

(c) *The Role and Nature of Government*

The government, obviously, is a powerful instrument. But who controls the government and what are their objectives? Economists tend to assume automatically that the major objective of government is to accelerate economic development. On reflection, however, it is not certain that this is so. No one, for example, pretends nowadays that the purpose of a colonial government is to promote the material welfare of the subject peoples. Marx, certainly, had no illusions about this. He was quite convinced that colonial regimes were primarily interested in extracting a surplus for the benefit of an alien class. Writing about British colonialism in India, he said:

> There have been in Asia, generally, from immemorial times, but three departments of government: that of Finance, or the plunder of the interior; that of War, or the plunder of the exterior; and finally, the department of Public Works. . . . Now, the British in East India accepted from their predecessors the departments of finance and of war, but they have neglected entirely that of public works.[24]

Is the same true in Latin America? The answer, I think, is No. Certainly public works have not been neglected entirely. In fact, total gross investment in Latin America usually is about 18 per cent of G.N.P., and roughly one-third of this is in the public sector. In other words, state investment accounts for about 6 per cent of gross product. This, admittedly, is a small proportion, but it is not negligible. On the other hand, there is virtually no 'plunder of the exterior' today. The countries of Latin America, at least for the time being, are unlikely to engage in major military conflicts. Minor clashes sometimes occur, e.g. the 'football war' between Honduras and El Salvador, but these are not a major feature of international relations within the region. Such international violence as occurs in Latin America usually is conducted or instigated by the United States. Military budgets are relatively small in most Latin American countries, accounting on average for 15 per cent of government expenditure.

What about 'plunder of the interior'? Here the analysis becomes much more complex and the charge cannot readily be dismissed. To reach a judgement we need to know something about the attitude of government to public policy; the level of taxation, its structure and its incidence; the pattern of public expenditure and the groups which benefit from public expenditure.

Gunnar Myrdal has claimed that the recently independent countries of Asia 'are all "soft states"', both in that policies decided on are often not enforced, if they are enacted at all, and in that the authorities, even when framing policies, are reluctant to place obligations on people'.[25] In other words, the attitude of government is permissive: little is required of citizens; the authorities use the carrot rather than the stick. In Latin America, however, in contrast to Asia, governments are not in general 'soft'. The attitude of government to certain groups in the community is indeed permissive, but the general policy is one of 'firmness'.

Evidence of 'firmness' is not hard to find. Well over half the people in Latin America live under authoritarian regimes, and five of the South American republics now have military dictatorships, namely, Argentina, Brazil, Peru, Bolivia and Paraguay. These regimes, and others in the region, are not unwilling to use the stick to enforce their policies. In not a few Latin American countries peasant organisations have been disbanded, labour unions intimidated and student movements suppressed. In some instances a critical press has been censored or closed and outspoken individuals have been deprived of their civil rights, thrown into jail or forced into exile. In other words, governments have been willing, when they thought it necessary, to crush all effective opposition. The state could hardly be less 'soft'.

At the same time there is the corruption, black marketeering, tax evasion and non-enforcement of regulations which characterise Myrdal's 'soft state'. Similarly, the use of the armed forces to suppress mass opposition movements suggests that Marx's 'plunder of the interior' may be a common phenomenon. In short, Latin America may have succeeded in blending together certain characteristics of both colonial and post-colonial Asian governments.

It is hardly surprising that this should be so. We have argued at considerable length above that the central feature of the Latin American economy is monopoly power, i.e. the control of the scarce factors of production – land, capital and technology – by a small minority of property owners. This concentration of economic power is sustained and reinforced by a monopoly of political power. The two, in fact, go together: without political control the power of the monopolists would be gravely weakened. In several countries, as we have seen, the interests of property owners are safeguarded through military dictatorship.[26] In at least one country (Nicaragua) power has been retained by a single wealthy family. In another country (Colombia) the two traditional parties representing the interests of landlords and industrialists have formally agreed to alternate control of the executive and share power in the legislature. In two others (Guatemala and Bolivia) the majority did come to power for a short period, but counter-revolutionary groups soon regained control. In yet another (Chile) internal tranquillity and the essence of the status quo have been maintained until recently by the timely introduction of small and incomplete reforms.

There can be little doubt that throughout most of Latin America political control is retained by those who own property and exercise monopoly power. This, obviously, affects the role and nature of government, since the objectives of the government must ultimately coincide with those of the dominant economic groups. One must then ask whether the dominant economic groups give a high priority to economic development. It certainly is not evident that they do.

It is unlikely, of course, that economic growth as such would be resisted, provided it occurred as a result of voluntary action by those who possess the surplus or arose from improvements in external conditions – such as an increase in export prices. On the other hand, if there were a conflict between growth and the maintenance of monopoly power, the growth objective would be relinquished. Similarly, the dominant minority – and the governments which represent them – can be expected to oppose measures to increase employment and improve the distribution of income, unless they are compelled to make these concessions in order to remain in power. In other words, our hypothesis is that economic development is not a major objective of Latin American governments.

This hypothesis has numerous implications for the organisation of government and the finance of development. First, one would expect that the public sector would be relatively small, the proportion of the surplus transferred to the government would be low and the total tax burden, i.e. the ratio of taxes to national income, would be slight. Next, one could anticipate that tax administration would be lax, particularly direct taxation of income and landed wealth. Similarly, governments would tend to rely on positive incentives to encourage those who control the surplus to invest it productively. Tax concessions and subsidies for the rich should be widespread. The state would be 'soft' with the monopolists and 'firm' with everyone else; the former would get the carrot and the latter the stick.

Institutional reforms are likely to be modest and infrequent. In particular, the property rights of locally owned enterprises are likely to be respected. Occasionally, however, foreign-owned enterprises may be nationalised, since this probably would strengthen rather than weaken indigenous entrepreneurs. Radical land reforms, like those of Mexico, Bolivia and Cuba, are unlikely to occur except as part of a revolution. It is surely no accident that in the other countries of the region progress in land reform has been so slow, despite universal recognition of its importance for development. Only in Chile and Venezuela, in fact, is a peaceful reform of any size under way, and in neither of these countries does agriculture account for more than 10 per cent of G.D.P. Reforms are possible only when they are no longer vital, and property can be expropriated only when property owners have shifted most of their assets elsewhere.[27]

Let us now consider the implications of our hypothesis for the way in which resources are transferred to the government. In a democratic society taxes can be regarded as semi-voluntary, in that they are voted upon by elected representatives, and the transfer of part of the economic surplus to the state can be regarded as an example of what Boulding calls 'the principle of self-coercion'.[28] Under a democratic regime one would expect that the tax system as a whole would be progressive and that a substantial proportion of government revenue would be raised through direct taxation. That is, the majority can be relied upon to insist that the rich should pay proportionately more than the poor. In an undemocratic regime, however, self-coercion would be replaced by coercion. One would expect, first, that the tax system would be regressive and, second, that it would rely heavily on indirect taxes. Third, one would expect that the system of taxation would be inelastic, so that the government would not automatically receive a growing share of the national income and economic surplus. Any rise in the ratio of taxes to national income would be the result of an increase in tax rates rather than a consequence of the way the system works.

One would also expect, fourth, that government enterprises would not be used to mobilise the surplus for economic development. On the contrary, one would anticipate that the nationalised industries, through their pricing and investment policies, would be used to subsidise private economic activity. Finally, governments can be expected to use inflation as a device for transferring resources from the private to the public sector. Under some circumstances the dominant minority would prefer inflation to taxation as a way of financing the government, since the monopoly power enjoyed by the minority may enable them to shift the incidence of price rises on to the weaker members of the community. Deception may succeed if coercion fails.

Our hypothesis that governments in Latin America are not concerned primarily with promoting development and equality also has implications for the way in which public revenues are spent. In particular, one would expect the proportion of government resources devoted to promoting development to be low. This would be reflected in a low ratio of state investment to total public expenditure. It might also be reflected in small budgetary allocations for education and health. Salaries of civil servants, on the other hand, should account for a large part of total expenditure. Moreover, one would expect state capital formation to be a small proportion of total investment and to be channelled largely into social overhead facilities. Finally, one would expect that government programmes in such areas as social security, health and education would favour upper and middle income groups.

To what extent are these various predictions supported by the facts? In Table 2 below a variety of quantitative indicators have been assembled which will enable us to test the hypothesis, at least in part.

In general, our expectations about the volume and composition of government revenue are supported by the data. A relatively small fraction of the economic surplus is transferred from the private to the public sector. On average, tax revenue is less than 15 per cent of G.N.P.

Moreover, even in comparison with other underdeveloped countries, Latin America makes relatively little effort to channel resources to the government. According to a study of fifty-two countries by Lotz and Morss, all but six of the seventeen 'low tax effort countries' are in Latin America. On the other hand, five Latin American countries are in their 'high tax effort' category.[29] As anticipated, direct taxes play a small role in raising revenue; indirect taxation accounts for about 75 per cent of total tax revenue. Furthermore, in a few countries the dependence on indirect taxes has increased. In Peru, for instance, indirect taxes rose from 61·7 per cent of total taxes in 1960 to over 75 per cent in 1965.

A tax system which relies so heavily on indirect taxes is almost certain to be highly regressive. Line 4 of Table 2 indicates that the system is

Table 2. The Role of the Public Sector in Promoting Development

Revenue indicators

1. Total tax revenue as per cent of G.N.P. (unweighted average of 19 countries)	14·7
2. Per cent of countries in 'low tax effort' category on Lotz–Morss scale	58·0
3. Indirect taxes as per cent of total taxes (unweighted average of 16 countries)	75·0
4. Total income elasticity of the tax system (unweighted average of 6 countries)	0·96
5. Incidence of taxation in the agricultural sector (ratio of agriculture's share of total taxes to agriculture's share of total output, unweighted average of 19 countries)	0·38
6. Surplus after depreciation of 24 public enterprises in Latin America as per cent of enterprise activity	−21·9

Expenditure indicators

7. Public investment as per cent of total investment (average for 1960–6)	35·1
8. Public investment as per cent of total government expenditure (unweighted average of 6 countries)	36·9
9. Civil servants' salaries as per cent of government current expenditure (unweighted average for 8 countries, 1963)	52·0
10. Per cent of total population covered by social security	
Uruguay, Chile, Argentina	30·3
6 other countries	5·3

Sources:

Lines 1 and 2: J. R. Lotz and E. R. Morss, 'Measuring Tax Effort in Developing Countries', in *I.M.F. Staff Papers* (1967).
Lines 3 and 7: Chapter 1, Tables 9 and 7.
Line 4: U.N., *Economic Survey of Latin America, 1967.*
Line 5: Chapter 4, Tables 6, 8 and 10.
Lines 6 and 10: Chapter 3, Tables 8 and 10.
Lines 8 and 9: Chapter 2, Tables 3 and 4.

inelastic, even after taking changes in tax rates into account. In other words, there appears to be a slight tendency for the government's share of national income to decline as the national income rises.

One of the remarkable things about the tax system in Latin America is the extent to which agriculture is undertaxed. Under a proportional tax system agriculture's share of total taxation would be equal to its share of total output. Yet line 5 shows that agriculture's contribution to tax revenue is only 38 per cent as large as its share of the national income! At least on the surface, it would seem that in many countries a strong case could be made for sharply raising the tax burden in agriculture.[30] This is unlikely to occur, however, as long as those who monopolise the land retain political power.

Industry is taxed more heavily than agriculture, but this is offset by substantial subsidies. Tariff protection is the most obvious subsidy, but the provision of cheap inputs by public sector enterprises also is important. Nationalised industries in Latin America tend to set the price of their products too low, and this results in a transfer of the surplus from the public to the private sector. As can be seen in line 6 of the table, the accounting losses of public enterprises are enormous. The obvious solution is to raise prices, but, once again, this is unlikely to occur as long as those who benefit from the present situation dominate the government.

Let us consider briefly the pattern of government expenditure. As anticipated, public investment is a small proportion of both total investment and total government expenditure, being slightly more than one-third in each case. Over half of current expenditure goes on civil servants' salaries. Although a quarter of government expenditure is on health, education and the social services, this amounts to less than 4 per cent of the national income. Finally, with the exceptions of Argentina, Chile and Uruguay, the proportion of the population covered by social security schemes is negligible. Thus the evidence seems to be consistent with the hypothesis that the governments in Latin America have not assumed responsibility for accelerating material progress and reducing inequality.

(d) Conclusion

Although growth depends on many things besides the rate of accumulation of capital, rapid and sustained material progress requires a high savings rate, and this is unlikely to occur unless public savings are high in comparison with private savings. A strategy of rapid growth, hence, is almost certain to imply a large public sector and a high ratio of government taxation to national income. Public savings may either be used directly by the government to finance state investment or they may be transferred to the private sector. If the latter policy is pursued, the government in effect will be taxing the population as a whole in order that private capitalists may accumulate wealth.

In so far as the fiscal system is regressive and is based on indirect taxation, a policy of high public savings and low state investment will accentuate income inequalities. Thus, if one wishes to combine rapid material progress with diminished inequality, a policy of high taxation, high public saving and high state investment should be adopted. Moreover, an improvement in the distribution of income is likely to require an increase in transfer payments (e.g. on social security) plus additional current expenditure (e.g. on education and health), which increase still further the need to raise the tax burden.

There are, or should be, three major purposes of taxation and public expenditure policy in Latin America. First, a large fraction of the economic surplus should be made available for capital accumulation. Second, the composition of consumption should be altered in favour of those categories which raise the productivity of labour and accelerate the pace of technical change. Third, the benefits of growth should be distributed to the poorest members of the community so that income inequalities diminish, i.e. the incomes of the poor should grow faster than the income of the nation as a whole. There is no logical reason why these purposes cannot be achieved simultaneously, nor is there any technical economic reason which prevents the appropriate policies from being implemented; the obstacles are essentially political.

Professor Gerschenkron has shown that, historically, the greater the degree of 'relative backwardness', the more prominent the role of government in promoting growth and development.[31] The problem in Latin America is that the government is not a good instrument for mobilising the surplus, and the reason for this is that those who control the government are unwilling to make sacrifices in order to accelerate development, particularly if faster material progress undermines their monopoly position. This has been well explained by John Mellor:

> . . . the highest income groups in low-income countries can already command most of the material goods of developed nations plus the readily available personal services of a low-income society. Such

groups have little to gain from a dynamic process of economic development. . . . The higher income people may even lose ground as development raises wages in the personal services sector without compensating increases in productivity in the sector.[32]

Indeed, one can go further. Increasing scarcity of labour and higher real wages would not only raise the costs of personal services, they would also destroy the basis of the landlord's economic power. The monopolisation of land confers power and wealth only in so far as land is the scarce factor of production. (The concentration of land ownership in the United States is of no significance precisely because it is labour that is relatively scarce there, and not land or capital.) If rapid growth occurs, this would tend to weaken the power of landlords, and hence they will oppose it. Moreover, if this rapid growth occurs as a result of investment by the state, the power of private industrialists will be weakened, and they too will therefore oppose growth.

We are suggesting, in other words, that slow growth in Latin America is deeply rooted in the economic and political structure of the region. This can be demonstrated with a simple model.[33]

Per capita income in Latin America increased 1·3 per cent a year in the period 1960–6, while the population increased 3·0 per cent a year. Let us assume the population growth rate (p) remains unchanged and that the government raises the desired rate of growth of *per capita* income ($\bar{y}$) to 3 per cent. This implies a planned rate of growth of national income (g) of 6 per cent.

$$g = \bar{y} + p$$

We can now determine whether such a growth rate is feasible given current levels of taxation, the savings habits of the private sector and the amount of foreign aid available.

If the net incremental capital:output ratio (λ) is 4:1 the required net investment ratio (k) will be 24 per cent.

$$k = \lambda g$$

In equilibrium, this investment can be financed out of public savings (s_g), private savings (s_p), or foreign savings (a).

$$k = s_g + s_p + a$$

Net capital inflow for the region as a whole is unlikely to exceed 2·5 per cent of national income in the future. Thus the remaining 21·5 percentage points of investment must be financed locally out of private and public savings.

The share of private savings in the national income depends upon the tax burden (t) and the propensity of households and private corporations to save out of disposable income (α).

$$s_p = \alpha\,(1 - t)$$

If $t = 0{\cdot}15$ and $\alpha = 0{\cdot}10$, as seems to be typical of the region, private savings will be about 8·5 per cent of the national income. That is, foreign aid plus private savings can together finance a net investment rate of about 11 per cent. The remaining 13 per cent must come from the public sector. This clearly is not feasible, given that the tax burden is 15 per cent, because only 2 per cent of the national income would be available to the government to finance current expenditure. In other words, in the absence of radical reform, rapid material progress in Latin America as a whole is not possible.[34]

How large a fiscal reform would be necessary in order to achieve the growth objective? That is, how heavy should the tax burden be? The answer to these questions will, of course, vary from one country to another, but it is possible to make rough estimates of the order of magnitude for the region as a whole.

At present public consumption is about 11 per cent of G.N.P. This should be raised substantially. In particular, the quantity and quality of the state education system need to be increased. Whether this can be done within the existing political context is, perhaps, a little doubtful, although the Christian Democratic government in Chile has made considerable progress in education in the last six years. In most countries a vicious circle operates – those without education are not allowed to vote and those who cannot vote have no means of exerting pressure on the government to provide mass education. It will be difficult to break this circle in countries where the education of the masses is 'a discommodity to the rulers, as it imperils their political power'.[35] Yet if rapid growth and diminished inequality are to occur, the circle must be broken – not only in education but in health, housing, civic amenities, etc. Expansion and improvement of these programmes plus the finance of other current expenditure items probably would require about 18 per cent of the national income, the proportion prevailing in the United Kingdom.

The ratio of taxation to national income necessary to achieve the development objectives depends upon the desired share of public consumption (cg) and the amount of public savings required for the residual financing of the national investment programme. Given the rate of accumulation of capital, public savings (and taxation) will be lower the greater is the inflow of foreign capital and the larger is the propensity to save of the private sector. The aggregate tax ratio can be calculated from the following equation:

$$t = \frac{cg + (\bar{y} + p)\lambda - (a + \alpha)}{(1 - \alpha)}$$

Assume the values of the independent variables are as follows:

$$cg = 0.18 \qquad\qquad \lambda = 4$$
$$\bar{y} = 0.03 \qquad\qquad \alpha = 0.10$$
$$p = 0.03 \qquad\qquad a = 0.025$$

These values imply that the ratio of tax revenue to national income must be about 32·8 per cent,[36] i.e. more than twice as high as the unweighted average for the region as a whole. The difference between the ideal and the real tax ratio is a measure of the inadequacy of present governments in financing development and an indication of the challenge which faces governments in the future.

The objective is not beyond reach. Although the tax ratio in most Latin American countries is very low by the standards we have set, in some countries the ratio is high and rising. In both Brazil and Chile the tax burden rose from about 15·5 per cent in the period 1948–50 to approximately 30 per cent today. In Uruguay, unfortunately, the tax burden has declined over the last fifteen years from about 25 per cent to roughly 23 per cent. The decline in the tax ratio has been accompanied by a decline in *per capita* income. In Argentina the tax burden declined from 20 per cent in the early 1950s to about 15 per cent in the years of stagnation during the late 1960s; it has since recovered much of the ground previously lost. The other countries of the region, however, are far from the standard of 32·8 per cent we have established. In fact, to reach that standard they would have to raise the tax ratio by 100 per cent or more. This is most unlikely to occur within the foreseeable future.

Our analysis indicates that most Latin American countries are incapable of sustained rapid development. The monopoly structure of the economy perpetuates inequality and leads to the concentration of the economic surplus in the hands of a tiny minority. Despite this, private savings are a low proportion of the national income. The monopolists clearly prefer a quiet life to rapid development. Moreover, their control of the government enables them to impose their preferences on the community at large. In general, only a small fraction of the surplus is channelled to the government, and most tax revenues are raised through a highly regressive system of indirect taxation. Progressive direct taxation is unenforceable, even when it is enacted, because of the power of the wealthy. Hence the tax burden falls largely on the poor. The benefits of public expenditure, on the other hand, accrue largely to those who are more prosperous than the average. In other words, the government's tax and expenditure policies tend to accentuate inequality rather than diminish it. Finally, the amount of investment the public sector is able to finance out of budget surpluses is insufficient to raise the total investment rate to a level which would generate rapid material progress. Ultimately, the government reflects the balance of forces within the polity, and in Latin America the concentration of political power is such that the government, far from transforming the economy, becomes one of the major institutions maintaining the *status quo*. Monopoly, inefficiency, inequality and slow growth are likely to persist as long as the political character of the region remains unchanged.

NOTES

1. The classification that follows has been strongly influenced by the work of Rafael Baraona. See his *Tenencia de la Tierra y Desarrollo Socio-Economico del Sector Agricola en Ecuador* (CIDA, 1965). My understanding of how the *latifundia* system operates has been increased by the many conversations I have had with Alejandro Schejtman.

2. Inter-American Committee for Agricultural Development (CIDA), *Tenencia de la Tierra y Desarrollo Socio-Económico del Sector Agricola en Guatemala* (1965), p. 79.

3. A. G. Frank, *Capitalism and Underdevelopment in Latin America* (1967), p. 113.

4. Victor Tokman, 'Land Tenure and Socio-Economic Development of the Agricultural Sector in Argentina in the Post-War Period', D.Phil. thesis, (Oxford, 1969), p. 70.

5. A. C. Harberger, 'Monopoly and Resource Allocation', in *American Economic Review* (May 1954). See also D. Schwartzman, 'The Burden of Monopoly', in *Journal of Political Economy* (Dec 1960).

6. H. J. Bruton, 'Productivity Growth in Latin America', in *American Economic Review* (Dec 1967).

7. A. C. Harberger, 'Using the Resources at Hand More Effectively', in *American Economic Review* (May 1959).

8. Keith Griffin and John Enos, *Planning Development* (1970), ch. 6.

B

9. Keith Griffin, 'Reform and Diversification in a Coffee Economy: The Case of Guatemala', in P. P. Streeten (ed.), *Unfashionable Economics: Essays in Honour of Lord Balogh* (1970).

10. L. L. Johnson, 'Problems of Import Substitution: The Chilean Automobile Industry', in *Economic Development and Cultural Change* (Jan 1967).

11. Ifigenia N. de Navarrete, *La Distribucion del Ingreso y el Desarrollo Economico de Mexico* (1960).

12. See ECLA, *Estudio Sobre la Distribución del Ingreso en América Latina* (1967).

13. Notice that the share of the top 10 per cent of households declined by 15·3 per cent, whereas the share of the bottom 40 per cent declined by 26·6 per cent.

14. Simon Kuznets, 'Quantitative Aspects of the Economic Growth of Nations, VII, The Share and Structure of Consumption', in *Economic Development and Cultural Change* (Jan 1962), pt ii, p. 5. Also see H. Houthakker, 'On Some Determinants of Saving in Developed and Underdeveloped Countries', in E. A. G. Robinson (ed.), *Problems in Economic Development* (1965).

15. Simon Kuznets, 'Quantitative Aspects of the Economic Growth of Nations, V, Capital Formation Proportions: International Comparisons for Recent Years', in *Economic Development and Cultural Change* (July 1960), pt ii, pp. 55–6.

16. Luis Landau, 'Determinants of Savings in Latin America' (Project for Quantitative Research in Economic Development, Report no. 13, mimeographed, Harvard, 1966).

17. Ibid. p. 17.

18. N. Leff, 'Marginal Savings Rates in the Development Process: The Brazilian Experience', in *Economic Journal* (Sept 1968). The reliability of Leff's data, particularly for the period before 1947, has been questioned, however. See Chapter 5 below.

19. N. Kaldor, 'Economic Problems of Chile', in *Essays on Economic Policy* (1965), ii, 261.

20. M. J. Sternberg, 'Chilean Land Tenure and Land Reform' (Ph.D. thesis, University of California, Berkeley, 1962), ch. iv.

21. P. K. G. Panikar, 'Rural Savings in India', in *Economic Development and Cultural Change* (1961–2).

22. A. Sturmthal, 'Economic Development, Income Distribution and Capital Formation in Mexico', in *Journal of Political Economy* (June 1955), 194.

23. Ibid. p. 195.

24. Karl Marx, 'The British Rule in India', in K. Marx and F. Engels, *On Colonialism* (1960), p. 37.

25. *Asian Drama* (1968), p. 66.

26. The current military dictatorship in Peru is an interesting case. If our hypothesis is correct, only a few foreigners and some members of APRA need fear for their property.

27. In Peru, the terms of compensation under the agrarian reform law are designed to assist landowners in transferring their assets from agriculture to industry. In so far as the agrarian reform is implemented, it will have the effect of converting *latifundistas* into industrial monopolists.

28. Kenneth E. Boulding, *Economics as a Science* (1970), p. 79.

29. J. R. Lotz and E. R. Morss, 'Measuring Tax Effort in Developing Countries', in *I.M.F. Staff Papers* (1967).

30. In some countries, e.g. Chile, the burden on agriculture may be greater

than the tax figures suggest, because food prices may be controlled by the government and kept low intentionally in order to subsidise urban industry.

31. A. Gerschenkron, *Economic Backwardness in Historical Perspective* (1966).

32. *The Economics of Agricultural Development* (1967), p. 6.

33. Cf. R. Musgrave, *Fiscal Systems* (1969), pp. 221–6. Musgrave uses his model to estimate tax requirements.

34. Since half of the required investment is a consequence of rapid population growth, many economists have begun to give higher priority to family planning than to tax reform. There is no doubt that in some circumstances an expanding population can retard material progress, but it is not clear that it has done so in Latin America. In fact there is a positive, but statistically insignificant, correlation between growth of *per capita* income and growth of population in the region:

$$y = -0.82 + 0.83p; \; R^2 = 0.11$$

My suspicion is that demographic expansion is a relatively minor barrier to progress in most of the region.

35. Carl S. Shoup, *Public Finance* (1969), p. 129.

36. The calculations based on the model must not be accepted uncritically. They are intended merely as an illustration. The model suffers from two defects. First, it is assumed that consumption expenditure (e.g. on health, education and birth control) has no effect on the rate of growth of *per capita* income. Second, it is assumed that the ratios and parameters of the system are independent of one another. Yet it is obvious that the tax burden (t) may affect the savings propensity of the private sector (a), or the amount of foreign capital received (a) may alter the capital–output ratio (λ), and so on.

1. Development Finance in Latin America: Basic Principles

LESTER C. THUROW

LATIN AMERICA is a diverse continent and the countries within it encompass a wide variety of economic and social conditions. In 1966 *per capita* G.N.P. ranged from \$890 in Venezuela to \$87 in Haiti. Some countries are populated mostly by European immigrants; others by native Indians and mestizos. The church is politically strong in some; weak in others. In planning economic development one must take such variations among and within countries into account. At the same time there are a series of economic problems that are common to all Latin American countries. This chapter focuses on the common problems, but this does not imply that the variations from the common picture can be disregarded.

(a) Theory

Any society, regardless of its political orientation, is faced with at least five major allocation or distribution decisions.[1]

1. Society's resources must be allocated between future consumption (current investment) and present consumption. To make this decision society must balance the welfare of its current citizens and the welfare of its future citizens. When this decision is made society has made one of the major decisions determining its rate of economic growth: it has determined the level of investment. Investment, however, must be broadly interpreted as any factor which leads to increases in future consumption. Thus in very poor countries investment may include the food and health care necessary for individuals to be productive. In balancing the welfare of current and future citizens society must look at the rate of return which can be earned on investment projects, the income of current and future citizens, and at its own rate of time preference.

2. Present consumption privileges must be distributed among society's current population. Here society is forced to compare and balance the

welfare of different individuals, but it must also consider the incentive effects that consumption privileges provide. Income is a store of potential consumption, but it also serves as a work incentive. It may be necessary to balance the demands of equity against the demands of efficiency. Such a trade-off cannot be determined theoretically. Moving towards a more equitable income distribution may lead to more or less work. The actual response depends upon the shape of the desired income distribution and upon the response of different individuals in society.

3. Present consumption privileges must be allocated between public consumption and private consumption. Here society must consider the relative benefits that flow from private consumption goods and public consumption. In any society, many goods will be publicly provided. Some goods, such as clean air, can only be provided publicly. There is no market mechanism for selling clean air, even if this were desirable. Other goods, such as education, health care and housing, have external effects on society which must be considered when determining purchases of these goods.

4. Investment resources must be allocated between public investment projects and private investment projects. The allocation may partly depend on the relative efficiency of public and private investment projects, but the preferences of a society for private or public production are the dominating factor. Private market imperfections or problems of achieving and financing activities characterised by economies of large scale may mean that public enterprise is more efficient than private; desires to prevent an unequal distribution of economic or political power may lead one to prefer public production.

5. Investment resources must be allocated between human investment projects and physical investment projects. Some investment should go into skills, education and training. Some investment should go into plant and equipment. But it should be kept in mind that expenditures on both human capital and physical capital may include consumption elements. Both an education and a new tractor may contain an element of consumption.

While the five allocation decisions facing society are theoretically separable, they are in reality interconnected. Although, for instance, the distribution of human capital and earned income need not determine society's income distribution, redistribution taxes and transfer payments have severe political limitations. Thus the desired income distribution may in reality determine the amount and kind of investment in human capital.

All five of these allocation decisions are essentially political decisions rather than narrow economic decisions. The political process must balance the welfare of one individual against the welfare of another individual, the utility of one type of good against the utility of another type of good, or the benefit of one institutional framework for production against another institutional framework. The political process must resolve the tough conflicts between equity and efficiency that may exist. There are no narrow economic grounds upon which these decisions can be made.

Even a government that decides to place the maximum reliance on private decision-making is forced to become involved in establishing the desired income distribution or in sanctifying the income distribution which is produced in the market. No economic system can guarantee that the process of production will generate the distribution of income which its members desire. Unless such a distribution has been established, the economy is ultimately inefficient. Thus every government has an income redistribution function to fulfil. Unless it has fulfilled this function, private allocation decisions between savings and investment, public and private consumption, public and private investment, and human or physical investment are incorrect allocation decisions. They are based on the wrong distribution of economic voting power.

Even if income were optimally distributed at each moment of time, society would still need to intervene to ensure that income was optimally distributed over time. Since society is concerned with the welfare of future citizens as well as current citizens, society cannot rely on private savings decisions to allocate resources to the future even if income is optimally distributed among present citizens. Individual decisions probably will be primarily concerned with the welfare of the individuals making the decisions and not with the welfare of future individuals. Thus private economic decisions, made when individuals are acting as private individuals, need not coincide with the decisions that the same individuals make when acting as citizens and public individuals. Consequently, society may be forced to modify private savings decisions even if income is ideally distributed.

The problem of balancing the welfare of different individuals is a problem of politics. Formal economics provides no help in making allocation decisions among individuals. The validity of the welfare weights that spring from the political process depend upon the validity of the political decision-making process. Thus political reform is logically prior to economic reform. There are no 'right' economic policies until the 'right' political priorities have been established.

Most economic reforms that have been suggested for Latin America, such as those in the Alliance for Progress, are some expert's view of what the 'right' priorities would be if Latin American countries were run in accordance with procedures that gave relatively equal weight to the welfare of each individual (or perhaps higher weight to those with lower incomes). The policies recommended by these experts may or may not be sensible, but they are essentially irrelevant as economic policies if actual political priorities spring from a very different structure of weighting individual welfare.

Given the oligarchs and military officers who so often control Latin American politics, current economic policies might or might not be the right set of policies to maximise welfare as the rulers see it, but the reform proposals that have been suggested most certainly are not the right set of priorities. To expect any group to adopt policies which would reform themselves out of political and economic power is to expect too much. This occasionally happens, but from stupidity and not from conscious planning.

Thus political reform or revolution must precede economic reform. In its absence, any planning for economic growth which would create a wide distribution of wealth and a high standard of living for the entire population must take on the air of contingency planning rather than policy-making.

Economic theory provides a stylised ideal of how these difficult allocation decisions are to be made. This ideal has no empirical content, but it is well to keep it in mind since the theory provides a convenient checklist of the major items that must be considered.

Theoretically, society balances the welfare of different individuals by using its social welfare function. The social welfare function simply establishes the relative weights that are to be given to the welfare of particular individuals. In practice the social welfare function is the preferences of a country's rulers. Given the welfare weights attached to different individuals, it is possible to determine how many resources should be devoted to the welfare of future citizens (investment) and how many resources should be devoted to the welfare of present citizens (consumption). Knowing the resources available for present consumption and the relative importance of the welfare of its present citizens, society can then distribute consumption privileges (income) among them.

The allocation between private consumption goods and public consumption goods is made by looking at the utility or satisfaction that individuals derive from the two types of goods. Present consumption is divided in such a manner as to ensure that the marginal utility of private consumption equals the marginal utility of public consumption.

The allocation between private and public production is made by establishing the benefits society attaches to different institutional frameworks. Given these methodological benefits, investment resources are allocated between public and private investment until the marginal returns to private and public investment are equal.

The outcome of all these decisions is important when attempting to establish tax policies. Tax policies can be regarded as composed of four layers. First, there is a set of taxes and transfer payments necessary to establish society's desired income distribution. There may be large gross flows, but the taxes and transfer payments necessary for redistribution are exactly equal. There are no net flows from private individuals to the government. This layer of taxes might be called 'redistribution' taxes.

To redistribution taxes must be added a second set of taxes, the taxes necessary to achieve the optimum division between public consumption and private consumption. In the aggregate these taxes will equal public consumption expenditures, but they must be raised in such a manner as to preserve the optimum distribution of consumption. To do this taxes must be distributed in accordance with the benefits received from public consumption. This layer of taxes might be called 'benefit' taxes.

To these two layers of taxes a third must be added, 'investment' taxes. These are the taxes necessary to ensure that total savings equal desired total investment. They must, of course, be raised in accordance with the distribution objectives. The third set of taxes will not, however, be equal to public investment. Public investment funds may come from private savings or public savings may be lent for private investment. The third set of taxes must in the aggregate fill the gap between desired savings and the savings which individuals or firms undertake.

Finally, 'stabilisation' (Keynesian) taxes must be added to hold the economy at the desired degree of utilisation of capital and labour resources. They must, of course, be raised in such a manner that they will not disturb the desired distribution of income.

The balance of payments may provide a constraint on all of these allocation decisions. If foreign goods are necessary complements to domestic investment or to domestic consumption, balance of payments constraints may force alterations in allocation decisions. Economic policies may be used to overcome balance of payments constraints, but in the short run there may be no such instruments. Thus, if society wishes to allocate 20 per cent of its resources to investment, it may be unable to do so because it cannot finance the necessary complementary foreign goods. If this happens, society may have to reallocate its resources between consumption and investment or within the investment sector from one investment project to another.

(b) The Scene

In 1966 Latin American *per capita* G.N.P. was $440, ranging from highs of $890 in Venezuela and $826 in Argentina to lows of $87 in Haiti and $182 in Bolivia (see Table 1). *Per capita* G.N.P. is reported to have

Table 1. 1966 *Per Capita* G.N.P. (U.S. $)

Argentina	826
Bolivia	182
Brazil	333
Chile	588
Colombia	336
Ecuador	221
Mexico	493
Paraguay	220
Peru	259[a]
Uruguay	611[a]
Venezuela	890
Haiti	87[a]
Panama	542
Dominican Republic	265
Costa Rica	426
El Salvador	276
Guatemala	301
Honduras	227
Nicaragua	360
Average	440

[a] 1965.

Source: U.N., *Statistical Yearbook, 1967* (New York, 1968), p. 583.

been growing at an annual rate of 1·3 per cent from 1960 to 1966 (see Table 2), but this is not enough to prevent the income gap between Latin America and other rich countries from growing wider, much less to close that gap. Over the same period *per capita* G.N.P. in the U.S. grew by 3·7 per cent per annum to $3697 and in the U.K. it grew by 2·4 per cent to $1925. Measured in relative terms, Latin America is becoming poorer. It is falling farther and farther behind.

Moreover, the rate of growth achieved is not adequate to close the gap between the rich and poor in Latin America. Seventy million rural Latin Americans have estimated *per capita* incomes of $60 to $70 per year. The poorest 60 per cent of the population have only 30 per cent of total income and the richest 2 per cent have 30 per cent of total income.

Table 2. Annual Rate of Growth of Total and *Per Capita* G.N.P., 1960–66

Country	Total (%)	Per Capita (%)
Argentina	2·6	1·1
Bolivia	5·2	2·9
Brazil	3·8	0·7
Chile	4·0	1·6
Colombia	4·5	1·3
Ecuador	4·0	0·6
Mexico	6·3	2·9
Paraguay	3·5	0·5
Peru	5·8	2·7
Uruguay	1·2	−0·1
Venezuela	5·2	1·7
Haiti	−0·9	−2·9
Panama	8·1	4·8
Dominican Republic	2·3	−1·3
Costa Rica	5·2	1·2
El Salvador	6·4	3·2
Guatemala	6·3	3·2
Honduras	5·5	2·2
Nicaragua	7·8	4·5
Average	4·3	1·3

Source: ECLA, *Economic Survey of Latin America, 1966* (U.N., New York, 1968), p. 16.

Some countries, of course, are doing significantly better than the Latin American average, but only two countries, Nicaragua and Panama, had a *per capita* rate of growth which exceeded that of the United States and their *per capita* G.N.P.s were only $360 and $542, respectively, in 1966. Generally, it would be accurate to say that there are no success stories in Latin America. No countries are succeeding in catching up and the absolute rates of growth are very low. Some countries, such as Haiti, Uruguay and the Dominican Republic, actually retrogressed from 1960 to 1966.

A major economic problem in Latin America is apparent in Table 2.

Although *per capita* growth rates are low, the rate of growth of output is quite high, viz. 4·3 per cent. Thus much of the blame for a poor economic performance is due to a very high rate of growth of population. Given a population growth rate of 3 per cent, rapid *per capita* economic growth is impossible with the limited resources available for investment in Latin America. An expanding population simply cannot be equipped

Table 3. Real Economic Growth of Latin America by Sectors, 1961–1966 (%)

	G.N.P.	Agriculture	Mining	Manufacturing	Construction
1961	5·0	4·4	3·0	7·8	2·5
1962	3·8	4·0	6·2	3·8	0·8
1963	2·3	1·9	3·3	1·7	2·7
1964	6·3	3·9	6·0	10·2	6·8
1965	5·1	6·8	2·8	4·9	−0·4
1966	3·1	−0·8	−0·1	5·0	6·8

	Electricity, gas and water	Transportation and communication	Trade and finance	Public administration and defence	Other services
1961	10·0	5·9	6·6	3·4	3·9
1962	10·7	3·3	3·4	0·9	3·4
1963	6·2	3·4	1·9	3·4	4·2
1964	9·4	6·6	6·3	3·2	4·6
1965	7·8	4·4	6·1	3·3	4·3
1966	8·8	3·2	4·1	3·4	4·1

Source: ECLA, *Economic Survey of Latin America, 1966* (U.N., New York, 1968), p. 26.

with the necessary human and physical capital. To equip such an expanding labour force would require major reductions in current consumption, and existing governments are unable or unwilling to do this.

This dismal picture is not altered by looking at sectors of the economy rather than countries (see Table 3). In the important agricultural sector output grew 3·4 per cent per year, but only 0·44 per cent per year in *per capita* terms. 70 per cent of the 3·4 per cent increase in agricultural output could be traced to increasing the area under cultivation and only 30 per cent to actual increases in the productivity of agricultural resources. In terms of employment, 46 per cent of the work force was engaged in agriculture in 1965 (see Table 4). This percentage is decreasing, but even so agriculture absorbed 28 per cent of the new workers who came into the labour market between 1960 and 1965.

Table 4. The Distribution of Employment, 1965

	Number ('ooos)	%	Per cent absorption 1960–1965
Total	76,416	100·0	100·0
Agriculture	35,221	46·1	28·1
Mining	753	1·0	0·8
Manufacturing	10,546	13·8	11·3
Construction	2,969	3·9	3·3
Basic services	3,991	5·2	6·6
Trade and finance	7,220	9·5	13·2
Government	2,895	3·8	5·1
Miscellaneous services	9,649	12·6	19·2
Unspecified	2,749	3·6	7·8

Source: ECLA, *Economic Survey of Latin America, 1966* (U.N., New York, 1968), pp. 31 and 32.

Any attempt to increase production in Latin America must focus on agriculture. Agriculture is a major fraction of the entire economy, it is organised in an inefficient and inequitable manner, and structural re-

Table 5. Ratio of G.D.P. per Urban Inhabitant to G.D.P. per Rural Inhabitant

Country		Country	
Argentina	2·3	Venezuela	6·2
Bolivia	5·4	Haiti	6·3
Brazil	3·2	Panama	4·4
Chile	4·0	Costa Rica	4·6
Colombia	2·1	El Salvador	5·5
Ecuador	3·2	Guatemala	4·7
Mexico	3·7	Honduras	2·9
Paraguay	3·9	Nicaragua	2·8
Peru	4·6	Average	3·7
Uruguay	0·8		

Source: ECLA, *Economic Survey of Latin America, 1966* (U.N., New York, 1968), p. 327.

forms might permit a more rapid economic growth. Since output per inhabitant is almost four times as high in urban areas as it is in rural areas (see Table 5), human resources need to be transferred from rural to urban areas. To transfer human resources, however, agricultural output must increase so that food supplies will be large enough to support much larger urban populations. This can be done in part by transferring capital resources from urban to rural areas and in part by altering rural institutions and creating incentives to increase production.

Land reform may offer a method for rapidly increasing agricultural output. In the typical Latin American country output per agricultural worker is much higher on large multifamily farms, but output per acre is much larger on small farms (for an illustration of the magnitudes involved, see Table 6 on Argentina). Countries with surplus populations

Table 6. Value of Agricultural Production in Argentina (*Minifundia* = 100)

Size of farm	Per hectare of farmland	Per hectare of area under cultivation	Per agricultural worker
Minifundia	100	100	100
Family farm	30	51	250
Medium size multifamily farm	51	62	471
Large size multifamily farm	12	49	622

Source: ECLA, *Economic Survey of Latin America, 1966* (U.N., New York 1968), p. 350.

in both urban and rural areas should not be concerned with maximising output per employed worker. They simply should attempt to maximise total output. Land reform would help to achieve this objective. Output per worker probably would fall, but total agricultural output would rise and in the process more of the population would be employed. Existing data indicate that there might be very large increases in both output and employment. Typically, more than half the agricultural land area in Latin American countries is in the form of large *latifundia*.

Manufacturing has been growing at about 5·6 per cent per annum, but this is hardly enough to absorb Latin America's large rural and urban poor. In fact, from 1960 to 1965 the percentage of the work force employed in manufacturing actually dropped (see Table 4). In 1965 manufacturing employed 13·8 per cent of the work force, but in the preceding five years it absorbed only 11·3 per cent of the new workers coming into the labour market. Service industries provided the major source of new employment.

The declining proportion of the labour force employed in producing goods and the increasing proportion of the labour force employed in services is disturbing. The same trend is visible in advanced countries, but at much higher income levels. Thus there is an open question as to how much of this service employment is genuine employment and how much is disguised unemployment. Since output per worker and the rate of growth of output per worker is typically higher in goods-producing industries, shifts towards services do not augur well for future rates of economic growth.

Between 1960 and 1966 there have been practically no changes in the division of resources between present and future consumption, between private and public consumption and between the proportion of investment made by public and private concerns (see Table 7). Gross investment has remained at approximately 18 per cent of G.N.P. over the period. 35 per cent of this was invested publicly and 65 per cent privately. As regards consumption, public consumption amounted to 13 per cent of total consumption and private consumption accounted for the remaining 87 per cent. In comparison, private investment was 15 per cent of G.N.P. in the U.S. in 1968, 17 per cent of G.N.P. in the U.K. in 1966, and 12 per cent of G.N.P. in Latin America.

Table 7. The Allocation of Resources

	Consumption:			Fixed investment:			Per cent of total resources devoted to investment
	$ (billions)	% Public	% Private	$ (billions)	% Public	% Private	
1960	63·8	13·0	87·0	13·5	34·8	65·2	18·1
1961	66·9	13·2	86·8	14·3	34·3	65·7	18·3
1962	68·9	13·4	86·6	14·7	33·3	66·7	18·3
1963	71·2	13·5	86·5	14·0	35·0	65·0	17·1
1964	75·1	12·9	87·1	15·2	36·2	63·8	18·0
1965	78·1	12·5	87·5	15·6	36·5	63·5	18·2
1966	81·0	12·5	87·5	16·7	35·9	64·1	18·1

Source: ECLA, *Economic Survey of Latin America, 1966* (U.N., New York, 1968), p. 28.

Defence expenditures, perhaps rather surprisingly, are a small percentage of total government expenditures (see Table 8). On average they were 15·2 per cent in 1966, with a range from 5·9 per cent in Costa Rica to 25·5 per cent in Haiti. After the military coups in 1967 and 1968, this percentage may rise sharply in the future. Education, health and social service expenditures account on average for 24 per cent of government expenditure or considerably more than defence expenditures. Not many developed countries could make such a claim.

Table 8. Government Expenditures in 1966

	Total U.S. $ (millions)	Education (%)	Health and Social services (%)	Defence (%)
Argentina	2,297	13·1	11·0	10·6
Bolivia	207	...	...	...
Brazil[a]	4,911	8·9	3·5	20·9
Chile	1,174	18·3	10·1	9·9
Colombia	631	17·4	5·4	24·4
Ecuador	175	15·0	6·8	15·5
Mexico	1,564	24·3	16·8	10·6
Peru	833	22·2	4·6	15·8
Venezuela	1,702	13·3	21·1	10·4
Haiti	28	11·7	12·0	25·5
Panama	10	25·0	13·5	...
Dominican Republic	189	13·8	9·3	17·1
Costa Rica	91	27·6	12·7	5·9
El Salvador	93	22·8	21·2	9·9
Guatemala	136	24·5		10·8
Honduras	63	25·3	14·9	9·8
Total	14,202	14·4	9·6	15·2

[a] Does not include state governments.

Source: U.N., *Statistical Yearbook, 1967* (New York, 1968), p. 635.

Tax receipts (see Table 9) are notable for three reasons: (1) Expenditures consistently exceed tax revenues. Such expenditure–revenue gaps are common to developing countries. Consequently inflation becomes one of the major instruments in acquiring resources for the public sector. (2) With the exception of Brazil and Venezuela there is a very heavy reliance on export or import taxes. These large countries lower the average percentage for Latin America as a whole to 16 per cent but there are 8 countries with percentages above 30 per cent. (3) Domestic indirect taxes account for 53 per cent of total taxes while direct taxes account for only 31 per cent. In the U.S. direct taxes account for 65 per cent of government revenue and indirect taxes account for 35 per cent (in 1968). In the U.K. direct taxes account for 64 per cent and indirect taxes account for 36 per cent of total revenues.

Domestic tax-raising capabilities are of primary concern since Latin American countries must rely on their own revenue-generating capabili-

Table 9. Sources of Tax Revenue, 1966

	Total U.S. $ (millions)	Direct taxes (%)	Domestic indirect taxes (%)	Foreign trade indirect taxes (%)
Argentina	1,974	17	63	20
Bolivia	157	5	77	18
Brazil	3,573	27	65	8
Chile	797	42	45	13
Colombia	615	44	26	30
Ecuador	139	15	33	52
Mexico	1,963	45	38	17
Peru	675	22	50	28
Venezuela	1,645	47	46	7
Haiti	28	9	42	49
Panama	115	36	45	19
Dominican Republic	163	17	38	45
Costa Rica	84	22	17	61
El Salvador	79	20	37	43
Guatemala	121	13	57	30
Honduras	61	24	43	33
Total	11,889	31	53	16

Source: U.N., *Statistical Yearbook, 1967* (New York, 1968), p. 635.

ties. With falling foreign aid budgets and rising repayment schedules on old debts, the net inflow of capital resources from abroad is falling and already has reached low levels. In 1966 Latin American exports of goods and services exceeded imports of goods and services by $1·2 billion ($12·0 billion versus $10·8 billion), but the net balance on current account was only $0·9 billion (see Table 10). For the four years from

Table 10. Foreign Resources (*billions of U.S. dollars*)

Year	Balance on current account	Interest payments and repatriated profits
1960	1·1	1·2
1961	1·2	1·3
1962	1·2	1·5
1963	0·3	1·4
1964	0·7	1·7
1965	0·5	1·8
1966	0·9	2·0

Source: ECLA, *Economic Survey of Latin America, 1966* (U.N., New York, 1968), p. 24.

1963 to 1966 the balance on current account amounted to $0·6 billion per year. Exports of goods and services have been growing rapidly (5·3 per cent per year from 1960 to 1966) and have increased faster than imports of goods and services, but this has been counterbalanced by rapidly rising repatriation of profits and interest payments. These rose from $1·2 billion in 1960 to $2·0 billion in 1966. Consequently, most Latin American countries have a very limited capability of increasing imports of goods and services. Since machinery needs to be imported for industrialisation, balance of payments problems place a severe constraint on general economic development. Given the inelastic demand for most Latin American products on world markets, there is no way that this constraint can be lifted by action on the part of Latin American governments.

Latin America has not met the 5 per cent per year target for economic growth during the U.N.'s Decade of Development, but its aggregate growth rate (4·3 per cent per year from 1960 to 1966) is not too bad. When one considers growth on the more meaningful *per capita* basis, however, it is clear that Latin America has a poor growth record of only 1·3 per cent per year. Given that Latin America already is devoting a rather high percentage of its income to investment and now faces the prospect of very limited external financing of development projects, there is no alternative to slowing down the rate of population growth if the region wishes to achieve rapid *per capita* growth of income. Government revenue systems do, however, need to be reformed to ensure that savings (public and private) increase as a share of output. With tax systems heavily dependent on indirect domestic taxes and taxes on foreign trade, revenues do not automatically generate increased public savings.

Although population control is perhaps the most important prerequisite for rapid growth of incomes, in the rest of this chapter we will concentrate on the problem of raising revenue in the Latin American countries. The focus is on increasing public savings for investment purposes. Given the already inequitable income distribution in Latin America, it is difficult to argue for plans which encourage private savings by making the income distribution more inequitable. Moreover, there is a question as to how much private saving is domestically invested and how much is invested in Europe and North America.

(c) Generating Tax Revenue

Descriptive generalisations can be made of the factors which determine the amount of tax revenue different countries raise.[2] At very low income levels (below a *per capita* income of $300), foreign trade is most easily taxed. At higher income levels ($300 to $750), cultural differences seem to be the major determinant of the level of taxation and above this level political 'will-power' seems to be most important. The question here, however, is not what causes countries to raise the revenue they actually raise, but what revenue countries should raise.

How revenues should be generated depends on the development strategy being followed. Although any actual strategy is a mixture of types, strategies and their implications can be most easily examined by considering two polar strategies. These might be called the 'incentive maximisation' strategy and the 'resource accumulation' strategy.

The incentive maximisation strategy is based on the assumption that individuals are rational and hard-working income maximisers. They will rapidly increase their own output if they are given a reasonable opportunity to do so. At present they are not increasing their output because they face a set of prices and other obstacles which make it economically irrational to invest and increase their own output. Thus the major function of development policy is to liberate the entrepreneurial skills of the population in agriculture and the small urban entrepreneurs, since these constitute the largest groups in the economy.

To accomplish this liberation governments must initially put resources into agriculture in the form of low cost credit facilities and perhaps, in addition, alter land tenure conditions. Similar policies to protect and encourage initiative would be necessary in the backward areas of manufacturing. Credit policies would be used to lower costs and protection would be used to raise output prices. Given this shift in prices affecting agriculture and small business, entrepreneurs in both areas will invest, save and quickly start to generate surpluses which could and would be reinvested, or governments could siphon off some of the surpluses for public investment projects.

Thus the strategy is to tip initially the terms of trade in favour of agriculture, build up an agricultural base which can support a rapidly growing urban population, and then tip the terms of trade in favour of other sectors, principally manufacturing, of the economy. Given favourable incentives and an agricultural market for their goods, modern firms will grow rapidly.

In this strategy the principal role of government is to remove obstacles to growth and to shift the terms of trade between sectors of the economy with tax policies. Thus taxes should initially fall heavily on the existing urban populations and then be gradually shifted to the rural populations as their production increases.

A revitalised and liberated agriculture provides the basis on which modern manufacturing can grow. With growing productivity in agriculture, labour becomes available and an increasing urban population can be fed. The growing agriculture and small business sectors also provide a demand for goods and services which modern manufacturing can meet.

Some government overhead capital investment is necessary in this strategy, but governments do not become the main sources of investment funds or investors. Most investment is made from private savings and directed privately. The function of foreign aid is to give the government of the developing country the necessary resources to tip the terms of trade in favour of agriculture initially and to provide necessary complementary inputs such as fertilisers or fertiliser factories.

In the incentive maximisation strategy, government tax policies must be carefully adjusted to prevent them from interfering with private incentives. The essence of the argument is that equity should be sacrificed to maximising efficiency (work incentives, investment incentives and saving incentives), so that higher standards of living and greater equity can be achieved at some point in the distant future. Thus tax policy should be concerned primarily with increasing incentives, and questions of current equity should be ignored.

The 'resource accumulation' strategy, on the other hand, is based on different assumptions and reaches the opposite conclusion. Initially resources must be taken out of agriculture and the backward sectors of business and transferred to modern manufacturing. This strategy is based on the assumption that the rural worker and small businessman do not respond adequately to changes in the prices they face. Rural workers may in fact have a backward-bending supply curve. As agricultural prices rise they may work less rather than more. By taxing rural workers and lowering their income you may make them work more, rather than less. If their income does rise, they may simply consume more rather than invest.

According to this strategy the problems in the modern sector of the economy arise not from lack of entrepreneurial incentives, but simply from insufficient resource accumulation. If enough resources can be generated, they can be invested to yield high returns and consequently produce a high rate of growth.

Such a strategy assumes that excess labour is flowing out of the rural areas without any improvements in rural productivity. An increasing urban population must be fed by accumulating resources from agriculture. Investment demand is not a problem because a government-managed investment programme can provide the necessary demand for investment goods. Thus, investment in the modern sector rather than consumption and investment in agriculture and small business provides the demands for goods and services necessary to make investment in the modern sector profitable.

Hence the terms of trade are initially turned against agriculture in order to generate resources and only after the modern sector is growing rapidly and encounters labour constraints are resources put into agriculture.

In this development strategy tax policies are easier to design and serve a different function. Equity dominates efficiency because taxes are believed to have little or no impact on investment incentives, savings incentives and work incentives. The problem is simply to raise the desired resources in an equitable manner. Governments must be involved in managing investment since savings and investment are to be raised to levels incapable of being sustained by private business.

Both strategies may be correct. The problem is to determine which strategy is correct for which country, or what mix of strategies is best. Historically there are examples of economic development using both strategies. The U.S. and the U.K. relied on private savings and investment, but initially the terms of trade were tipped against agriculture in the market. Japan and the U.S.S.R. relied more on public saving, but they also used government tax policies to accumulate resources from agriculture and initially tip the terms of trade against agriculture. Among highly developed countries it is harder to find examples of the terms of trade initially being tipped in favour of agriculture, but perhaps Taiwan is a modern example. Canada and Australia are in this category, but these are rather special cases since they are essentially high income agricultural economies.

The choice between these two strategies depends on the answer to several empirical questions: (1) What is the response of peasants and small businessmen to changes in prices? Do they work harder when the price of what they sell goes up or when their incomes go down owing to increased taxation? How high is the marginal propensity to invest?

In Latin America the answers to these questions would seem to point to the resource accumulation strategy. The marginal propensity to invest in Latin America seems rather low and income effects seem to dominate price effects. (2) How should the relative merits of equity in raising taxes be compared with the benefits from higher incomes in the future? This is a problem of value judgements, but I believe that current equity cannot be ignored in the raising of government revenue. (3) What is the relative importance of improving productivity (the relation between inputs and output) and increasing the number of inputs? To the extent that productivity and technical progress are embodied in physical capital and human capital, the two problems cannot be separated. To increase productivity it is necessary to increase inputs or to invest. Although there are plenty of productivity gains to be achieved in any economy with organisational improvements, politically and administratively these are generally very hard to secure. Developed countries have not had notable success in direct attacks on obsolete work rules or inefficient industries. The greatest stimulus to a high rate of growth of productivity seems to be a high rate of growth of output. Changes are made in a context of growth rather than as a method of starting economic growth. Thus desires to increase productivity and eliminate inefficient industry or producers may also lead one to select the resource accumulation strategy.

(d) Specific Taxes

The choice of development strategy determines the choice and form of tax policies. Given the political problem of instituting and adjusting tax laws, there is also a high premium to be placed on a system of taxes which will generate automatic growth in revenues as the economy grows. If possible the tax system should generate an increasing share of government revenue in total output as output rises. Automatic tax increases that come from the operation of the tax laws and economic growth are much easier to tolerate politically than frequent discretionary tax changes that raise the same amount of revenue. It should also be remembered that with the possible exception of export and import taxes, there are no free taxes. All taxes lower someone's income and are going to be resisted by those who will receive lower incomes.

(i) *Taxes on Foreign Trade.* Export and import taxes may or may not lower domestic incomes. This depends on the relevant elasticities of the supplies and demands for exports and imports. If there are elastic demands for export goods, export taxes will be shifted backwards to domestic producers. Exporters, rather than foreign purchasers, will bear the burden of the tax. Most Latin American countries are faced with an elastic demand for their exports because of competition from other Latin American countries or because of competition from some other area of the world. Thus export taxes in most cases are not free taxes. They affect domestic incomes.

The incidence of import taxes also depends on the elasticity of demand. The more inelastic the demand, the more the incidence of any tax falls on the domestic country rather than on incomes in the foreign countries. With most Latin American imports being complementary investment goods, complementary production goods or complementary consumption goods, the elasticity of demand for imports is almost certainly low. As a result, import taxes also are essentially domestic taxes.

Reliance on import taxes also creates a special revenue problem during growth. Efforts to stimulate import-competing industries result in fewer imports and less government revenue. Thus there can be a direct clash between revenue needs and development tactics. Without import revenues, the resources for creating import-competing industries may not be available.

Tax abatement to stimulate foreign investment is another frequently used device. The usefulness of this device depends on the price elasticity of investment with respect to taxes. If the elasticity is high, reducing taxes on foreign investment may yield many more investment resources than would be achieved by direct taxation, although it will also lead to foreign rather than domestic control of the nation's resources.

For any particular Latin American country the foreign investment elasticity with respect to tax abatement is probably high. Except for extractive industries, of which there are a great many in Latin America, firms do not have strong preferences as to whether they are located in one country or another. While this may be true for individual countries it is probably not true for Latin America as a block and is definitely not true for the underdeveloped world as a block. Basic decisions to invest abroad are probably only marginally affected by tax rates. Thus the fallacy of composition leads to incorrect tax policies for each individual Latin American country. Each country would benefit from tax abatement individually but this leads to collective abatement by all countries and losses for all countries. There is no way out of this box, however, unless general agreements can be secured to prevent countries from giving tax abatements to foreign investors.

(ii) *Income Taxes*. Although progressive income taxes are undoubtedly the best taxes in terms both of preserving equity and of growing automatically with the economy, they put a severe strain on the administrative capabilities of an underdeveloped country. A good income tax system will operate successfully only under certain conditions:[3] (1) The existence of a predominately monetary economy. (2) High standards of literacy. (3) Honest and good accounting records. (4) A high degree of voluntary compliance. (5) A political system in which the rich are not dominant. (6) An honest and efficient administration. Finally, income taxes work best under a system of punishments which throws people in jail for tax cheating rather than under a system that merely fines them. Compliance is never really voluntary and only those countries which make tax cheating a criminal rather than a civil offence have a 'high degree of voluntary compliance'.

All of the above factors regrettably lead one to conclude that income taxes cannot be the main instrument of taxation in Latin America. This does not mean, however, that the present systems of income taxes cannot be improved. Present income taxes generally are regressive and have exemptions that are much too high. Latin American exemptions are typically higher than American or U.K. exemptions. A lack of progression and high exemptions may be a correct tax policy under the incentive liberation strategy, but it is incorrect if one is following a 'resource accumulation' strategy.

(iii) *Value Added Taxes*. Value added taxes have an advantage over corporate income taxes in that they are easier to administer. Administrative ease arises from the self-enforcement aspects of value added taxes. Corporate profit taxes require a complete and honest set of corporate records. Value added taxes only require knowledge of the value of products purchased from other companies and the value of output sold. Since purchasing companies want to maximise the reported value of inputs purchased from other companies on their tax forms and selling companies want to mimimise the reported value of output sold, the records of one company can be used to check the records of another company. Since private interests are directly opposed there can be no collusion at the expense of the government. Value added taxes have the additional advantage of at least growing as fast as the economy. A 're-source accumulation' strategy implies that high rates would be appropriate, while a strategy of 'incentive liberation' would lead one to suggest low rates.

(iv) *Property Taxes or Wealth Taxes*. In all countries wealth, or property, taxes become in effect taxes on land and buildings. In all countries there are problems of assessment. This might be solved by using some variant of Harberger's suggestion that individuals self-assess their own property and that they be forced to sell property if someone is willing to pay more than 120 per cent of their self-assessment.[4] This scheme is as applicable to developed as to underdeveloped countries, and it has been adopted in neither for the same reasons. Politically, no one is willing to adopt harsh penalties for underassessment. Moreover, in the smaller Latin American countries in which land is monopolised by a few wealthy families who are linked by ties of marriage, there would be no necessity of assessing the value of property correctly, since there would be few potential buyers – apart from the government (which they control) and foreigners (who probably would not be allowed to purchase large tracts of land).

In countries such as those in Latin America, where property and particularly land are underutilised, property taxes would ideally be based on potential yield rather than actual yield. This complicates the problem of tax administration, but it means that taxes in principle could become a major instrument for encouraging owners to fully utilise their property. There is also the problem of keeping up with changes in the potential yield of property and land. The faster technical progress occurs, the harder this becomes. One solution is to assess individual pieces of property in terms of their potential yield *vis-à-vis* some standard type of property (an average acre of land). Then as the potential yield of this standard type of property rises, the potential yield of all property is adjusted in the same proportion. High potential assessments and tax rates would be desirable under both of our strategies.

Ideally in the Latin American context potential yields would be set at very high rates to encourage land reform, but political realities mean that this is no more probable than direct land reform itself.

(v) *Sales Taxes*. In countries with wide disparities in standards of living, sales taxes can become progressive rather than regressive if high rates are placed on luxury items, but the same problems restrict the use of both sales taxes and income taxes. They both demand elaborate and honest records. Consequently, sales taxes need to be placed at the manufacturing and wholesale level to reduce the number of taxpayers and the amount of record-keeping. Both strategies would call for high rates on luxuries, but the incentive liberation strategy would juggle rates to create favourable incentives. For example, agricultural inputs might be subject to low rates.

(vi) *Public Service Taxes*. Public overhead capital such as roads, ports, trains, electricity, communications and a host of other items are essential factors in the production of output, yet Latin American countries typically do not collect users' charges which cover costs, much less make profits.[5] In the 'incentive liberation' strategy, prices should be raised to a level which equates supply and demand for these essential services. Typically this will involve prices which will earn profits for government enterprises which provide public overhead capital. In the 'resource accumulation' strategy, users' charges for public overhead capital should be set as if the government were a discriminating monopolist. The government extracts each person's consumers' surplus from the use of these services. In either strategy, profits from public capital would be part of public savings which would be available for public or private investment.

(vii) *Compulsory Savings*. One of the major objections to the 'incentive liberation' strategy is that it ignores equity among the present generation of taxpayers. This problem can be partially eliminated by transforming taxes into compulsory saving. Individuals are forced to pay taxes but in return they are given bonds which can only be redeemed at some date in the future. Essentially consumption privileges are made more equitable than the initial distribution of income. This does not eliminate the equity problem since individuals are being inequitably forced to save, but it may reduce it. What little evidence there is, however, would suggest that the political objections to compulsory saving are almost as great as those to taxes. Chile attempted a compulsory savings plan in 1968 but it met with fierce resistance. Given the fierce resistance to such plans, their impact on work incentives might be just as adverse as those of taxes. If this is the case there is little to be gained from compulsory savings rather than taxation.

(viii) *Efficiency Taxes*. Under the 'incentive liberation' strategy there may be a series of taxes (positive or negative) levied to alter the prices facing entrepreneurs. Thus if labour is underutilised while capital is in short supply, taxes may be placed on capital equipment to encourage a substitution in the capital–labour ratio in favour of labour. To encourage the use of fertiliser, fertiliser prices may be subsidised. Whether these are good or bad taxes depends on whether the desired responses are engendered. The 'resource accumulation' strategy implies that taxes should be imposed on products with inelastic demands. Revenue is collected and purchasing decisions are not greatly affected.

(e) Utilisation of Resources

Often Latin American countries possess resources that are not used because they lack complementary goods. For example, factories may operate at less than capacity because they lack some foreign import. The major underutilisation of real resources, however, is unemployment and underemployment of labour. One reason labour is not fully used is that there is not enough capital at conventional capital–labour ratios to employ all of the existing labour force.

Taxes may be levied on physical capital to encourage a shift in the capital–labour ratio, but no one would argue that the elasticity of the capital–labour ratio with respect to the relative prices of capital and labour is high enough to solve unemployment in this manner. A lack of technical expertise and the need to adopt foreign techniques, rather than developing techniques suited to the capital–labour endowments of Latin America, means that the capital–labour ratio probably has a low price elasticity with respect to the relative prices of capital and labour.

The difference between private employment costs and social employment costs may also lead to underemployment of labour from society's viewpoint. In countries which do not allow individuals to starve, individuals must be fed whether they work or do not work, but private industry need only pay its employees. Thus the private costs of hiring an individual might be high while the social costs (private costs minus subsistence costs) might be low. In this case a wage subsidy might be an appropriate policy.

Several problems arise when trying to utilise human resources fully. It is clear that total output would increase if methods for using unemployed labour could be found. More important, increasing personal incomes is a social end in itself. Furthermore, greater employment and higher incomes would probably lead to greater equity, and this may induce governments to search for ways of fully employing its labour forces. Consequently governments may (and indeed should) develop projects which use labour at a capital–labour ratio that is radically different from those adopted in the private sector of the economy. In general, Latin American governments need to organise labour-intensive programmes for rural investment, as the Chinese have managed to do.

Although such projects may have low social opportunity costs in underdeveloped countries, they usually are not undertaken because of their high budgetary costs. In this respect governments are like firms. To employ people they must pay the conventional monetary wage. They must be able to accumulate financial resources from the rest of the economy in order to do this. Since politically the unemployed can be forced to subsist at lower standards of living than would be tolerable if they were working on government projects, massive public employment programmes depend upon a government's power to lower the real standards of living of those employed elsewhere in the economy. Thus public employment projects with low social costs may have high budgetary and political costs. They also demand a high degree of organisational skill.

This explains why Latin American countries, with the exception of Cuba, do not attempt to fully utilise their labour resources, but it does not diminish the economic gains that could be obtained from a fuller utilisation of economic resources. In terms of acquiring resources for development, there are more resources to be acquired here than anywhere else.

(f) Conclusion

In the process of economic development economics must play a subsidiary role. Designing workable economic development plans requires considerable effort and knowledge, but it is not an impossible task. The most difficult task is policy implementation and this is essentially a political task. The problem of implementation is not confined to poor countries. Rich countries have not been noticeably successful in raising the incomes of poor regions or groups within their borders. The economic means for reducing poverty exist but political will-power is lacking. Any economic system automatically creates vested interests which make the political costs of transition to a new system very large. This is especially true in countries where economic power is closely associated with political power. A revolution in the distribution of economic power requires revolution in the distribution of political power. Similarly, economic development requires development finance, but it also requires an ability to acquire the political resources necessary to effect economic change.

NOTES

1. For a longer discussion on the allocation decisions which any society must make, see Richard A. Musgrave, *The Theory of Public Finance* (McGraw-Hill, New York, 1959), ch. 1.

2. Harley H. Hinrichs, *A General Theory of Tax Structure Change during Economic Development* (Harvard Law School, 1966).

3. Richard Goode, 'Personal Income Tax in Latin America', in *Fiscal Policy for Economic Growth in Latin America* (O.A.S., Johns Hopkins Press, Baltimore, 1965), p. 159.

4. Arnold C. Harberger, 'Issues of Tax Reform for Latin America', ibid. p. 119.

5. See Chapter 3 below.

2. Economic Surplus and the Budget

JORGE ARRATE and LUCIO GELLER

FISCAL policy is a global concept which includes both the structure and policy of government income as well as the structure and policy of public expenditure. Quite often fiscal policy is identified with only one of its two features – either public expenditure or revenue – and thus the overall view is lost.

One of the reasons for this separation, perhaps, is different interpretations of the causes of growth of the public debt in developed and backward countries. The deficiency of government revenue over expenditure is such a general phenomenon that it is hard to find exceptions to it. The roots of this phenomenon differ according to the type of country under consideration. Thus, for instance, in developed countries growth in the public debt appears to be caused by the increase in public expenditure relative to *per capita* product; by the increase in social expenditure, considered a responsibility of the state, relative to other public expenditures; and by the lag that apparently exists between the approval of public expenditures and their financing.[1] In these countries fiscal policy tends to be concerned largely with public expenditure policy, as it is expenditure policy which is responsible for the increase in the public debt.

In backward countries it is evident that the problem of growing public indebtedness – both internal and external – is related more to the financing of public expenditure than to the level and rate of growth of expenditure. In these countries the economic, political and administrative structures result in inelastic revenue systems. This is a consequence both of the type of taxes imposed and of administration of the fiscal system. In backward countries the most urgent fiscal policy problems have to do with tax potential and this preoccupation has increased lately because it has become recognised that the state must assume a major role in financing development.

Notwithstanding the differences in emphasis in the two types of countries, it should not be forgotten that income and expenditure policies should be analysed jointly. This would appear to be obvious, but the ease of doing so depends very much on the method of analysis. The method chosen should reflect the social, political and economic context in which the analysis occurs.

(a) Fiscal Policy, Effective Demand and Economic Surplus

The analysis could centre on the concept of effective demand. The Keynesian approach to fiscal policy emphasises the impact of public expenditures on effective demand and studies the variables that explain public income – autonomous variables and variables that depend on income. Public expenditures act as one of the autonomous elements of overall expenditure – autonomous in the sense that they are not affected by variations in the level of the national product – and consequently government spending affects the employment and price level of the economy. Tax revenues, on the other hand, reduce private expenditure and, therefore, decrease overall expenditure. It is thus evident that if the unit of analysis is effective demand, government income and expenditure policies are likely to be concerned with stabilising the economy. This means that in the short run the government is likely to be concerned with reducing the level of unemployment or, once inflexibilities begin to appear, restricting aggregate demand so that inflation does not accelerate. In the long run the objective of Keynesian fiscal policy is stable growth and full employment, stable growth being understood to mean equality between the increase in effective demand and increase in productive capacity, and full employment being understood to mean growth in productive capacity at a rate which absorbs the increase in the labour force. Stable growth requires regulation of the overall magnitude of public income and expenditure, whereas a full employment policy requires that fiscal policy discriminate between consumption and investment. In a developed economy, where the factors of production are quite mobile, the concept of effective demand can form the basis of fiscal policy.

Alternatively, the method of analysis could centre on the concept of economic surplus. Through its income and expenditure policies the public sector helps to determine the magnitude of the economic surplus as well as its destination. We define the economic surplus as the difference between the available social product and the consumption of workers and their families. The available social product is equal to the gross social product less amortisation.[2] In turn, the gross social product corresponds to total material production plus services directly connected with production, such as transportation and trade.

Once the economic surplus has been defined, it can be seen that taxation plays a double role: on the one hand, taxes may increase the magnitude of the surplus to the extent that they affect consumption of workers and their families; on the other hand, taxation may transfer to the public sector part of the surplus appropriated by the owners of capital. That is, taxes may affect the amount and composition of the capitalists' expenditure – the capitalists' consumption and private investment – as well as the magnitude of the economic surplus.

An increase in the tax effort, i.e. the ratio of tax revenue to the social product, will be limited by the growth of the economic surplus and by the possibilities of transferring the surplus from the private sector to the public sector. There are several ways to increase the surplus, viz. by reducing real wages, by increasing the productivity of labour while keeping real wages constant, and by raising the level of employment.

Although the economic surplus may increase as a result of tax policy, the economic surplus available for *development* in a given period will almost certainly be less than the total economic surplus, because part of the surplus will be used to finance more consumption than is strictly necessary. It is frequently argued that the economic surplus available for development could be larger if efficiency in the public sector were higher. While it is true that more rational spending on general social expenditure items is an important objective, it seems clear that, in the long run, the increase in the economic surplus available for development will occur through an increase in the total economic surplus rather than through a decrease in general social expenditures.

Part of the economic surplus available for development is likely to be devoted to expenditures that do not lead to an increase in the productive capacity of the economic system. The expenditures that do constitute productive use of the economic surplus by the public sector are new productive investments in state enterprises and investments that serve development indirectly (schools, universities, hospitals, certain types of housing, etc.); most expenditure on scientific and technological research and on increasing the number of professionals, trained workers and people who can read and write; as well as expenditure on social services, such as health services, which directly affect the productivity of the labour force.

We have already noted that policy directly affects the surplus available for development, since taxes affect private expenditure decisions.

Taxes represent an appropriation of the economic surplus by the state and constitute a transfer of resources from the private to the public sector. This transfer of resources may result in a reduction of consumption by the capitalists, but it may also result, at least in part, in a reduction in the productive use of the surplus in the private sector. Thus it is important to consider the factors that determine the amount of the surplus that the public sector should appropriate.

First of all, it is essential to consider to what extent the public and private sectors use the surplus for development purposes. Secondly, it is necessary to estimate the social yield of productive expenditure in the public sector and to compare this with the social yield in the private sector. In making this comparison, not only should market prices be corrected for any distortions that may exist, but dynamic factors should also be considered. For instance, the classification of activities into expanding and passive industries according to their income elasticity of demand presupposes the present unequal distribution of income. To the extent that private investment responds to the existing pattern of demand, the continuation of the present distribution of income becomes a necessary condition for the continuation of a high level of investment in the new industrial sectors. At the same time, the unequal income distribution is both a cause and an effect of the composition of investment. It is something of a paradox that in the backward countries the passive industries are those that serve the needs of the majority of the population. This must be taken into account when calculating the social yield of investment expenditure in the two sectors. Lastly, the immense size of the development task confronting Latin America virtually compels the public sector to appropriate a large part of the surplus. Many of the investments needed to overcome the obstacles to growth are characterised by economies of scale. The national private sector is unable to mobilise the large amounts of savings needed to finance these projects. Thus if the projects are to be carried out at all, they must be financed either by foreign capital or by the public sector. Foreign financing has many disadvantages,[3] and in any case is unlikely to be available in the amounts required, so that in practice the responsibility must remain in the public sector.[4]

One conclusion that emerges from our analysis is that an appreciation of the role of the state in determining the magnitude and destination of the economic surplus requires a classification of public income and expenditure based on different criteria from those traditionally used. Specifically, the division of expenditure between public consumption and public investment is of little use, in that public consumption includes many expenditures that promote development, while public investment includes certain investments that contribute nothing to productive capacity. For this reason the statistics collected and classified by national and international institutions seldom are ideal for the type of analysis we wish to make.

(b) Public Appropriation of the Economic Surplus

The public sector can capture part of the economic surplus via the profits obtained by public enterprises, via charges for administrative services which exceed the costs of these services, and via taxation. In Latin America, as the figures of Table 1 indicate, taxation is the public sector's largest source of income. The uses to which this income is put are determined by public expenditure policy, which may emphasise either general social expenditures or activities which directly or indirectly promote development.

Table 1. Taxation as a Per Cent of Total Government Revenue in Six Latin American Countries

	1955	1960	1965	1966
Argentina	64·6	78·8	70·6	70·8
Brazil	79·7	83·9[a]	85·2[b]	85·5
Chile	84·6	94·5	92·8	92·1
Guatemala	90·7	90·7[c]	91·7[d]	94·1
Mexico	87·0[e]	91·9	...	92·8
Venezuela	94·6	95·6	96·2	95·8

[a] Average for 1960–1 and 1964–5.
[b] Average for 1964–5.
[c] Average for 1960–2.
[d] Average for 1963–5.
[e] Figure for 1956.

Source: ECLA, *Estudio Económico de América Latina* (1967).

From the viewpoint of the real behaviour of the economy, several factors may operate which restrict the public sector's ability to capture the surplus. The analysis of these factors and of their relative importance constitutes the study of taxable capacity and tax effort. We shall understand taxable capacity to mean the potential of the public sector to absorb resources from the private sector in the form of taxes, or in other words, the capacity of the private sector to bear a given level of taxation.

C

We shall understand tax effort to mean the actual absorption of the resources of the private sector via taxation. The comparison between an economy's tax effort and some indicator of taxable capacity gives an idea as to whether the tax effort is low, average or high.

In a static analysis, tax potential depends upon the size of the economic surplus and the possibilities of compressing the consumption of the workers. Taxes may simply capture part of the surplus, transferring it from the private to the public sector, or they may, in addition, reduce the level of consumption previously attained and thereby increase the total surplus available for development.

The most commonly used indicator of a country's tax effort is the ratio of taxes to national product. When the numerator and denominator are known the ratio can be calculated and comparisons between countries can be made. In Table 2, the ratio of taxes to national product for several Latin American countries appears, together with other information. The ratio in Latin America varies between 9 and 22 per cent. The same ratio is approximately 37 per cent in France, 35 per cent in Western Germany, 29 per cent in the United Kingdom and 26 per cent in the United States.

It may happen, however, that countries with a high ratio of taxation to national product are exerting a relatively low effort in comparison with their taxable capacity. For instance, if two countries have an identical ratio of taxes to national product it does not follow that they are both making the same effort in terms of taxes collected, inasmuch as differences in *per capita* income, in the economy's degree of monetisation, in the relative size of the foreign sector, in the sectoral origin of the national product and in income distribution all affect a country's taxable capacity.

Of the factors mentioned, *per capita* product normally is used as the major indicator of an economy's level of development and taxable capacity. It is certainly associated with a higher degree of monetisation, a smaller proportion of illiterates in the population and better possibilities for implementing tax laws and preventing evasion. Hence, when comparing two countries with an identical national product, the one with the smaller population could be expected to be capable of a greater tax effort.

The larger the relative size of the industrial sector in the national product, the greater the taxable capacity, since generally speaking industrialisation is associated with more monetisation and more regular accounting practices, thus facilitating the control of evasion. Similarly, the larger the foreign sector, the greater the administrative control and the larger the number of 'tax handles'. Likewise, a country whose income distribution is very unequal would have a greater taxable capacity than one whose income distribution is more even, since it may be easier to tax the rich than the poor.

The available empirical evidence regarding the importance of these factors or other similar ones at different levels of taxation is not conclusive, however, and sometimes even is contradictory. Although generally speaking there appears to be a consensus that most of the factors mentioned lose explanatory power when analysing differences in tax ratios in high *per capita* income countries, there is no agreement as to the relative importance of these factors in low income countries.[5]

The method usually followed in analysing the relationship between tax effort and tax capacity attempts to explain the differences between tax ratios through cross-section statistical regression procedures for a large sample of countries at different levels of development. In simple terms, each country is typified by certain variables, *per capita* income and the size of the foreign sector, for instance, and the expected tax ratio is determined from the magnitude of these variables. The comparison of the expected ratio with the actual ratio gives an idea as to whether or not the country in question is making an adequate tax effort. Sometimes the countries in the sample are classified according to their development level, creating subgroups (e.g. of rich and poor countries), and the same procedure is repeated for each subgroup separately. Some of the results obtained with this method are shown in Table 2.

The purpose of these comparisons is to reach policy conclusions. A low tax effort would imply that a country is not allocating enough resources to the public sector, and if the public sector is supposed to play an indispensable role in promoting development, low tax effort would imply that the economy's growth prospects were being harmed. These comparisons also are used by nations and organisations which provide foreign aid to underdeveloped countries. It has become fashionable recently to make aid conditional upon 'self-help' measures in the recipient country, and particularly upon measures designed to mobilise a country's internal resources. The presumption is that more foreign assistance would be channelled to those countries that show they are making a greater tax effort.[6] In terms of policy, the logical recommendation to a country wishing to accelerate development is to reform the tax system and allow the public sector to capture a larger share of the surplus. This would not only increase locally financed development expenditure, it would also lead to an increase in foreign aid.

Recommendations for reform derived from analyses like those we have been discussing encounter serious obstacles, however. Although there are countries that appear to be able to collect more taxes, they do not in practice do so. The reason for this has more to do with politics than economics. In particular, the high income groups in Latin America hold most of the economic and political power, and they have generally opposed introducing new taxes or increasing rates on already existing taxes. As shown in Table 2, out of seventeen Latin American countries considered, only five collect more taxes than would be expected given their *per capita* income and the importance of foreign trade. Of the remaining twelve, three are average and nine are in the low tax effort category.

A more important argument against the indiscriminate use of indicators of tax capacity and tax effort is that they provide no information about the way tax revenue is used. It cannot be said that one country makes a greater tax effort than another unless one compares the uses to which each puts the income collected. The magnitude of the surplus appropriated by the public sector is only one aspect of the problem; the use to which the surplus is put is another. As indicated before, the surplus captured by the public sector can have two basic destinations: it can be devoted to general social expenditures or it can be used for development. The information furnished by an analysis of a country's tax effort does not enable one to make a complete diagnosis of an economy's problem. It is equally important to determine what part of public revenue is devoted to accelerating development. Tax effort and development effort are not necessarily equivalent. Their equivalence depends on the destination of the funds collected through taxation.

(c) *Public Use of the Economic Surplus*

In terms of the analytical framework we are using, only part of the economic surplus available for development will be effectively used for that purpose. Let us recall that we consider the following expenditures to have a positive effect on productive capacity: new directly productive investments, investments that serve development indirectly (investment in education, health and so on) and expenditures which increase useful knowledge or spread it more widely.

The traditional organisation of data on public expenditure in Latin America does not allow one to conduct a refined analysis within our theoretical framework. Normally, two types of public expenditure classifications are available: (1) an 'economic' classification which distinguishes between capital expenditure and current expenditure, and (2) a 'functional' classification which focuses on the sectors in which expenditures occur – defence, housing, education, health, etc. When using this information, it must not be forgotten that, first, not all capital expenditures in the public sector represent a use of the surplus for development, and, second, many current expenditures on the social services may contribute to future increases in productive capacity. The analysis which follows, using information classified in the traditional manner, attempts to illustrate this fact. At the same time we shall advance some broad hypotheses on the 'developmentalist' or 'stagnationist' nature of public expenditure in Latin America.

Table 2. Ranking of Latin American Countries by the Tax: G.N.P. Ratio and by an Indicator of Tax Effort[a]

Country	Ranking according to T./G.N.P.	Ratio T./G.N.P.	Ranking according to effort[b]	Level of effort
Uruguay	1	21·8	2	High
Brazil	2	21·4	1	High
Chile	3	20·9	3	High
Argentina	4	20·1	6	Average
Dominican Republic	5	17·9	5	High
Ecuador	6	16·7	4	High
Peru	7	16·0	7	Average
Panama	8	15·1	8	Average
Costa Rica	9	13·8	10	Low
Nicaragua	10	13·5	9	Low
Colombia	11	10·9	12	Low
El Salvador	12	10·9	14	Low
Paraguay	13	10·2	13	Low
Mexico	14	9·9	15	Low
Honduras	15	9·9	16	Low
Haiti	16	9·6	11	Low
Guatemala	17	9·3	17	Low

[a] The averages are for the years 1962–4 or 1963–5.
[b] High, average or low tax effort is measured on the basis of deviations from the line of regression in an equation that considers *per capita* income and the size of the foreign sector as variables, adjusted for a sample of 52 low income countries.

Source: Jorgen R. Lotz and Elliot R. Morss, 'Measuring Tax Effort in Developing Countries', in *I.M.F. Staff Papers* (Nov 1967).

Table 3 contains data on the relative magnitudes of current and capital expenditure in six Latin American countries. Current expenditure includes wages and salaries paid by the public sector, purchases of goods by the government, transfer payments, interest on the public debt, etc. Capital expenditure not only includes real investment, it also includes so-called financial investments (purchases of stocks and shares, the granting of loans, etc.) and amortisation of the internal and foreign debt.

Table 3. Distribution of Government Expenditure between Current and Capital Account in Six Latin American Countries

Country	Current expenditure (%)	Capital expenditure (%)
Argentina (average 1964–6)	70·3	29·7
Brazil (average 1964–6)	67·3	32·7
Chile (average 1964–6)	65·6	34·4
Guatemala (average 1963–5)	59·3	40·7
Mexico (1966)	59·4	40·6
Venezuela (average 1963–5)	56·3	43·7

Source: ECLA, *Estudio Económico de América Latina* (1967).

Part of current government expenditure clearly does have a positive effect on development. On the other hand, another part, and possibly a substantial part in many Latin American countries, is devoted to maintaining a large and growing bureaucracy. This, of course, is a response of populist governments to pressures from the middle class demanding job opportunities.

Table 4 summarises some information on the division of current public expenditure between wages and salaries and other items. Not only do wage payments account for a large proportion of total current expenditure, but they have been increasing quite rapidly as well. Between 1960 and 1963 wages grew more rapidly than all other current expenditures in nearly every one of the countries studied. In Table 4 payments to the social security system, including payments to the social security system for civil servants, are classified as 'other expenditures', and thus the real importance of wage payments is understated by the data. In Chile, for instance, between the years 1964 and 1967 remuneration of public employees accounted for about 25 per cent of total public expenditure and social security payments accounted for approximately another 22 per cent.[7]

Despite the pressures exerted on the public sector to allocate a large proportion of its resources to current expenditures, the state accounts for a significant share of total investment. The reason for this is that private investment is low. In addition, in some cases the type of invest-

Tables 4. The Importance of Wages and Salaries in Current Public Expenditure in Eight Latin American Countries

Country	Indices[a]				Percentage of total current public expenditure			
	1960	1961	1962	1963	1960	1961	1962	1963
Uruguay								
Remunerations	100	128	171	165	42	52	58	63
Other expenditures	100	86	90	71	58	48	42	37
Brazil								
Remunerations	100	138	139	157	54	50	63	60
Other expenditures	100	160	97	126	46	50	37	40
Peru								
Remunerations	100	112	126	137	55	56	53	56
Other expenditures	100	109	131	132	45	44	47	44
Mexico								
Remunerations	100	110	119	134	45	43	41	42
Other expenditures	100	120	140	151	55	57	59	58
Bolivia								
Remunerations	100	132	129	134	49	54	51	51
Other expenditures	100	108	118	123	51	46	49	49
Venezuela								
Remunerations	100	112	...	117	62	65	...	63
Other expenditures	100	101	...	116	48	35	...	37
Argentina								
Remunerations	100	114	121	109	44	47	50	51
Other expenditures	100	100	97	84	56	53	50	59
Chile								
Remunerations	100	102	112	99	34	33	33	32
Other expenditures	100	105	117	103	66	67	67	68

[a] The deflator used was the cost of living index.

Source: Organisation of American States, Department of Economic Affairs of the Pan-American Union, *Latin America: Problems and Perspectives of Economic Development, 1963–1964* (Johns Hopkins Press, Baltimore, 1966), p. 196.

ments needed for development require such large amounts of capital that private national entrepreneurs are unable to finance them. Between 1960 and 1966, on the average for Latin America, public investment accounted for approximately one-third of total investment.[8] None the less, there is considerable variation around this average from one country to another.[9] Table 5 provides data from several Latin American countries. It can be seen that in Chile the share of public investment is well above the average, whereas in Argentina it is considerably below average. The characteristics of each country are different, as is the ideology of each government, and these have an obvious effect on the allocation of public revenue.

Table 5. Public Investment as a Percentage of Total Investment in
Six Latin American Countries

Country	1960–2	1964–6
Argentina	22·4	28·5
Brazil	34·5	61·8
Chile	59·5	66·5
Guatemala	26·8	23·1
Mexico	32·7	31·3
Venezuela	43·7	39·6

Source: ECLA, *Estudio Económico de América Latina* (1967).

The functional classification of public expenditure also is of some use in analysing the characteristics of the public sector. Here again the differences between countries are considerable.[10] In 1966, for example, expenditure on defence varied between approximately 6 per cent in Costa Rica and 25 per cent in Haiti.[11] This type of expenditure obviously belongs in the non-productive category, because it contributes nothing to development. Brazil, one of the countries considered to be making a major tax effort,[12] spends a high proportion of public revenue on defence, and hence its development effort is not as great as its tax effort.

Expenditure on education and health could make a contribution to development, depending upon their nature and specific destination. In the case of education, for instance, it is difficult to determine to what extent educational expenditure in Latin America contributes to development and to what extent it should be considered consumption. It could be argued that, to the extent that social benefits derived from education are positive, educational expenditures should help to increase productive capacity. But, evidently, the educational system may adapt well or poorly to the social needs that arise from the dynamics of growth. There are reasons to believe that the educational system in Latin America has not played a 'developmentalist' role. The educational system has not been able to reduce Latin America's technological dependence on the industrial countries. Nor has it been able to remove the bottlenecks of trained labour and professional skills that seem to be a permanent feature of the economy. These deficiencies suggest that the educational system is oriented more towards the satisfaction of consumption than towards increasing the potential for production.

Despite the very broad nature of our analysis, some conclusions have emerged. First, public expenditure is heavily biased towards current expenditure, especially towards the payment of wages and salaries and the financing of social security. Next, real investment constitutes only a part of public capital expenditure; the remainder corresponds to the purchase of stocks and shares, the provision of loans and grants, and amortisation of the public debt, both foreign and internal. From a functional viewpoint, the relatively high percentage of expenditure on defence, and the serious doubts as to the real nature of expenditure on educational and social services suggest that many of the government's resources are wasted and contribute little or nothing to development. This impression is strengthened, in some cases, upon examination of the functional distribution of real public investment. Thus in Chile, for example, the figures reveal that in 1967 only 6 per cent of public investment was channelled to the industrial sector, 5·3 per cent to mining and 10·8 per cent to agriculture.[13]

(d) Tax Policy in a Backward Country

Throughout the preceding discussion we have tried to use the concept of economic surplus as the basis of our analysis. One of the conclusions reached was that taxable capacity could increase in the long run provided the economic surplus continues to increase. The absolute and relative size of the economic surplus will increase as a result of higher levels of employment and as a result of rises in the productivity of labour which are not totally translated into higher real wages. Such productivity increases result from changes in technology and from the increased skill of the labour force, which in turn are due to a greater division of labour or greater expenditure on education.

These changes in the technical conditions of production constitute one of the most important laws of economic development. At the same time, the failure of these changes to take place quickly is one of the causes of structural backwardness in Latin America. The role of fiscal policy in this context is to contribute towards increasing the economic surplus through public investment, so as to raise the technological level of the entire economy and, more precisely, to accelerate the rate of advance in those sectors in which the country has a present or potential comparative advantage.

Changes in productive techniques which originate in the public sector have an additional advantage in that they prevent the economic surplus from being transferred to the rest of the world via 'unequal exchange'. The prices that result from the present system of international trade, in which capital is free to move and profit rates are equalised in the various countries, necessarily induce a transfer of the economic surplus from the backward to the developed nations. This transfer of the surplus occurs because profit rates are the same in all countries despite the fact that the productivity of labour, real wage rates and the rate of technical progress are very different. The historical conditions in the backward countries and the low rates of technological progress that characterise them have led to a structure of relative prices that fails to reflect the true social costs of production. This unequal exchange occurs in both the domestic and the world markets and is a consequence of the distorted price system. Elimination of this unequal exchange is possible to the extent that the different internal economic activities gradually reach technical levels corresponding to those of the developed countries; in other words, the development process itself will gradually eliminate the problem.[14] Meanwhile, leakages abroad can be reduced with the help of fiscal policy, namely, by imposing export and import taxes that alter the terms of trade in favour of the backward countries. This solution, however, is only a short-term one.

The transfer of part of the economic surplus is accentuated by the monopolistic behaviour of foreign enterprises that dominate the foreign trade sector and some domestic markets. These monopolistic elements channel the economic surplus abroad through a deterioration of the terms of trade or through profit remittances. The problem becomes particularly acute when the activities of these firms lead to an internal transfer of the surplus from the technologically backward sectors, in the hands of nationals, to technologically modern sectors, generally in the hands of foreigners. In order to prevent these transfers foreign companies must become the target of a specially designed tax policy.

In short, from the point of view of development, a backward country's fiscal policy should address itself to the following objectives: first, to guarantee a steady increase of the economic surplus; second, to capture a growing proportion of that surplus for the public sector; third, to minimise leakages of the surplus abroad. These last two points will be discussed in what remains of this section.

(i) *The Elasticity of Government Revenue*. The capture of a growing proportion of the economic surplus for government purposes should be reflected in indicators that compare the percentage change in tax revenue with the percentage change in the economic surplus. The conventional classification of the national accounts does not allow us to calculate the tax elasticity as we have defined it, and we have to be content with other more traditional indicators, like those shown in Table 6.

Table 6. The Income Elasticity of Taxation in Six Latin American Countries,[a] 1960–66

Country	Elasticity in relation to G.D.P.	Elasticity in relation to total expenditure
Argentina	0·832	0·823
Brazil	1·109	1·096
Chile	1·103	1·060
Guatemala	0·719	1·004
Mexico	1·183	0·925
Venezuela	0·827	1·631

[a] Calculated from the slope of the line of regression.

Source: ECLA, *Estudio Económico de América Latina* (1967).

According to data for the period 1960–6, the tax effort increased in only three cases: Brazil, Chile and Mexico. These three countries had a marginal tax effort that exceeded their average. Nevertheless, it should not be inferred that this marginal effort was very great, especially if one also considers the rate at which public expenditure increased. In Brazil and Chile additional taxation helped to reduce the imbalance between revenue and expenditure, even though in Chile central government expenditure increased its share of the gross domestic product. On the other hand, in Mexico increased taxation failed to keep pace with the increase in public expenditure. In Argentina, Guatemala and Venezuela the tax effort was poor, particularly in Argentina, where public expenditure grew faster than gross domestic product.

The major factors in determining the elasticity of government revenue are the structure and progressiveness of the tax system, the political possibility of raising tax rates and imposing new taxes, and the possibilities of introducing stricter administrative controls.

As regards the first factor, let us consider direct taxes. If the system of personal income taxes incorporates the principle of progressivity, personal direct taxation will have an elasticity that exceeds unity and a rise in either real or money incomes (e.g. as a result of inflation) will result in a more than proportionate increase in government revenue from this source. A system of corporate taxation, even if the rates are uniform, may contribute to an elastic tax structure. This will be particularly true if an increase in the productivity of labour leads to a rise in profits rather than in wages, or if the process of inflation redistributes income in favour of corporate profits. A tax on capital also would tend to produce an elastic tax structure if the process of growth is accompanied by a rise in the capital–output ratio. Taxes on capital, however, are difficult to enact and enforce in societies where property owners are politically dominant. Moreover, it can be argued that taxes on capital create disincentives for private investment.

The objective of an expenditure tax is to reduce consumption and increase the funds available for investment. In other words, its objective is to increase the rate of private savings. If it were widely applied its elasticity would be uncertain and would depend on the extent to which its objective was attained. Indirect taxes would tend to be elastic only if they fall heavily on goods with a high income elasticity of demand. In Latin America this implies taxing those articles consumed by the upper 10 per cent in the income distribution. These groups tend to have a diversified and elastic pattern of demand because of the high level of *per capita* income they have reached and because of their habit of emulating the consumption standards maintained by prosperous groups abroad.

Tariffs and multiple exchange rate systems tend to be inelastic taxes because development in Latin America has occurred through a process of import substitution. Export taxes also are inelastic because the emphasis on industrialisation has led to a neglect of the possibilities for expanding exports.

In summary, the elasticity of the tax system depends on the average of the elasticities of the different taxes. An examination of the composition of taxation – i.e. direct, indirect and external taxes – is not sufficient to indicate the elasticity of government revenue. There are reasons to believe, however, that wherever the share of direct taxes is low or falling, the tax system as a whole tends to be inelastic. One can compensate for this, of course, by raising tax rates.

In Chile, for instance, as the data in Table 7 indicate,[15] the weighting of the different types of taxes did not change very much between 1960 and 1966. There were, however, some important changes that are not reflected in the table, such as the introduction in 1965 of a tax on the presumed minimum income. At the same time, the tax bases were readjusted periodically and automatically in order to keep up with inflation. Similarly, taxes on the foreign trade sector were modified and changes were introduced in the method of taxing the foreign-owned copper companies.

In Brazil the income tax was altered in order to increase its progressiveness; the existing sales tax was replaced by a simpler one and customs duties were reduced. In Argentina, in 1967, important fiscal reforms were introduced. New taxes were imposed, rates on existing taxes were increased, and exporters were taxed through a system which captured the windfall profits obtained from the devaluation of the exchange rate. In Mexico, between 1962 and 1964, an overall and progressive system of personal income taxation was designed, and a progressive scale for the tax on corporations was established. The abolition of certain taxes, such as estate duties and excess profits tax, was offset by an improvement in administration and collection, and by an increase in the number of taxpayers.[16]

Table 7. The Tax Structure in Six Latin American Countries, 1960 and 1966

Country	Direct taxes (%)	Indirect taxes (%)	Taxes on foreign trade (%)
Argentina			
1960	25	38	37
1966	26	49	25
Brazil			
1960	34	54	12
1966	29	62	9
Chile			
1960	23	43	34
1966	27	40	33
Guatemala			
1960	11	43	46
1966	14	54	32
Mexico			
1960	38	35	27
1966	47	37	16
Venezuela			
1960	10	8	82
1966	14	9	77

Source: ECLA, *Estudio Económico de América Latina* (1967).

(ii) *Public Revenue and Foreign Enterprises*. We have already remarked that foreign enterprises are a vehicle for transferring the economic surplus abroad through profit remittances. Many national enterprises in

Latin America also act as mechanisms for transferring the surplus, through payment of profits abroad in exchange for patents, trademarks or foreign technical expertise.

The leakage of the surplus abroad is very pronounced when foreign enterprises control certain mining enclaves. The high productivity of labour in the mining export sector is not only the result of applied modern technology but also a consequence of the high quality of the natural resources which the foreign companies exploit. As a result the economic surplus in the export sectors is a very large proportion of value added. At the same time this surplus tends to leak abroad. One of the reasons for this is that generally speaking the prices paid by the large international firms are internal transfer prices, and these can be manipulated to suit the convenience of the parent corporation. Moreover, the reinvestment of profits obtained from a given activity is not automatic but depends on conditions in the world market and on the investment alternatives in different countries that the multinational enterprises confront. As a consequence of the scale of these enterprises, and their method of operation, it is difficult to tax them effectively or predict the revenue yield.

Table 8. Venezuela and Chile: Taxation of Oil and Copper

| | Percentage share of: | | | | Taxes in the mining sector as a per cent of | | | |
| | G.D.P. | | Total exports | | Total tax revenue | | Output of the sector | |
Year	Oil	Copper	Oil	Copper	Oil	Copper	Oil	Copper
1955	29·9	...	94·1	64·5	63·2	19·4	33·2	...
1960–2	30·0	5·4	92·4	61·2	70·2	12·1	45·7	35·8
1964–6	27·9	5·7	92·5	49·4	69·7	14·3	46·9	43·4
1966	26·4	6·9	91·5	54·7	66·8	16·6	47·6	46·9

Source: ECLA, *Estudio Económico de Américo Latina* (1967).

Notwithstanding the foregoing comments, the copper and oil enclaves that are exploited by foreigners in Chile and Venezuela, respectively, pay more taxes on average than the other productive sectors and enterprises. Taxes account for about the same proportion of the output of the sector in both cases, as can be seen in Table 8. However, the share of oil in Venezuela's gross domestic product and total exports is larger than the share of copper in Chile's G.D.P. or exports, and this explains why the proportion of taxes paid on oil, in comparison to total tax income, is about four times larger than the corresponding proportion of taxes paid on copper. Chile now hopes to increase further the proportion of the copper surplus retained in the country. It remains to be seen whether the announced programme of gradual nationalisation is successful in doing this.

(e) Redistribution and Economic Growth: The Limitations of Fiscal Policy

One of the basic tasks of fiscal policy in Latin America is to increase the economic surplus. At the same time the ability of the public sector to do this is severely limited by the social and political forces that act upon it. The responsibilities of the public sector for promoting development are very great, as are the difficulties under which fiscal policy must operate, and this constitutes one of the most evident contradictions in the countries of the region.

Industrialisation in Latin America has been strongly affected by the unequal distribution of income. Inequality has produced a pattern of demand in which great weight in total consumption is given to the tastes of the higher income groups. The industrial structure that has emerged from the process of import substitution has, of course, reflected this pattern of demand. The small size of the domestic market has led to monopolistic concentration and a strong tendency in favour of a highly diversified pattern of production. That is, the industrial structure is geared to satisfying a small but very diversified market dominated by high income groups who are in a position to acquire manufactured items, and especially durable consumer goods.

Several factors tend to reinforce this system. First, pressure for incentives and assistance from existing and potential industrialists, national and foreign, has led the state to adopt an industrial policy which takes as given the existing distribution of income and pattern of demand. Second, the process of industrial concentration has increased the links between industrialists and other financial and merchant interests, and as a result mechanisms have been created which ensure that as new groups enter the urban consumer society the pattern of demand which supports the present industrial structure is maintained. Advertising, the growing ease with which consumer credit is granted, and the creation of financial institutions concerned with promoting purchases of consumer durables are common phenomena. They have all been used to diffuse a particular pattern of consumption.

Furthermore, this entire process, in accentuating consumption demand, tends to restrict the ability of the public sector to capture a larger share of the surplus through higher personal taxes. The potential savings of consumers are transferred to private enterprises rather than to the government. Once the surplus is in the hands of private firms, it becomes increasingly difficult for the state to collect it. Indeed, industrial groups insist constantly that the state should assist and promote manufacturing activity, and the government is reminded incessantly that it must not strangle the private sector. Only exceptionally can the government rely on the foreign trade sector to provide additional revenue. Relatively slow growth in the volume of trade and instability in the prices of many primary commodities make it impossible for a large public investment programme to be financed by export taxes and tariffs.

Unfortunately, the surplus appropriated by the public sector often has been badly used. The low income groups have, of course, pressed strongly for a rise in their standard of living, and in some cases the ruling groups have made minimal concessions. In particular, demand for employment opportunities in the civil service has put a strain on public expenditure. The reform-oriented governments have concentrated in many cases on the social aspects of development, such as housing, education and health. To a certain extent these policies have been successful in maintaining a modicum of social peace, but the use of the resources of the public sector for social expenditure has severely limited its capacity for implementing an aggressive policy of economic development that is more in accord with the needs of the majority of the population.

Although public expenditure has been devoted to the social services, it does not follow that this policy has led to a more equal distribution of income. On the contrary, in many cases public expenditure on the social services has increased inequality. For instance, the provision of free university education could redistribute income only if it were part of a system which provides equal educational opportunities for the bulk of the population. Otherwise, free university education becomes a subsidy to the well-to-do who are in a position to prepare their children for a university career. Similarly, a social security system will not redistribute income if the contributions of the government are financed out of regressive taxation or if the costs of the contributions of the employers are shifted on to the workers (through lower wages) or on to consumers (through higher prices).

It is clear that there are serious limitations in the extent to which public policy can accelerate economic growth or improve the distribution of income, and it is in the context of these limitations that government activity in Latin America should be viewed. Concepts such as taxable capacity, tax effort, the elasticity of government revenue, the composition of expenditure and the level of state investment cannot be interpreted correctly if account is not taken of the historical inheritance of poverty, the dependence of the underdeveloped countries on the exterior, the political situation and the pressures for rapid social development. In the final analysis, it appears that the role of the public sector in promoting development in Latin America is severely limited by the same socio-economic structure which the public sector is supposed to modify.

NOTES

1. For a more detailed examination of some of these hypotheses, see Richard Thorn, 'The Evolution of Public Finances During Economic Development', in *The Manchester School of Economic and Social Studies*, xxxv, 1 (Jan 1967).

2. Strictly speaking, the concept of amortisation should be replaced by that of renovation. Amortisation refers to the maintenance of the capital stock; renovation refers to the replenishment of capital goods in order to maintain the social product constant. Consequently, the amount of renovation is generally less than that of amortisation, inasmuch as the former includes technological progress incorporated into the capital goods. In order to clarify these and other concepts related to the economic surplus, see Charles Bettleheim, *Planification et croissance accélerée* (Maspero, Paris, 1946), ch. 6.

3. See Chapter 7 below.

4. Several of the ideas set forth in this paragraph, and enlarged upon to some extent in the final section, are being developed by economists in international organisations and in the Institute of Economic Research and Planning of the University of Chile. Among them we should mention Jorge Bertini, Carlos Matus, Anibal Pinto, Charles Rollins, Sigmundt Slawinsky, Maria C. Tavares and Pedro Vuskovic. Although some papers have already been published, most of them have not yet been circulated widely. See, for instance, Pedro Vuskovic, 'Concentración y Marginalización' (Graduate School of Latin American Economic Studies (Escolatina), Santiago, 1969, mimeo).

5. See the following econometric studies in which different ways of grouping the countries allow the authors to reach different conclusions: Richard Musgrave, *Fiscal Systems* (Yale University Press, New Haven, 1969); Jorgen R. Lotz and Elliot R. Morss, 'Measuring Tax Effort in Developing Countries', in *I.M.F. Staff Papers* (Nov 1967); Harley H. Hinrichs, 'Determinants of Government Revenue Shares among Less Developed Countries', in *Economic Journal* (Sept 1965).

6. In practice, however, most foreign assistance is allocated on the basis of political rather than economic criteria.

7. República de Chile, *Balance Consolidado del Sector Público de Chile, año 1966–1967 y período 1964–67* (Imprenta Prisiones, Santiago, Chile, 1969), p. 60.

8. See Chapter 1, Table 7.

9. See Chapter 3, Table 1.

10. See Chapter 1, Table 8.

11. It is possible that these percentages may be even higher. The exclusion of expenditures on police and other accounting devices probably understate the real magnitudes.

12. See Table 2 above.

13. República de Chile, op. cit. p. 118.

14. This subject is developed in Carlos Romeo, 'Comercio exterior, inter-cambio desigual, desarrollo economico' (draft of a thesis for the University of Chile; written in Cuba).

15. The data in Table 7 differ from that of Chapter 1, Table 9 because different criteria for classification have been used.

16. See ECLA, *Estudio Económico de América Latina* (1967), ch. 4.

3. Public Sector Activities

LAURENCE WHITEHEAD

THE previous chapter has dealt with taxation and general government expenditure – i.e. with the financing of 'public goods' (defence, public administration, etc.) – so this chapter will confine itself to the remaining activities of the public sector. 'Public goods' are provided for the community as a whole, are indivisible, and cannot therefore be charged to individual users in proportion to their use. But in many countries the state also supplies goods and services which can be allocated to individual consumers, in which case the price the state charges for its activities can be a major source of finance, as well as a powerful instrument of government control over income distribution, sectoral balance, market structure, etc. Sometimes the prices charged by the public sector for its activities involve a tax element (e.g. individual 'purshasers' of social security benefits may be unable to escape payment if they decide the service costs them too much), but the fact that the state incurs a specific obligation to a particular customer, in exchange for his payment, differentiates this type of public sector transaction from general taxation. This chapter examines public enterprises and social security funds to see how their pricing policies contribute to financing development. It concludes by considering how public development banks raise loans on behalf of public enterprises. But before we turn to the statistics available on the Latin American public sector we should briefly review some hypotheses put forward in the existing literature.

(a) Public Enterprise in the Development Process

There are very few underdeveloped countries outside the communist bloc with governments that wish public enterprise to predominate over private in the process of development. (Since the exceptions to this rule are outside Latin America we shall ignore them here.)[1] Even in revolutionary Mexico, as early as 1941 the Finance Minister expressed ideas which have now become a typical view of 'Third World' governments: 'The state does not want to take the role of enterpriser, but rather to help private enterprise to take charge of transforming the economy of the country.'[2] Admittedly for a while evidence from India was used to argue that neither public nor private enterprise need predominate in a developing country – there was a third way based on harmonious co-operation in a mixed economy. A. H. Hanson was a prominent advocate of this view:

> In industry, it is the state's clear intention to occupy the 'commanding heights' and to exercise firm control over the whole range of productive undertakings, but private enterprise is by no means ruled out – *small* private enterprise, indeed, is being actively encouraged – and the perspective offered is one of considerable *variety* of industrial organisations, with state, joint, co-operative and individual enterprises all playing their allotted parts in the fulfilment of the plan. . . . With future, as well as present, emphasis thus placed on public enterprises the Indian state should not labour under the necessity, as Mexico and Turkey do, of relying on economic inequalities to promote an adequate rate of capital formation . . . the Indian mode of economic development will be an influential example for the whole 'underdeveloped' sector of the 'neutralist' bloc. It may even help to resolve the present profound crisis in socialist thought.[3]

No one would still adhere to the doctrine of the 'third way' in this extreme form (Hanson himself recanted in the preface to the second edition of his book),[4] but the belief in some sort of parity between the state sector and private enterprise in developing countries still retains its popularity. The evidence seems to suggest, however, that in most cases public enterprise is run largely in the interests of the private sector.

This becomes apparent once we examine why particular activities are included in the public sector, while others are the preserve of private enterprise. Myrdal explains why public utilities are generally state-run:

> . . . changes in technology have tended to greatly increase the requirements for public utility investments. It is generally assumed in all the South Asian countries that these investments must be a state obligation for a number of reasons: the magnitude of the individual investment; the monopoly character of public utilities and the need to control the prices of their services in order to prevent what in effect would be private taxation; and the improbability that under these circumstances private enterprise and finance would be willing and able to do the job.[5]

Even where the state sector extends beyond the field of public utilities it does not normally present a threat to private enterprise:

> A main reason for state investments in power, transport, and other public utilities has been to promote private enterprise. Where, as in India and Pakistan, the state has also ventured into industry on a large scale, it has done so mainly in fields where, for various reasons, private industry could not be expected to take the initiative. Furthermore it has taken this step mainly in order to make supplies of raw materials or capital goods available to private industry.[6]

To take nationalisation further than that is likely to precipitate a political crisis, as Hanson correctly observed:

> Nearly always one of the essential interests at stake is whether the government shall control business or business control government. Political crisis in a mixed economy, therefore, is very likely to occur at a point where the government has extended public enterprise and pushed economic *dirigisme* somewhat beyond the boundaries of the area within which the business community feels such 'interferences' are tolerable, if not actually helpful.[7]

It would be wrong to overestimate the political power of business interests acting in isolation, but neither should one ignore the fact that most of the non-communist governments in the Third World who have allowed the public sector to threaten private enterprise have subsequently been overthrown and their policies largely reversed. (Perón in Argentina, Goulart in Brazil, Paz Estenssoro in Bolivia, Nkrumah in Ghana, Bandaranaike in Ceylon, Sukarno in Indonesia, etc. The most important exceptions are Arab states.) While each case has a variety of causes the hostility of private enterprise was usually a contributory factor.

Not only is the state sector normally limited to those activities which are complementary to the needs of private enterprise, the pricing policy of nationalised concerns also is frequently tailored to the interests of its consumers in the private sector rather than to the investment needs of the state sector. For Gaitskell rapid state accumulation is very difficult in a democratic society:

> The fact that [in Britain] since 1945 the public sector of industry, far from financing its development out of its own profits, has been borrowing extensively from private sources, is not just accidental. While one reason for this is that the nationalised industries happened

[sic] for the most part to be in a weak financial and physical condition when they were taken over, even more important are the economic and political obstacles in the way of higher prices and profits in these industries. . . . In a democracy it is not so easy for the nationalised undertakings to charge high prices in order to provide a larger volume of savings.[8]

Nor is it much easier where private enterprise has been combined with undemocratic forms of government. Myrdal's discussion of this issue certainly suggests that in South Asia it is the interests of private enterprise, rather than the democratic nature of the political system, which account for the limited profits available for new investment in the state sector:

> . . . the investment and pricing policies pursued by public enterprises are usually such that, by holding down prices, they swell the profits of the private sector. Thus when put into practice, the vaguely socialist notion that public enterprises must render services at low prices in fact boosts considerably the returns on private capital. Instead of being used to supplement government revenue and help to mop up purchasing power, the public sector functions to inflate private profit.[9]

However these political forces work, they must be quite powerful in South Asia since

> throughout most of the region goods and services from the public sector have been priced so low that the rates of return on capital invested have been lower than the ('too low') rates of interest prevailing on the capital market.[10]

If it is true that resources are often transferred from the public to the private sector in this way, then a reduction of these transfers is a real alternative to the present reliance on administrative controls over the private sector. Myrdal considers that the government often gives such strong incentives to the private sector (he calls cheap inputs, tax holidays and subsidised credit 'positive operational controls') that these then have to be offset by clumsy 'negative operational controls' ('bullying, administrative restrictions on capital issues, investment and production, the denial of foreign exchange, the rationing of consumer goods, and the imposition of excise duties').[11] 'This is like driving a car with the accelerator pushed to the floor but the brakes on,'[12] he comments.

One major effect . . . must be *extraordinarily high profits for those private enterprises that succeed in running the gauntlet of discretionary positive and negative controls.*[13]

This being the case, private industry would have an interest in seeing that state enterprises adhere to a low price policy not only because it would keep down their costs but also because, in doing so, it would tend to increase the need for negative discretionary controls.[14]

Myrdal's description of public enterprise in South Asia suggests some hypotheses we can test against the Latin American data. Even if the public sector does contribute a large proportion of a nation's investment, it may generate only a small proportion of the country's 'investible surplus'. This phenomenon is often attributed to the inefficient organisation and poor management which are said to characterise public enterprises, and no doubt in many cases this is an important factor. But there is also the tendency of many governments to socialise concerns only when they become chronic loss-makers (such as the railways) and are therefore no longer lucrative to private business, but must be kept running in the interests of the (predominantly private) economy as a whole. If we exclude railways from the public sector, that normally leaves a group of enterprises which are potentially highly profitable and dynamic (albeit monopolistic and capital-intensive). If this potential is not realised we should ask how the 'surplus' generated by this sector is transferred to private industry. Where such transfers occur on a large scale we have a pattern of growth dominated by a highly lucrative private sector, which can deploy the investible surplus of the whole economy according to the normal short-run profitability considerations, while grudgingly paying limited amounts of tax to subsidise the deficits of the 'inefficient, inflated' public sector. Such a system might not be the best way to maximise the growth of output in the long run, or even the growth of output from the private sector. But very probably it would maximise the growth of private sector profits in the short run – a consideration which private enterprise cannot be expected to ignore.[15]

Of course it is not inevitable that resources generated by the public sector should be transferred to the private sector of a 'mixed' economy. There are cases where the reverse has happened (such as the Soviet Union in the 1920s). Transfers in the opposite direction tend to end with the elimination of the private sector of the economy altogether, but there may be substantial intervals of coexistence before this happens. Generalising from Russian experience, Preobrazhensky, a Soviet economist writing in the twenties, distinguished three types of relationship between public (which he called 'socialist') and private sectors of the economy:

> (1) when the state economy receives less value from the nonsocialist milieu than it gives . . . we shall have a steady decomposition of large-scale socialist production, and a gradual selling off of its product below cost. . . .
>
> (2) prices of the products of state industry are so calculated that . . . neither of the economic systems exploits the other. This solution is in general possible only as a very brief episode . . . what [socialism] loses in speed in the period of primitive accumulation, in the sense of development of its technical economic base, owing to its extreme poverty in capital, it is *obliged* to make up for by intensified accumulation at the expense of the non-socialist milieu. One of the most important means of this accumulation . . . is non-equivalent exchange of values with the non-socialist milieu.
>
> (3) . . . a price policy consciously calculated so as to alienate a *certain* part of the surplus product of private economy in all its forms.[16]

Thus Preobrazhensky apparently believed that either the public sector must 'exploit' the private sector (a process leading eventually to complete socialisation of the economy) or vice versa (in which case there would be a 'steady decomposition of large-scale socialist production'). An equilibrium between the two sectors (of the kind practically taken for granted by spokesmen of the 'mixed economy') could, in his view, only be a very brief episode. Of course he was thinking of a revolutionary situation in which state and private sectors were pitted against each other for political, as well as for economic, reasons. In a mixed economy private enterprise may well tolerate subsidies that save the state sector from actual 'decomposition', provided this sector represents no threat to the institution of private property. An 'equilibrium' of sorts may develop between the two sectors – personnel may be exchanged, information pooled and policies harmonised. The state sector might even be allowed to price its products so that investment needs were covered without government subsidies. But even so Preobrazhensky could still be correct in essentials – in a mixed economy the best profit opportunities may be reserved to the private sector, and the 'exchange of values' between the two sectors may generally be 'non-equivalent' to the detriment of the public sector. Let us consider the Latin American case.

(b) Latin America's Public Sector

Table 1 shows the proportion of national investment accounted for by the public sector in thirteen Latin American countries. These figures are only very rough indicators, since they are taken from a variety of sources which use varying definitions of the concepts employed. The figures are not all for the same year, and in some cases the year selected may be unrepresentative of the longer period trend.

Despite these reservations Table 1 clearly shows that public investment is an important part of total investment in most Latin American countries. The glaring exception is Peru. The Central American countries are also on the low side, obtaining only about a quarter of their investment from the public sector. But over a third of total investment is accounted for by the public sector in Bolivia, Brazil, Ecuador, Mexico and Venezuela. Public investment exceeded 3 per cent of G.N.P. in twelve of the thirteen countries for which there are data in Table 1, and in Bolivia, Brazil, Ecuador, Mexico and Venezuela it exceeded 5 per cent. Governments with this kind of direct command over the investible resources of a nation have, in theory, a powerful lever for directing and stimulating economic growth.

Much of this public investment, however, is devoted to infrastructure and social welfare – schools, hospitals, etc. Clearly we should distinguish between this type of investment and government investment in productive enterprises, which are capable of generating a new investible surplus, and of trading with the private sector. Table 1 attempts to summarise the national accounts data on public enterprise. Information is only available for eleven of the thirteen countries in the table; and public enterprises, however defined, are negligible in six. It is interesting to note that, apart from Ecuador, public enterprise is most important in those Latin American countries which have experienced social revolutions – Mexico and Bolivia appear in the table, and of course Cuba would show a very large proportion of its national investment to be undertaken by public enterprises if data were available for the island. Public enterprise is of only secondary significance in Brazil and Uruguay.

To carry the analysis further we have to look closer, first at the national accounts of two countries which do give a more detailed macroeconomic breakdown of their public enterprise sector (Brazil and Mexico), and secondly at the company accounts of the major firms.

We have information on the Brazilian public enterprise sector only

Table 1. Public Investment in Thirteen Latin American Countries

Country	Year	Public investment: % of all investment	Public investment: % of G.N.P.	Of which public enterprise investment: % of all investment	Of which public enterprise investment: % of G.N.P.
Argentina	1959–61	21	4·8	...	...
Bolivia	1960	46	7·0	35	5·9
Brazil	1960	38	5·8	10	1·5
Colombia	1960	15	3·1	...	...
Ecuador	1960	47	6·5	24	3·3
Honduras	1959	27	3·6	negl.	negl.
Mexico	1960	42	5·7	24	3·3
Nicaragua[a]	1960	23	3·5	negl.	negl.
Panama[a]	1960	21	3·7	negl.	negl.
Paraguay	1961	21	3·8	negl.	negl.
Peru	1960	9	1·9	negl.	negl.
Uruguay	1960	18	3·2	7–10	1–1·5
Venezuela[a]	1960	60	11·2	negl.	negl.

[a] As % of G.D.P.

Sources:

Argentina: Carlos Diaz Alejandro, *Devaluación de la Tasa de Cambio en Un País Semi-Industrializado* (Buenos Aires, 1966), p. 112.

Bolivia: Secretaria Nacional de Planificación y Co-ordinación, *Planeamiento II – Cuentas Nacionales 1958–66*. Calculated from tables I-A and VI-A.

Brazil: *Revista Brasileira de Economia* (March 1962), National Accounts Table VI and p. 105. However Nathaniel Leff, *Economic Policy-Making and Development in Brazil 1947–64* (1968), p. 39, estimates public investment at 59 per cent of all investment, if Brasilia is counted in the public sector.

Colombia: Calculated from Banco de la Republica, Departamento de Investigaciones Economicas, 'Cuentas Nacionales 1950–60' (mimeo, Bogota, n.d.), ff. 10, 14.

Ecuador: Calculated from *Memoria del Gerente General del Banco Central del Ecuador* (1963), p. 224 and annex II, p. ix, table 4.

Honduras: Calculated from U.N., *Analisis y Proyecciones del Desarrollo Economico, IX, El Desarrollo Economico de Honduras* (1960), p. 54.

Mexico: Roberto Anguiano Equihua, *Las Finanzas del Sector Publico en Mexico* (1968), tables 1 and 2, and NAFIN, *Statistics on the Mexican Economy*, pp. 41, 45.

Nicaragua: Calculated from U.N. *Analisis y Proyecciones del Desarrollo Economico, IX, El Desarrollo Economico de Nicaragua* (1966), p. 43.

Panama: Calculated from Joint Tax Programme of O.A.S. and I.D.B., *Fiscal Survey of Panama* (1964), p. 8.

Paraguay: Calculated from Joseph Pincus, *The Economy of Paraguay* (1968), pp. 266, 274.

Peru: Calculated from IV Asamblea del Instituto Inter-Americano de Estadística, *Cuentas Nacionales y Planificación del Desarrollo* (Banco Central del Peru, n.d.), p. 118.

Uruguay: Calculated from Banco de la Republica Oriental del Uruguay, Departamento de Investigaciones Economicas, *Cuentas Nacionales* (1965), tables B5, B14 and B74–6.

Venezuela: Calculated from B.I.D., Division de Desarrollo Economico y Social, *Datos Basicos y Parametros Socio-Economicos de Venezuela 1950–65*, tables I, IB, 9 and 27A.

for the period 1956–60. Table 2 shows the income generated by twenty-one government enterprises classified into three categories. The twenty-one include the main nationalised companies, and also government enterprises such as the Post Office. Since the figures are in current cruzeiros, year-by-year increases largely reflect inflation, not growth in real income. It is possible that inflation also distorted the profitability position shown in the table – this would happen, for example, if depreciation charges were not valued at replacement cost.

Table 2. Income Generated by Twenty-One Brazilian Public Enterprises
(in thousand million current cruzeiros)

	1956	1957	1958	1959	1960
Industry					
Wages and salaries	3·4	4·4	5·5	7·2	10·4
Profits	3·5	5·6	8·2	15·3	21·1
Banks and financial intermediaries					
Wages and salaries	5·7	7·4	9·3	12·4	16·8
Profits	1·7	3·6	6·1	9·3	10·9
Transport and communications					
Wages and salaries	15·0	18·0	19·5	22·8	32·7
Profits	−10·8	−13·9	−13·9	−17·1	−23·6
All sectors					
Wages and salaries	24·1	29·8	34·4	42·4	59·9
Profits	−5·6	−4·7	0·4	7·5	8·4

Source: *Revista Brasileira de Economia* (March 1962), 101.

However, taking these twenty-one enterprises as a group, the table suggests that they were incurring deficits equal to about a quarter of their wage and salary bill in 1956, whereas by 1960 they were earning a modest surplus equal to 14 per cent of wages and salaries. Throughout the period the source of the deficit was the transport sector, which consistently paid a larger wage and salary bill than all the other public enterprises put together, and which with equal regularity incurred losses exceeding two-thirds of its wage bill. To a limited extent the improved performance of the public sector as a whole came from public banks and financial intermediaries, since they generated a growing share of public enterprise income, with profits rising twice as fast as wages (also, as we can see in Table 3, their share of total banking activity rose considerably, while private banking shrank to a minority position by 1960). However the chief impetus to higher profitability in the public sector came from state industrial enterprises such as Petrobras, Companhia Siderurgica Nacional, etc. Industry generated just over a third of public sector income in 1956, whereas by 1960 its share had risen to almost a half. Profits grew twice as fast as the wage bill, until by 1960 the profits generated by state industry at last exceeded the deficits generated by the state transport sector.

Table 2 does not, of course, indicate any tendency towards the 'decomposition' of public enterprise in Brazil. On the contrary public enterprise, taken as a whole, moved from deficit into surplus. Table 3 reinforces this impression, demonstrating that the state sector provided a growing proportion of output, rising from 7·5 per cent to 9·9 per cent of the income generated by the three sectors under consideration, despite the declining importance of the state transport sector.

Table 3. Per Cent of Sectoral Income Generated by Public Enterprise in Brazil

	1956	1957	1958	1959
Industry	3·9	4·9	5·2	6·3
Banks, etc.	39·0	44·0	49·7	53·0
Transport and Communications	7·4	6·0	7·1	5·7
Three sectors combined	7·5	8·4	9·3	9·9

Source: *Revista Brasileira de Economia* (March 1962), 103.

But the question is not simply whether the state sector earns a surplus on its current operations. The crucial issue is whether the state sector can generate a surplus large enough to finance the bulk of its long-run investment needs. If it fails to extract the required investible surplus from the private sector in this way, then it must run up debts, either with foreign creditors or with domestic creditors (if they can be induced to lend) or with the government (the latter being an inflationary course, unless the government is willing to offset enterprise deficits by a tax surplus). Public investment largely financed in either of these last three ways is extremely precarious. Of course in some sectors (such as electricity) investment needs may be expanding so fast that considerable credit may be needed from outside. There is nothing wrong with this provided prices are set high enough to guarantee a decent return on the capital invested. But taking the public sector as a whole, we should expect it to earn sufficient profits from its transactions with the private sector to finance most of its investment from internal sources.

On these criteria the public transport sector is clearly a hopeless failure. The government has nationalised those transport enterprises which face secular decline and can no longer even remotely cover operating costs, let alone finance their investment needs. Public transport is not run with the intention of generating a surplus – rather it is subsidised to provide employment where private enterprise would produce redundancy, and to provide electorally popular cheap transport for the urban population. Efforts to reduce the losses on this sector would be at the expense as much of the low income masses as of the profitable sectors of private enterprise, and might well be socially costly (e.g. in terms of increased traffic congestion in major cities).

By contrast, publicly owned industry (which sells chiefly to private firms rather than to consumer households) has been obtaining growing surpluses. They were sufficient by the end of the period to cancel out the transport deficit. The public sector has succeeded in expanding its share of the industrial sector (see Table 3). From Table 2 we can see that averaging the three years 1958–60, nationalised industry's wage and salary bill was only 17 per cent of the bill for public enterprise as a whole, whereas it generated 44 per cent of the public sector's income. Of course public industry is concentrated in those very capital-intensive activities which do not offer a quick return to private capital, and where the investment outlay is very large. Thus to sustain the rate of expansion indicated by Table 3 required a marked concentration of public enterprise investment in the industrial sector, notably greater than the concentration of income, although still inevitably less than the concentration of profits. 'On average, during the period 1958–1960, investments by industrial enterprises were 54·3% of all investment by Federal Government Enterprises.'[16a]

Table 4. Sources of Finance of State-Owned Industrial Enterprises in Brazil in billion current cruzeiros, cumulated 1956–60

Internal sources	49·7
Subsidies	15·9
Suppliers' credits from abroad	6·5
Credit from national banks	6·2
All sources of finance	78·3
Gross capital formation	60·4

Source: *Revista Brasileira de Economia* (March 1962), 107.

Unfortunately the Brazilian statistics do not enable us to disaggregate public enterprise financing into industrial, banking and transport components. All we have is Table 4, which appears to support Myrdal. It aggregates data from the same half-dozen industrial enterprises which already appeared (as the 'industry' subgroup) in Table 2. These enterprises were unable to finance all their investment from internal sources (which amounted to 49·7 billion cruzeiros). They needed 28·6 billion in government subsidies and loans. On the other hand gross savings were sufficient to finance over 80 per cent of gross capital formation. This suggests a conclusion which will be confirmed later on (see Table 7): even the most profitable sectors of public enterprise are rarely able to fully finance their investment needs.

Another drawback of these data on Brazilian public enterprise is that they only refer to the period 1956–60. This may give a misleadingly favourable impression – there may have been some deterioration in the financial position of the public sector in the period 1961–4 when the rate of inflation accelerated and economic growth declined. Likewise after 1964 the stabilisation efforts of the new military regime may have particularly affected public investment.

Turning to Mexico, Table 5 summarises the performance of Mexican public enterprise from 1950 to 1964.

Table 5. Public Investment in Mexico, as per cent of G.N.P.

	1950	*1960*	*1964*
Public gross fixed capital formation	6·5	5·7	8·0
Of which: agriculture	...	0·44	1·05
fuel and energy	...	1·62	2·04
industry	...	0·07	0·33
communications and transport	...	2·03	1·68
administration and social	...	1·53	2·91
Investment by public enterprises	...	3·32	...
Of which: agriculture	...	0·08	0·12
fuel, energy, industry and commerce	...	1·86	2·41
communications and transport	...	0·75	0·74
administration and social	...	0·63	...
Public enterprise profits (before investment)	...	1·69	2·75
Deficit of public enterprises alone (after investment)	−0·65	−1·2	−1·3
Deficit of whole public sector (plus = surplus)	+0·05	−1·9	−3·4
Met by: internal loans	...	0·6	1·2
foreign loans	...	1·3	2·2

Source: Roberto Anguiano Equihua, *Las Finanzas del Sector Publico en Mexico* (UNAM, 1968), table 2, pp. 72, 90, 94, 105, 320. Note that public enterprise profits and deficits may be misleading, because they include transfers between the government and the enterprises, and repayment by the government of loans incurred by the public enterprises. Total public investment in 1960 is given as 5·7 per cent of G.N.P. rather than the 6·2 per cent shown in table 2 of Anguiano's book. The difference consists of government purchases of real estate and shares, etc., i.e. types of public investment which do not constitute gross fixed capital formation.

As with the Brazilian data, the period covered is too short to permit extrapolation, particularly since 1964 was a boom year for the Mexican economy. But the table does show the importance of public investment in Mexico, and indicates that around half this investment is undertaken by public enterprises. Once again public enterprise steps in where the prospects of a quick return on investment are not too good. Private enterprise controls most of the lucrative opportunities in manufacturing, while public enterprise undertakes the 'lumpy' infrastructural investments needed to create a suitable environment for the private sector. The existence of public investment in agriculture may seem surprising at first glance, but this is almost entirely investment in irrigation, and serves to create highly profitable private farms in the arid northern states. The beneficiaries of the scheme do not contribute much to its financing.

Profits appear to be an important and rapidly growing source of finance for Mexico's public enterprises (although, as explained in Table 5, they may be inflated by transfers from the federal government), but they are insufficient to finance the investment programmes of these enterprises. Thus public enterprise deficits (after investment) rose from 0.65 per cent of G.N.P. in 1950 to 1.3 per cent of G.N.P. by 1964. The deficit of the public sector as a whole rose much more dramatically, reaching 3.4 per cent of G.N.P. by 1964 (an exceptional year), and roughly two-thirds of this deficit was financed by *foreign* borrowing. It is doubtful whether private enterprise could have secured foreign credit on the scale needed by Mexico's public enterprise without falling under the control of private foreign companies.

Of course global figures for Mexican public enterprise may conceal very important variations between types of enterprise. The Brazilian data have shown how the whole public sector may appear in an unfavourable light simply because of financial difficulties in public transport. Unfortunately we do not have a comparable classification of Mexican public enterprises, but we can find some similarities to the Brazilian case. For example, Table 6 compares the budgets of the state petrol company (PEMEX) and the state railways for 1967.

PEMEX is the most important public enterprise not only in Mexico but in Latin America as a whole. In fact it is the largest indigenous enterprise of any type in Latin America, and was listed as the 67th largest industrial enterprise outside the United States in 1967.[17] In 1960 it was responsible for over one-tenth of total public investment, and in 1964 for 15 per cent – in that year this enterprise alone was responsible for investing 1·22 per cent of Mexico's G.N.P. It was not a profit-making concern until 1961, and even since then it has relied heavily on loans to finance some of its investment needs. But PEMEX is clearly not in any process of 'decomposition', although equally clearly it is not exploiting Mexican private enterprise in the way its market power might permit. It is perhaps Latin America's most successful

Table 6. 1967 Budgets of PEMEX and Ferrocarriles Nacionales de Mexico, in millions of pesos

	PEMEX	Ferrocarriles Nacionales
Income from own sources	10,112	2,960
Government subsidies	...	1,412
All income	10,112	4,372
Operating costs	7,229	2,430
New investment	2,105	490
Amortisation of debt	615	601
Other expenditure	163	932
All expenditure	10,112	4,372

Source: R. Anguiano Equihua, *Las Finanzas del Sector Publico en Mexico* (UNAM, 1968), pp. 65, 122.

instance of the working of a 'mixed economy'. On its own it is insufficient to disprove the Preobrazhensky thesis (and we shall see in a moment that it is a rather exceptional case), but it does show that in the most favourable circumstances a reasonably equal and permanent relationship can be established between a public enterprise and the private sector.

By contrast Mexico's railways inevitably show up rather poorly. But even they manage to cover three-quarters of their current expenditure from their own income (Brazil's public transport losses were two-thirds of the wage bill, it will be recalled), and to spend almost a quarter of their income on new investment plus the repayment of past debts. The subsidy they receive from the government amounts of 0·45 per cent of G.N.P. – a substantial amount, of course, but one that compares favourably with the Brazilian subsidy of over 1 per cent of G.N.P. transferred to all types of public transport (not only the railways) each year from 1956 to 1960. Mexico's railways are not immune to the secular problems afflicting all railway systems in this era of road transport, but they have been quite successful in adapting to the challenge.

Brazil and Mexico are the two largest nations in Latin America, but if we wish to generalise about the region as a whole we cannot confine ourselves to them. We lack a macroeconomic breakdown of the public sector for the other countries of the region, or statistics showing how public enterprise accounts have developed over time, but fortunately we do have an analysis of the company accounts of twenty-four public

Table 7. Average Financing Needs of Sixty-Four Public Enterprises in Underdeveloped Countries, of which twenty-four are Latin American enterprises
(in per cent of enterprise activity, where activity $=\frac{1}{2}$(revenue + expenditure))

	Number of enter-prises	A. *Surplus on current operations*	B. *Surplus after depreci-ation*	C. *New invest-ment*	D. *Surplus after all invest-ment* (B−C)	E. *Govern-ment transfers*
Railways						
Latin America	4	−57·1	−84·1	5·3	−89·4	90·6
All	12	−13·5	−40·5	0·5	−41·0	35·3
Other Transport						
Latin America	4	−3·8	−33·8	16·4	−50·2	44·5
All	11	+10·9	−19·1	0·2	−19·3	17·8
Petrol						
Latin America	5	+43·3	+23·3	50·0	−26·7	−1·6
All	7	+33·8	+13·8	36·9	−23·1	−0·7
Electricity						
Latin America	3	+21·0	0·0	93·2	−93·2	59·6
All	13	+27·2	+6·2	108·2	−102·0	33·7
Communications						
Latin America	2	+26·7	+6·7	31·6	−24·9	14·5
All	8	+5·7	−14·3	17·7	−32·0	28·6
Other Industry						
Latin America	6	−6·6	−30·6	24·4	−55·1	45·7
All	13	−6·3	−30·3	107·8	−138·1	63·3
All Sectors						
Latin America	24	+2·1	−21·9	34·4	−56·6	42·3
All	64	+8·0	−16·0	50·3	−66·3	32·9

Source: *I.M.F. Staff Papers* (March 1968), 108, 110, 111, 113, 115. New investment in column C is the excess of total investment (given on p. 111) over depreciation (the difference between columns A and B).

enterprises drawn from seven Latin American countries: seven Colombian enterprises, six Argentine, four Mexican, three Bolivian, two Brazilian, one Chilean and one Peruvian. Furthermore, these Latin American accounts have been compared with the figures for forty other public enterprises in nineteen other underdeveloped countries.[18] Naturally, combining the accounts of such a range of enterprises produces distortions – each year's accounts of each enterprise is given an equal weight in Table 7, so that enterprises whose accounts were available over a long period are overrepresented compared to those whose accounts were available for only a few years, and small concerns

D

are overrepresented, and large concerns underrepresented, in the averages. Even so the results obtained by this method are probably broadly reliable.

Column A of Table 7 shows that, taking all sectors of public enterprise together, the average surplus on current operations is extremely low, viz. 2·1 per cent of 'activity' (as defined in the table) in Latin America, and 8 per cent of activity for all underdeveloped countries. After deducting the depreciation needed simply to keep these enterprises running at their present levels of activity in the future, column B shows on average a very substantial deficit: 16 per cent of annual activity for underdeveloped countries as a whole, rising to 21·9 per cent for Latin America. These enterprises must indeed be setting excessively low prices for their products,[19] and are obviously only saved from the rapid process of 'decomposition' predicted by Preobrazhensky by large government subsidies. Of course this poor overall position is considerably influenced by the miserable performance of railways and other public transport, but column B shows that on average public industry is also charging such inadequate prices for its products that it is decapitalising at the annual rate of 30 per cent of activity. The state petrol companies are the only sector earning a respectable surplus on current transactions. But, as column C shows, the new investment needs for petrol are more than double the investible surplus shown in column B. As for electricity, here the new investment needs are roughly as large as the level of enterprise activity, and there is no prospect of any significant self-financing of investment on this scale. New investment also exceeds 30 per cent of activity in Latin American communications enterprises, and approaches 25 per cent of activity in Latin America's rapidly decapitalising industrial public enterprises. Thus, taking the twenty-four Latin American enterprises as a group, we find that although their current deficits alone reach 21·9 per cent of activity they are undertaking new investment costing 34·4 per cent of activity, (New investment for all sixty-four public enterprises rises to the astronomical level of 50 per cent of activity, pushed by the extraordinary investment ratios of nationalised industry outside Latin America.) With new investment ratios at this level it is easy to see why private enterprise is leaving gaps for public enterprise to fill. Even with profit-maximising price policies these are not activities where one can expect large, rapid returns on a limited capital outlay. As it is, with pricing policies which on average barely cover operating costs before depreciation, column D shows that these public enterprises are, on average, hopelessly incapable of financing their massive investment needs out of their own resources. Post-investment deficits averaged 56·3 per cent of activity for Latin American enterprises, and 66·3 per cent for under-developed countries as a whole! These deficits rose to 90 per cent not only for Latin American railways but also for Latin American electricity companies. Even Latin American state petrol companies, the only group to earn respectable profits on current transactions, were running deficits equal to a quarter of annual activity, after new investment had been subtracted.

If we grant that these enterprises are almost all performing essential functions and that their present rate of expansion is broadly satisfactory, then unless we assume quite staggering inefficiency in all state enter-prises the conclusion is irresistible that they should be charging much higher prices for their output. Even if on average they raised their prices by 66·3 per cent they would almost certainly still be incurring some losses, because demand would fall and unit costs would rise in response to the price increase. Of course there is no reason why individual enter-prises should not finance large investment projects at least partly through loans, but taking a large number of public enterprises together one would expect them, on average, to meet most of their needs from internal funds. Thus for the sixty-four enterprises surveyed in Table 7 an 'equivalent exchange of value' between public and private sectors would require at least a 50 per cent rise in the average price of public enterprise outputs – and in many cases prices ought to be doubled. This gives us some measure of the degree of subsidy which public enterprise is currently conferring on the private sector in non-commu-nist underdeveloped countries. When spokesmen for private enterprise complain of the burden of taxation they are obliged to shoulder, they should be reminded of the offsetting government subsidies they are receiving in this way. Equally, when a government considers policies to restrain overall demand or cream off the 'excess' profits of the private sector, they should be reminded that a higher price for public enterprise products is a serious alternative to increased discriminatory controls.[20]

Of course public enterprises are very diverse, as we have seen, so that these conclusions cannot be applied automatically to individual cases. In some instances the chief cause of a deficit may genuinely be inefficient management or feather-bedding. If so the appropriate solu-tion must be reorganisation of the enterprise, rather than higher prices. In other cases there may be a social justification for a deficit-producing price structure – for example low public transport fares in urban areas may discourage socially costly dependence on private transport. Even here the argument would not, presumably, justify a deficit of indeterminate size: some specific level of subsidy would have to be agreed upon, and a price policy would be needed which ensured the financing of the residual cost. In yet other instances public enterprises may be justified in exploiting their monopoly power to the full by charging prices far above the cost-plus level. It might, for example, be in the national interest for a state electricity company to pursue this type of policy when selling to large, profitable foreign firms – e.g. mining companies. Thus a satisfactory price policy for public enterprises would need to consider not merely the influence of the overall price level on the rate of accumulation but also the way the price structure may affect the pattern of demand, the distribution of income and the balance of payments.

Meanwhile the present situation is that, far from using the pricing policies of public enterprises as a technique for capital accumulation, these concerns are being allowed to swallow up public savings simply in order to meet current operating costs. On average the twenty-four Latin American enterprises in Table 7 are converting public savings (which should be used for new investment) into current expenditure to the tune of 21·9 per cent of the value of their annual activity. We have seen that including new investment their financing needs amount to 56·3 per cent of activity, and we can also see from column E that three-quarters of this total is met by transfers from the central government. (Outside Latin America the deficits are even larger, but the government transfers are smaller.) In fact government transfers finance almost the whole deficit of Latin America's public transport enterprises, and about 90 per cent of the deficits incurred by industrial enterprises. The principal sectors where government transfers do not meet the deficit are electricity and above all petrol – i.e. the more solvent state enterprises, whose deficits arise only because of their rapid rates of expansion. As credit-worthy concerns they are able to raise loans from domestic and foreign sources. Where they do receive help from the government it may be in the form of a *bona fide* loan rather than a subsidy, in which case it would not appear in column E. We shall see later (in section (*d*)) how these enterprises raise their foreign loans.

Once we have seen the scale of government subsidies there is little we can add about this source of finance. Of course governments can refuse to pay the required subsidy unless efficiency is improved or specific new investment projects are postponed. Thus the scale of government subsidies is variable, but it varies according to complex, and usually secret, bargaining processes which are not amenable to economic analysis. Once the scale of the subsidy has been determined, then an economic issue arises – whether the subsidy should be recovered in some form of new taxation or through a budget deficit which might have inflationary consequences.[21] But since the government budget has been dealt with in Chapter 2 we shall pass over this issue here. In the next section we shall examine another way the government might finance limited public enterprise deficits, and then we shall look at the intermediaries chiefly responsible for raising the loan element in public enterprise financing – the development banks.

(c) *Social Security Funds: A Neglected Source of Forced Savings*

Social security funds are another type of public sector enterprise. Certainly they differ from other state concerns in a number of ways – their customers may not be able to opt out of the transaction, and must commit themselves to make regular payments over an extended period. The product sold is a set of future claims rather than a material good, and the market is the household sector of the economy rather than other productive enterprises. However these schemes resemble nationalised companies in recognising a specific obligation to each 'customer', related to the payment he makes. Therefore the price charged for the service provided will affect the total amount of public savings. Since the schemes consist in charging *at present* for benefits to be received *in the future*, and since in most of Latin America they are still rapidly expanding their coverage, they should be building up reserves. These resources could perhaps be used either to finance the investment needs of public enterprise, or some other aspect of public investment.

When more is paid into a social security fund than is disbursed the effect is identical to that of a tax measure. The insured population consume a smaller proportion of their income, and the forced saving secured in this way permits an equivalent amount of deficit-financed investment elsewhere in the economy without inflation. To transfer these resources one could, in theory, have the public enterprise issuing bonds in which the managers of the social security fund could invest their surplus. In practice this is an unlikely outcome at present: partly because capital markets are generally poorly developed in Latin America; partly because in an inflationary situation these types of paper issue are unattractive, especially if the contributors to the social security fund want their

Table 8. Social Security Fund Surpluses as a Percentage of Gross
Domestic Investment in eighteen Latin American Countries

	Gross accrued savings	Gross cash savings	Net cash savings
Argentina			
1959	5·5		
1961–3	4·6	0·2	
1963	5·2	0·9	0·9
Brazil			
1959	9·5		
1959–60	9·7	3·6	
1960	10·5	4·6	2·9
1963	6·3	−0·9	−3·5
Chile			
1957		19·9	
1960–2		13·1	
1962		14·7	14·7
Colombia			
1958		a	
1961–3		0·6	
1963		1·0	−2·3
Costa Rica			
1959		4·6	
1962	6·7	4·5	1·5
Cuba			
1954–5		7·3	
Dominican Republic			
1960–2		−0·1	
1962		0·6	−0·6
Ecuador			
1960		11·5	
1961–3		10·5	
1963		10·9	9·8
El Salvador			
1958		a	
1959–60		0·7	
1960		0·8	−0·1
Guatemala			
1959		0·6	
1963–4		0·3	
1964		0·7	0·7
Honduras			
1962		0·6	0·3
Mexico			
1959		2·4	
1961–3		3·5	
1963		3·4	0·7
Nicaragua			
1961–2/63–4	0·8	0·3	
1963–4	3·0	1·3	1·3

Table 8—*continued*.

	Gross accrued savings	Gross cash savings	Net cash savings
Panama			
1959		9·6	
1960–2		5·3	
1962		5·4	
Paraguay			
1961–2		1·5	
1962		2·1	1·1
Peru			
1959		*a*	
Uruguay			
1961–3	11·7	2·5	
1963	15·8	3·6	3·6
Venezuela			
1959		*a*	
1962		0·2	—0·3

a = Under 0·5 per cent.

Sources: I.B.R.D. report, *Financial Aspects of Social Security in Latin America* (1962), p. 57, and Franco Reviglio, 'Social Security: A Means of Savings Mobilization for Economic Development', in *I.M.F. Staff Papers* (July 1967), 326–8 and 337.

benefits guaranteed with a minimum of risk; but fundamentally because enterprises with ambitious investment programmes cannot secure genuine loans (as opposed to government subsidy/loans) if they are unable, on their present pricing policy, to finance even their current level of operations. Enterprises which wish to finance their expansion by credit simply must adopt realistic pricing policies. If not they will be unable to repay loans, so either the social security contributors will be defrauded or the government will have to take over the bad debts. For this reason social security surpluses should not be used as an *alternative* to the realistic pricing of public sector products, but they could be used as a *complementary* method of financing public investment.

But is this potential source of public savings in fact of any importance in Latin America? Table 8 provides indicators of the contribution made by social security surpluses to the financing of gross domestic investment in seventeen Latin American countries around 1960. Three alternative concepts are presented: (1) gross accrued savings, (2) gross cash savings and (3) net cash savings. The central concept is gross cash savings, which is simply the increase in social security reserves over the year. In some cases, however, it may be considerably less than gross accrued savings, which includes in the surplus payments overdue either from the government or the employers, and government contributions paid in securities rather than cash.[22] Of course these additions only represent *potential* savings, the savings which would occur if the social security funds were able to realise the debts owed to them. Table 8 shows that the potential savings generated by the social security system may be several times larger than the savings actually achieved. The major discrepancies between potential and actual savings occur in Argentina, Brazil and above all in Uruguay, where the discrepancy amounted to over 10 per cent of gross domestic investment in 1963, and may well have grown even larger since then. The inflation experienced by these three countries makes it worthwhile to postpone payment of social security contributions as long as possible, so that the real cost of the payment can be eroded by price rises. The third indicator shown in Table 8 is net cash savings – a concept defined by Reviglio[23] to mean gross cash savings less government subsidies financed by borrowing rather than taxation. This third concept is the one which measures the net contribution to national savings made by social security funds, since increased social security reserves clearly do not represent national savings if they are financed by government subsidies which, in turn, are financed by money-creation, rather than taxation. Although this is the correct concept in principle, the problem in practice is to distinguish between subsidies financed by taxation and those financed by government borrowing. Reviglio's solution, used in column 3 of Table 8, is to assume that social security subsidies are financed by borrowing whenever total government borrowing for all purposes exceeds the social security subsidy. Using this strong assumption, column 3 makes some significant alterations to the data in column 2, although the reduction in savings only exceeds 2 per cent of gross domestic investment in three cases – Mexico and Costa Rica, where the contribution to national savings dwindles into insignificance if government subsidies are deducted, and Colombia, where the contribution actually becomes significantly negative.

Having made these adjustments, it appears that only three of the countries listed in Table 8 were significantly contributing to national savings through their social security surpluses in the early 1960s – Chile, Ecuador and Panama. (Cuban data are available only for the pre-revolutionary period.) In many cases the small surplus is an inevitable consequence of the small scale of social security schemes (social security receipts were less than 1 per cent of G.N.P. in El Salvador,

Nicaragua, Venezuela and Honduras).[24] But in other cases social security receipts were a very large element in economic activity (receipts amounted to 12·6 per cent of G.N.P. in Uruguay in 1963, almost equalling total central government revenue from all taxes),[25] and yet the funds made no significant contribution to total savings, or even made a negative contribution. In Table 9 therefore we examine more

Table 9. Social Security Receipts, Expenditures, Savings, Assets and Coverage in Nine Latin American Countries
(ranked by percentage of G.N.P. taken in social security receipts)

		Total cash receipts (% of G.N.P.)	Expenditure (% of G.N.P.)	Gross cash savings (% of G.N.P.)	Total assets (% of G.N.P.)		Per cent of total population contributing
Uruguay	1963	12·6	12·1	0·45	19·3	(1962)	40·6
Chile	1962	10·4	8·5	1·85	9·5	(1960)	22·9
Ecuador	1963	4·6	3·0	1·60 (1·44)	20·6	(1961)	3·8
Panama	1962	4·4	3·0	0·91	19·8	(1961)	7·4
Brazil	1963	3·9	4·1	−0·15 (−0·58)	8·3 (1960)	(1962)	6·5
Costa Rica	1962	3·8	3·3	0·73 (0·24)	6·7	(1963)	7·7
Argentina	1963	3·7	3·5	0·18	7·8	(1961)	27·4
Bolivia	1963	2·8	2·8	0·06	...	(1962)	3·1
Mexico	1963	2·1	1·6	0·49 (0·10)	3·2	(1963)	3·2

Note: Where net cash savings differs from gross, then the net figure is given in parentheses.

Sources: Assets data from F. Reviglio, 'Social Security: A Means of Savings Mobilization for Economic Development', in *I.M.F. Staff Papers* (July 1967), 351; receipts, savings, expenditure and coverage data from F. Reviglio, 'The Social Security Sector and its Financing in Developing Countries', in *I.M.F. Staff Papers* (Nov 1967), 502, 503, 505 and 510 respectively.

closely the nine Latin American countries where social security receipts exceeded 2 per cent of G.N.P., and in which, therefore, a significant surplus could be generated by a suitably organised scheme, even without raising new sources of revenue.

Table 9 shows that Chile and Uruguay devote a much higher proportion of their G.N.P. to social security than any of the other Latin American countries. These two countries, plus Argentina, provide social security coverage for a large proportion of their total population, whereas the other six only provide it for a privileged minority of workers. (These three are also the most urbanised countries of Latin America, and those in which agricultural workers are a minority of the labour force.) Yet the largest schemes with the widest coverage do not make the biggest contributions to savings. Whereas Uruguay's receipts amount to 12·6 per cent of G.N.P. and no less than 40·6 per cent of her population are contributors (which means that including dependants practically everyone must be a beneficiary), social security only generated a surplus of 0·45 per cent of G.N.P. in 1963, while Ecuador generated net savings of 1·44 per cent of G.N.P. with receipts equalling 4·6 per cent of G.N.P. levied from a mere 3·8 per cent of the population. This contrast can be explained largely in terms of the maturity of the respective schemes – a newly established or rapidly expanding scheme can be expected to generate a large surplus in the initial stages, before the claims for benefits fall due. By contrast a long-established scheme, like that of Uruguay, has to pay benefits to the accumulated ranks of past contributors, while it cannot hope for growing receipts since all the work force is insured already and the population is increasing slowly. In fact as G.N.P. per head declines (this has been the trend in Uruguay over the last ten years) the real value of receipts is also likely to decline. Unless the real value of benefits is also reduced at a similar rate such a scheme can become a major source of public dissaving. It is notable that Ecuador's scheme, despite its smaller receipts, smaller coverage and its shorter existence, has already accumulated assets valued at 20·6 per cent of G.N.P., compared with Uruguay's total of only 19·3 per cent. We can safely assume that this divergence between the two countries has become a great deal more marked since 1963, as Uruguay entered an even more acute phase of inflation and economic decline. Clearly the maturity of a scheme is only a partial explanation – in a rapidly growing economy it is much easier to meet the growing burden of obligations as a scheme matures.

In a continent where only 13·1 per cent of the total population were protected by social security schemes in 1960[26] and where income per head has allegedly been rising at about 1·6 per cent a year[27] (and probably rising faster among the insured population), one would expect an important fraction of social security receipts to provide reserves for a later stage, when the expansion of coverage will slow down and obligations to current contributors will mature. Yet we find that only in Ecuador, Chile and Panama did increased social security reserves exceed $\frac{1}{2}$ per cent of G.N.P. (Table 9) or 5 per cent of gross domestic investment (Table 8). The same conclusion seems to apply to social security funds as to public enterprises – in theory they are a powerful source of capital accumulation, but in practice they are scarcely making any contribution to financing development. Indeed five of the eighteen countries listed in Table 8 were actually making a negative net contribution to savings in some years.

The position is much worse if we consider the possible backwash effects these schemes may have on other types of saving. Reviglio made light of these effects, quoting evidence from the U.S.A. and India to show that the reduction in personal and company savings brought about by the existence of a social security scheme is considerably less than the new savings created by the scheme.[28] He added that in Latin America the personal savings of the household sector are generally small, or even negative, and noted that 'since the right to the pension cannot be sold in the market it is not a substitute for other forms of investment which give liquidity for security, as well as prospects for future gains'.[29] So he concluded that 'it seems reasonable to think that a significant part of the savings represented by such surpluses could not have been realised without such programs'.[30] Unfortunately the direct evidence for this conclusion is lacking, and the expression 'a significant part' is therefore deliberately vague. If we guessed that this part was half of the social security surplus then we would have to halve the figures in column 3 of Table 9. In this case Chile's system would only be adding 0·9 per cent of G.N.P. to Chile's domestic savings, Ecuador's would be adding 0·8 per cent, and all the others would be adding much less.

Even this, however, is probably too optimistic. The I.B.R.D. report quoted in Table 8 attempts to disaggregate the likely backwash effects on savings according to the source of the social security receipts. Contributions paid by those of low income would be 'almost entirely at the expense of immediate consumption', they concluded, whereas contributions from the middle class would probably be partly offset by a reduction in voluntary savings. (Unfortunately in Latin America social security primarily benefits the middle and better paid workers, i.e. those most able to reduce their voluntary savings.) Employers' contributions were probably passed on in higher prices rather than absorbed by a reduction in company savings, the I.B.R.D. continued, and higher prices probably reduced consumption rather than savings.[31] So far so good – there would be some backwash effects from employers' and employees' contributions, but these might not be very large. However, the I.B.R.D. report showed that other sources of income were an important proportion of receipts in most Latin American countries, and here we can expect important offsetting effects on savings. Table 10 summarises the available data on other sources of income. It shows that government contributions (including earmarked taxes but excluding money paid into the funds in its capacity as an employer) exceed half of total receipts in five countries out of the twelve for which 1963 figures

Table 10. Sources of Income for Social Security Funds in Latin America
(per cent of total income)

	Employers and employees	Government	Income from capital	Other income[a]
Argentina				
1959	89·6	0·1	9·2	1·2
Bolivia				
1959	73·6	25·5	0·3	0·6
1963	75·4	23·1	0·8	0·6
Brazil				
1959	53·5	25·6	5·0	16·0
Chile				
1957	60·6	31·7	4·9	2·8
1963	55·9	32·8	1·9	9·4
Colombia				
1958	65·9	28·3	...	5·8
1963	41·1	57·6	...	1·3
Costa Rica				
1959	74·0	15·0	8·9	2·2
1963	52·4	36·7	9·7	1·2
Cuba				
1954–5	67·2	28·3	3·6	0·8
Dominican Republic				
1959	74·1	11·8	5·0	9·2
Ecuador				
1960	42·2	2·6	15·1	40·2
El Salvador				
1959	73·9	24·9	0·9	0·4
1963	43·9	55·9	0·1	0·1
Guatemala				
1959	84·8	13·6	0·7	0·9
1963	49·5	50·0	...	0·5
Haiti				
1953–4	32·4	36·0	0·3	31·3
Mexico				
1959	67·8	24·6	7·6	...
1963	68·5	25·7	5·8	...
Nicaragua				
1959	66·0	31·8	2·0	0·2
1963	37·6	59·8	2·5	0·1
Panama				
1959	69·0	6·9	21·3	2·8
1963	58·4	30·2	11·0	0·3
Paraguay				
1959	86·1	8·6	1·6	3·8
1963	74·7	17·9	4·9	2·6
Peru				
1959	73·5	21·7	3·8	1·2

Table 10—*continued.*

	Employers and employees	Government	Income from capital	Other income[a]
Uruguay				
1959	68·9	21·2	7·2	2·8
1963	82·7	6·8	0·1	10·4
Venezuela				
1959	77·8	18·2	2·1	2·0
1963	28·1	70·7	0·5	0·7

[a] Includes transfers among social security schemes which are normally balanced by items of a similar magnitude in the consolidated accounts of social security expenditure.

Sources: I.B.R.D. report, *Financial Aspects of Social Security in Latin America* (1962), p. 53. 1963 figures from ILO, *The Cost of Social Security, Sixth International Enquiry 1961–3* (Geneva, 1967). These figures are summarised in a slightly different form in Felix Paukert, 'Social Security and Income Redistribution', in *International Labour Review* (Nov 1968), 440–1, where fifty-three countries are compared.

are available, and for thirteen out of the nineteen countries included in the table we can find years when the government contribution exceeded a quarter of total receipts. Furthermore in Colombia, Venezuela and the five Central American countries there were dramatic increases in the proportion of receipts provided by the government between 1959 and 1963. In the words of the I.B.R.D. report:

> It may be assumed that at least some of the revenue from special taxes levied to meet the government's share of social security costs could be raised even if there were no social security schemes.[32]

In short, tax income which could otherwise have been channelled into investment was diverted into the social security funds, not merely to build up the reserves of these funds (which would constitute a redistribution of the resources available for public investment) but frequently also to cover current operating expenses (which involves a reduction in public savings and investment). As the schemes expand and government contributions to total receipts rise, more and more potential public saving is likely to be swallowed up in this way. Here is a backwash effect of the first order. Including it in the assessment, we would find that the small positive contributions to national savings shown in Tables 8 and 9 would almost all be wiped out, and almost every social security scheme in the continent would prove to be a significant absorber of public savings.

Of course these backwash effects are hypothetical. The quantity of dissaving on this count must be a matter of conjecture. But there is another factor offsetting social security saving, which we can quantify. 'Income from capital' represents savings generated elsewhere in the economy and then transferred to the social security sector – not new savings generated by that sector. Table 10 shows the percentage of receipts coming from this source. Transfers of this sort are most important in the two countries which stood out in Table 9 as channelling the largest proportion of their receipts into savings – Ecuador and Panama. Thus there is no need to make subjective estimates of the size of the backwash effects. Even without considering these effects, we can show that in the only countries where social security funds have been accumulating respectable surpluses, they have been doing so largely by transferring savings from other sectors of the economy. Not even the most successful schemes have been forcing their contributors to save more than they receive in benefits. All in all there is no evidence of social security schemes making any significant contribution to the financing of development in any Latin American country, and there is a strong presumption that in most cases they are having a negative impact. Unless there is a drastic change of policy, these negative effects can be expected to become worse as the existing schemes mature.

Should social security be used to finance development anyway? Why impose sacrifices on the workers, when property owners escape so lightly from the tax system? No doubt Latin American tax systems urgently need to be made more progressive, and any change in the social security system which was simply used to postpone such a reform should be deplored. But schemes expanding their coverage need to generate a large surplus in order to meet their future obligations. Contributors are not being exploited so long as the fund maintains its ability to pay them fair benefits. In the process social security systems can make a contribution to development as well, and if they raise the growth rate they will also raise the capacity of the economy to provide generous pensions to present contributors when they eventually retire. In any case it is not socially unjust to require contributors to help finance economic development, since in most underdeveloped countries the social security system is not a method of redistributing income from rich to poor. In Paukert's words:

Unlike developed countries, developing countries spend a large proportion of social security expenditure on government employees, while other schemes are rather fragmentary. Typically, the poorest sections of society are outside the impact of the various social security schemes.

A similar picture emerges when social security revenue is examined. . . . In the developing countries the lower income groups, which are not covered by social security, contribute indirectly through general taxation . . . [which] . . . is found to be much more regressive in developing countries than in developed countries. . . . Typically such people remain outside the system of social security, receive no benefits, and make no direct contributions. But they contribute through general taxes to social security programmes for groups with somewhat higher incomes.

Briefly stated, the position is that while income redistribution through social security in developed countries could be represented as a movement from the top to the bottom, in developing countries it resembles a movement from the top and bottom to the centre.[33]

Thus it is hard to argue on grounds of equity that the social security sector should not contribute more to national savings, although a higher priority might be to increase progressive income taxation, and the taxation of wealth and inheritances. But whether or not the social security sector is required to improve its savings performance, it can still have a significant effect on the pattern of national investment and the rate of growth. Column 4 of Table 9 shows that even in countries where social security makes no net contribution to national savings, it may accumulate assets valued at as much as 20 per cent of G.N.P. Thus the way these resources are invested may already be of national importance in a number of countries, and would become much more important if the rate of savings was stepped up. Table 11 shows the composition of social security assets in the seven Latin American countries where these resources were valued at more than 5 per cent of G.N.P.

The final column of the table shows that in most cases assets were largely held in financial claims of various kinds. The one country to hold most of its social security assets in physical form was Costa Rica in the 1960s. Reviglio explains that 'In Costa Rica, in the four years 1962–5, total investment of 50 million colons for hospitals represented a large part of the available resources.'[34] This is a useful form of investment from the national point of view, but unless the social security hospitals charge an economic rate for the services they provide it means that contributors as a whole are mostly consuming their social security benefits now, rather than saving to provide future benefits. Similarly Ecuador's scheme (which has accumulated assets worth 20·6 per cent

Table 11. Composition of Social Security Assets in Seven Latin American Countries

	Total assets as per cent of G.N.P.	Percentage of total assets held in:		
		Government bonds and direct loans	Mortgages and personal loans	All financial claims
Ecuador				
1959		5·0	41·4	88·9
1963	20·6	13·3	56·0	84·2
Panama				
1957		28·2	18·7	90·8
1964	19·8	28·0	15·2	88·2
Uruguay				
1963	19·3			
1964		67·4	10·4	100·0
Chile				
1955		3·5	31·5	80·6
1960		0·6	19·5	63·0
1962	9·5			
Brazil				
1960	8·3	53·2	3·6	97·0
Argentina				
1961		73·0	6·0	100·0
1963	7·8			
Costa Rica				
1955		17·4	33·9	84·9
1962	6·7			
1964		...	...	19·2

Sources: I.B.R.D. report, *Financial Aspects of Social Security in Latin America* (1962), p. 58, and F. Reviglio, 'Social Security: A Means of Savings Mobilization for Economic Development', in *I.M.F. Staff Papers* (July 1967), 351 and 354–5. Total assets excludes unfunded claims, except for Ecuador in 1959, where they amounted to 23 per cent of all assets, and for Brazil in 1960.

of G.N.P.) is channelling over half its resources to personal loans and mortgages which benefit only a privileged fraction of the contributors. It can be assumed that these loans are on more favourable terms than would otherwise be available (i.e. the proceeds of the assets are partly being consumed by the contributors) and that they are a stimulus to private consumption and dissaving, rather than to private investment.[35] In the other countries mortgages and private loans are less important, but wherever they are significant the same objections apply. The other important category of assets shown in Table 11 is public debt, in the form of either government bonds or direct loans to the government. Over half of all assets are held in this form in Argentina, Brazil and Uruguay. Indeed in 1964 the social security sector in Uruguay held no less than 52·6 per cent of the total internal public debt issued by the government.[36] Public debt is not an attractive form of asset in most Latin American countries, particularly in periods of inflation, but the government is often able to induce social security agencies to hold it despite terms which would be unacceptable to any independent enterprise. Thus, whereas Table 11 shows the assets of Uruguay's social security system to have equalled 19·3 per cent of G.N.P. in 1963, Table 10 shows that in the same year its income from capital was only 0·1 per cent of all income. Similarly in Argentina 'the real value of assets held by the social security sector, consisting mostly of public debt, declined by over 90 per cent in the period 1950–1961; in the same period, large erosions of the real value of the reserves occurred also in Brazil'.[37] This method of 'investing' social security savings is perhaps the hardest of all to justify, although it is the most common. Contributors are not even subsidising themselves – and in most cases the government's success in floating bonds which offer a negative real rate of interest simply permits a higher level of current expenditure without taxation. This confirms that social security surpluses should not be relied on, in isolation, to boost public investment. They can only be used as a *supplement* to a public sector which charges at least a cost-plus price for its outputs and adopts a development-oriented tax policy. In these circumstances, but only in these circumstances, the social security system could usefully invest in government or public enterprise bonds at a positive and realistic interest rate, and with guarantees against inflation.

Increasing the size of social security assets will contribute little to economic development unless the way these assets are managed is also reformed, so as to reduce the leakages into current consumption and channel the new resources into growth-promoting forms of investment. The I.B.R.D. report states that

> Little attention was given to the wider financial and economic implications of the policies of these institutions, such as the long term repercussions on the government budget, both on the revenue and the expenditure side, and the importance of their investments for

the economic development of the country as a whole. These implications were regarded more or less unavoidable, accidental or accessory.[38]

So long as this remains true little contribution to economic growth can be expected from the social security sector. And yet, consciously or unconsciously, as social security spreads and matures, the policies of these agencies will have a growing impact on the economic environment in which they operate. The evidence from this section suggests, unfortunately, that on balance this impact may be distinctly negative.

(d) Latin America's Development Banks

Undeniably, despite the pessimism of the last two sections, a considerable amount of public investment is somehow getting financed in Latin America. How are resources raised to maintain the level of public investment despite low taxes and give-away pricing policies? In Latin America public development banks play a large part in this process. This section will concentrate on three of the most important of these banks for which information is most readily available – the Banco Nacional do Desenvolvimento Economico of Brazil (B.N.D.E.), the Corporacion de Fomento of Chile (CORFO) and Mexico's National Financiera (NAFIN). These three institutions have been selected because they are key components of the public sector in their respective countries, and have been established long enough to permit broad assessments. NAFIN was set up in 1933 to stimulate an organised market for public bonds and private shares, and reorganised in 1941 as a government industrial investment bank. CORFO was created in 1939 (by the Popular Front government which had just come to power in Chile) initially as the government reconstruction agency to deal with the effects of the Chillán earthquake. It rapidly became

> a *sui generis* investment bank: it is an investment bank because it is *the* institution specialising in financing long-term investment; it is *sui generis* because it is run as a non-profit organisation and dispenses its vast resources without applying the traditional rules of profit-motivated investment banks.[39]

B.N.D.E. is the youngest of the three, set up by Vargas in 1952. It was created partly to provide an official intermediary capable of negotiating loans from international agencies on behalf of public and private

Brazilian enterprises. This function was of no importance at the time when NAFIN and CORFO were created, although in the postwar period it has also become one of their prime activities.

Table 12. Approximate Proportion of Investment Financed by Main Development Banks, in Brazil, Chile and Mexico

B.N.D.E. (Brazil)		CORFO (Chile)			NAFIN (Mexico)	
	Per cent of major public sector fixed investments		Per cent of gross domestic investment	Per cent of total public investment		New NAFIN resources as per cent of total investment
1957	35	1940	16·4	30·2	1941	6
1958	26	1945	6·3	17·3	1942–4	17
1959	24	1950	17·2	41·9	1944–6	6
1960	15	1954	18·4	25·8	1947–9	5
1961	12	1961	6·7	...	1950–2	5
1962	13	1962	11·0	...	1953–5	4
1963	24	1963	7·1	...	1956–8	2
					1959–61	11

Sources:

B.N.D.E. data from N. Leff, *Economic Policy-Making and Development in Brazil 1947–64* (1968), p. 40. The other public sector investments included in this total are roads, Petrobras and Brasilia. Obviously total public investment would be considerably larger than this, and B.N.D.E.'s percentage contribution would be correspondingly smaller.

CORFO data from M. Mamalakis, 'Veinticinco años de la CORFO', in *Ensayos Sobre Planificación*, ed. Griffin and Garcia (University of Chile, 1967), p. 415. A condensed version of this article was published in the *Journal of Development Studies* (Jan 1969).

NAFIN data calculated from Calvin Blair's study of NAFIN in *Public Policy and Private Enterprise in Mexico*, ed. Vernon (1964), p. 204, where 'new NAFIN resources' means the increase in the bank's 'total own resources' (the first column of Blair's table) in each period. These increases were expressed as a percentage of gross national investment as shown in the *Statistics on the Mexican Economy* (NAFIN, 1966), p. 45.

Table 12 provides very crude indicators of the amount of investment financed by these banks. The difficulty is that these banks channel resources into investment in a variety of ways, and it is not clear which of these should be included. In addition to direct investments there are equity purchases, various forms of loans (some of which practically amount to grants), and there are endorsements of loans from foreign creditors to domestic enterprises. These endorsements do not constitute any commitment of bank resources (unless the local enterprise defaults on the loan), but they may provide a significant source of bank income because the bank naturally charges a commission for this service. The figures for NAFIN shown in Table 12 refer only to commitments of the bank's 'own resources' – i.e. endorsements are not included, although they represented about a third of the funds channelled through NAFIN in 1967.[40] Unfortunately neither Leff nor Blair explain what aspects of bank activity they included in their calculations, so the figures for B.N.D.E. and CORFO may not be strictly comparable to those for NAFIN. One could also object to expressing NAFIN's 'new resources' as a percentage of total investment, since it cannot be assumed that these new resources exactly represent the bank's contribution to investment. With all these reservations, Table 12 does provide rough evidence that these three banks were remarkably important sources of finance in their respective countries.

Their importance is enhanced if we examine the type of investment in which they specialise. They concentrate on infrastructure and public enterprise and a large proportion of their resources comes from foreign credits. On B.N.D.E. Leff remarks that

> once the railways had been provided with new equipment in the early and middle 1950's, the great bulk of the Development Bank's resources went into four public sector projects – two in steel and two in electricity.[41]

Similarly Mamalakis notes that CORFO

> has dominated economic life since 1939. It controlled the lion's share of investment in machinery and equipment (more than 30% in ten years, during 1939/54), more than a fourth of public investment and as high as 18% (1954) of gross domestic investment.[42]

Likewise Blair notes that at the end of 1961

> NAFIN'S loans were nearly half as large as those of all private credit institutions, and they accounted for more than one third of total lending by Mexico's public credit institutions. Long term loans by NAFIN were considerably greater than those of the private lending agencies taken together.[43]

He adds that

> NAFIN's post-1947 emphases have led it inevitably to devote the bulk of its financial aid in recent years to the public sector. In part, concentration on public firms has been a by-product of the decision to invest heavily in the infrastructure, where railroads, electric power companies, and irrigation works are properties of the state. But the pattern extends beyond the infrastructure. At the end of 1959 . . . some seventy per cent of NAFIN's investment in manufacturing was . . . accounted for without including firms in which public-sector ownership was less than a majority . . . Of nearly 1·5 billion dollars in long-term foreign loans obtained with NAFIN's help in the interval 1942–60, more than four fifths can be identified as going to the public sector.[44]

All three banks had important domestic sources of income of course – B.N.D.E. received the proceeds of a special tax on personal and company income, CORFO benefited from an earmarked tax on copper company profits (although it also depended at times on inflationary credit from the central bank), and NAFIN is officially linked with the Banco de Mexico, so that it can obtain credit from them when necessary. (NAFIN has not needed to depend on government funds as much as the other two banks, because it has 'a profit record which would do credit to some of the best managed of private enterprises'[45] and is therefore far more credit-worthy both at home and abroad.)[46] In addition all three banks received income from their investments, although at least in CORFO's case these investments often yielded a loss rather than a profit.[47] It was their access to foreign credit, however, which made these three banks so important. Many of the investments they financed had a high foreign exchange component, and might not have been undertaken if foreign loans had not been available to supplement export earnings. Foreign creditors naturally preferred to lend to an agency whose credit was as strong as that of the government rather than to individual enterprises, and in all three countries the government allowed its development bank to supervise the allocation of available foreign loans for public sector investment. Table 13 shows the proportion of total public foreign indebtedness incurred by the development banks in each country. It shows that in Mexico almost 70 per cent of public foreign indebtedness has been incurred through NAFIN, and this indicates that nearly all foreign credits to Mexico have been channelled into public investment, whereas in Brazil and Chile a higher proportion may have been used in other ways (e.g. to finance current public expenditure). In all three cases the development bank appears to have been a principal source of the foreign credit available for financing the investments of public enterprises.

Table 13. Foreign Indebtedness in Brazil, Chile and Mexico, and the
Proportion Incurred by Development Banks
(million dollars at end of year)

		A. *Net foreign loans disbursed to public sector*	B. *Outstanding foreign debt of development banks*	(A) *as per cent of* (B)
Brazil	1962	2141·0	674·7	31·5
Chile	1962	565·4	133·5	23·6
Mexico	1967	2176·1	1512·8	69·5

Sources:
Column A data for Brazil and Chile from ECLA, *External Financing in Latin America* (1965), p. 204. Mexican figure from the Fourth Presidential Report of Diaz Ordaz, as published in *Novedades* (Mexico City), 2 Sept 1968.
Column B data: B.N.D.E. from the statistical supplement to B.N.D.E.'s *XII Exposicao sobre o Programa de Reaparelhamento Economico* (1963); CORFO from M. Mamalakis, in *Ensayos Sobre Planificación*, ed. Griffin and Garcia (University of Chile, 1967), p. 425; NAFIN from the *Informe de Actividades* 1967, p. 17 (note that this figure refers to 30 June 1967).

(e) Summary and Conclusion

We have presented some reasons for expecting public enterprises in 'mixed' economies to price their outputs so low that they generate quite inadequate surpluses to meet their investment needs. In such economies public enterprise commonly operates in precisely those sectors where the scale of these investments is largest and where private investment would be forthcoming only if offered high profits to compensate for the long gestation period of investments and their 'lumpy' character. By charging low prices for their outputs public enterprises are transferring public savings and foreign loans into subsidies to their consumers – subsidies which may raise the consumption levels of the popular classes (as happens when passenger fares are set very low on the railways), but more often swell the profits of the private sector (whether such profits go into private investment or consumption by the wealthy classes has not been investigated here). Artificially low prices for the outputs of the public sector also tend, obviously enough, to produce a misallocation of resources.

We then examined the evidence available for Latin America, and found that although state petrol companies represented something of an exception (in particular PEMEX), in most cases where public enterprises were important their pricing policies were indeed highly deficitary. On average, combining the accounts of twenty-four Latin American public enterprises, their expenditure including new investment exceeded their activity (the average of their income and expenditure) by 56 per cent, with the largest deficits occurring in electricity (because new investment needs are so huge) and railways (because prices come nowhere near to covering running costs). Three-quarters of these deficits was covered by government transfers, and much of the remainder was financed by foreign loans channelled through development banks whose credit-worthiness often reflected the government's willingness to service their debts, rather than the soundness of the enterprise they supported.

One method of reducing these deficits would be to close down a large part of existing public enterprise, and another would be to sharply increase their prices. Apparent escapes from this dilemma prove to be chimerical – foreign borrowing has diminishing returns as the servicing costs of past loans accumulate; transfers from social security funds, even if they did generate larger investible surpluses, would represent an unjustifiable squandering of contributors' assets unless the recipient of the funds pursued a more rational pricing policy; and continued government transfers are either a waste of public savings acquired through taxation, or a spur to deficit financing of government policy, which favours inflation. While both higher taxation and forced saving through deficit financing might be justifiable as *additional* means of financing development, they should not be used simply to offset the negative effect on public investment of the irrational pricing policies of nationalised concerns.

The conclusion appears inescapable – an urgent, and crucial, step in financing faster economic development in Latin America is the adoption of cost-plus pricing policies in the public sector. If this solution proves impossible it will demonstrate one of the political obstacles to rapid development that can arise in a 'mixed' economy.

NOTES

1. We could distinguish two types of exception: (1) Countries such as Burma, where 'industry was almost entirely of the resource-exploitative type such as mines, teak forestry and petroleum extraction, and was in the hands of foreign enterprises so large and well consolidated . . . as to impose a stranglehold on the entire modern sector of the economy'. In such circumstances it is understandable that a nationalist government would conclude 'that foreign economic domination should be broken and these enterprises placed in Burmese hands. In the absence of a sizeable group of indigenous entrepreneurs, socialism meaning nationalisation was the obvious policy choice.' (Gunnar Myrdal, *Asian Drama* (1968), ii, 833.) (2) Countries such as Tanzania, where the state sector predominates, not because the private sector is dangerously strong, but because it is hopelessly weak. As President Nyerere put it: 'The list of firms whose ownership has been affected by the Arusha Declaration is thus a very small one. It is small because, in the words of Norman Manley, "You can't nationalise nothing". The potential of Tanzania is still undeveloped, our real task is to develop it.' (*The Arusha Declaration* (TANU Publicity Section, Dar-es-Salaam, 1967), p. 23.)

2. S. A. Mosk, *Industrial Revolution in Mexico* (1950), p. 61.

3. A. H. Hanson, *Public Enterprise and Economic Development*, 2nd ed. (1965), pp. 199–201. A more realistic account of the relations between public and private sectors is provided by Michael Kidron, *Foreign Investment in India* (1965).

4. He decided that the third way he had described might sacrifice too much growth in the interests of equality: 'if, in a particular field, private enterprise is more growth creating than public, socialist and egalitarian ideologies should not be permitted to inhibit its expansion. The specific question of distribution may well be left to a later stage, when there is more to distribute.' (Hanson, *op. cit.* p. xxiv.)

5. Myrdal, *op. cit.* ii, 810.

6. Ibid. iii, 2103.

7. Hanson, *op. cit.* p. 202.

8. Hugh Gaitskell, *Socialism and Nationalisation* (Fabian pamphlet, 1956), p. 33. Since this was written British public enterprises have reduced their deficits.

9. Myrdal, *op. cit.* ii, 819.

10. Ibid. iii, 2104.

11. Ibid. ii, 903.

12. Ibid. ii, 925.

13. Ibid. ii, 926: his emphasis.

14. Ibid. iii, 2108.

15. This is not the place to analyse why the maximisation of short-run profit in the private sector may diverge from maximisation of long-run growth for the economy as a whole. In some Latin American countries an important proportion of private sector investible surplus gets tied up in luxury construction, for example. In theory, of course, there is always a tax policy capable of bridging such divergences, but in practice these may be impossible to apply, either for administrative or for political reasons.

16. Preobrazhensky, *The New Economics* (London, 1965), pp. 109–10. The mechanisms of 'primitive socialist accumulation' – i.e. the transfer of surplus from private to state sectors – are examined on pp. 95–104 of Preobrazhensky's book.

16a. *Revista Brasileira de Economia* (Mar 1962), 106.

17. *Fortune*, 15 Sept 1968, pp. 130–6, listed the 200 largest industrials outside the United States in 1967, ranking these firms by sales. Only firms who derived at least 50 per cent of their sales from manufacturing or mining activity were included in the list. The table also gives data on assets, net profits, invested capital and number of employees. PEMEX sales were $799 m. (compared with $8,376 m. for the largest company – Royal Dutch Shell) and the company earned a profit of $27 m. on an invested capital of $840 m. It employed 62,700 people.

Of the 200 firms listed by *Fortune* only six belonged to 'underdeveloped' countries. It is significant that the three largest were Latin American state petrol companies – PEMEX (ranked 67th with sales worth $799 m.); Petrobras (ranked 111th with sales worth $507 m.); and Y.P.F. of Argentina (ranked 133rd with sales valued at $422 m.). The remaining three were the C.U.F. Group – a Portuguese private enterprise (193rd); Bunge y Born, the Argentine private company (194th) and Hindustan Steel (199th), the Indian state company, whose losses in 1967 exceeded $29 m.

18. For a complete list of the enterprises examined in the table, see Andrew Gantt II and Giuseppe Dutto, 'Financial Performance of Government Owned Corporations in Less Developed Countries', *I.M.F. Staff Papers* (Mar 1968), 128–9.

19. Some would say the prices are not too low, it is efficiency which is too low. Certainly there may be evidence of inefficiency in many public enterprises, but it is not certain that they are less efficient than local private enterprises, many of which make healthy profits.

20. Gantt and Dutto do not consider the solution of higher prices. They prefer to restrain the growth of the public sector. '. . . the relative merits of tax reduction, or alternatively a less stimulative government budget should be contemplated as a substitute for additional subsidisation of government-owned corporations', Gantt and Dutto conclude, op. cit. p. 128.

21. Budget deficits are not necessarily inflationary even when resources are already fully employed. Suppose a deficit is used to finance further new investment by PEMEX. With a short gestation period and suitable pricing policies the investment could soon generate increased profits for PEMEX which would offset the inflationary budget deficit.

22. 'In some Latin American countries, when money has been scarce during inflation (or deflation), high premium rates, together with a low interest rate on overdue payments, have encouraged delinquency in the employers' payments. Employers in many developing countries lag in the payment of social security premiums and use the premiums as a source of financing for their own company operations; some of them not only fail to pay their own contributions but also retain the premiums withheld on employees' wages and salaries. Employer delinquency reaches unusual proportions in some countries, such as Argentina, Bolivia, Brazil, Paraguay and Uruguay. In Argentina (1964), accumulated overdue premiums were estimated at 45 billion pesos (compared with 92 billion for total receipts.' (F. Reviglio, 'Social Security Financing in Developing Countries', in *I.M.F. Staff Papers*, xiv (1967), 518–19.) A form of employer delinquency is also reported from Chile – a seminar on the Servicio de Seguridad Social (an organisation with over a million contributors) estimated that evasion of contributions due ran at 30–50 per cent of actual receipts. (See Juan Braun, in *Ensayos Sobre Planificación*, ed. Griffin and Garcia (University of Chile, 1967), p. 217.) In these countries the government is the largest employer of insured workers (36·3 per cent of insured workers are government employees in Chile,

31·8 per cent in Paraguay and 26·3 per cent in Uruguay) and it often leads the way in delinquency.

23. F. Reviglio, 'Social Security: A Means of Savings Mobilization for Economic Development', in *I.M.F. Staff Papers* (July 1967), 335.

24. Reviglio, in *I.M.F. Staff Papers*, xiv (1967), 502.

25. Ibid. p. 534 shows Uruguay's social security taxes equalled 92·8 per cent of central government ordinary tax revenue in 1963.

26. Ibid. 509.

27. Average for 1960–7 according to ECLA, *Estudio Económico de América Latina, 1967*, p. 3.

28. Reviglio, *in I.M.F. Staff Papers* (July 1967), 341–3.

29. Ibid. p. 343.

30. Ibid. p. 344.

31. I.B.R.D. report (1962), pp. 32–3.

32. Ibid. p. 33.

33. F. Paukert, 'Social Security and Income Redistribution', in *International Labour Review* (Nov 1968), 448–9.

34. Reviglio, in *I.M.F. Staff Papers* (July 1967), 353–4.

35. The Chilean system is easier to justify, but basically similar – 'since 1961 a large part of the available surpluses of the social security is transferred to the national housing administration (CORVI) to finance low-income and middle income housing for contributors to the social security system': ibid. p. 358.

36. Ibid. p. 356. Panama's social security scheme held 39·8 per cent of the country's total internal public debt in 1964; in Argentina (1961) 38·9 per cent; 31·5 per cent in Ecuador (1963); 20·2 per cent in Brazil (1962).

37. Ibid. pp. 361–2.

38. I.B.R.D. report (1962), p. 40.

39. M. Mamalakis, 'An Analysis of the Financial and Investment Activities of the Chilean Development Corporation, 1939–1964', in *Journal of Development Studies* (January 1969), 119.

40. Nacional Financiera S.A., *Informe de Actividades 1967*, p. 9.

41. N. Leff, *Economic Policy-Making and Development in Brazil 1947–64* (1968), pp. 39–40.

42. Mamalakis, in *Journal of Development Studies* (Jan 1969), 118.

43. C. Blair, in *Public Policy and Private Enterprise in Mexico*, ed. Vernon (1964), p. 194.

44. Ibid. p. 229.

45. Ibid. p. 201.

46. However the government, as the majority stockholder, has accepted a policy of low dividends and high reinvestment which may in some respects represent a transfer of government funds.

47. '. . . CORFO was lending without a dollar, or other, escalator clauses. As a result only a fraction of the real value of the loans was ever repaid by the recipient enterprises.' (Mamalakis, in *Journal of Development Studies* (Jan 1969), 122.)

4. The Role of Agricultural Taxation in Financing Agricultural Development in Latin America

ARTHUR L. DOMIKE and
VICTOR E. TOKMAN[1]

(a) Introduction

THE political problems associated with financing agricultural development are probably more difficult to resolve than those associated with any other sector. It is a commonplace that 'agriculture is special'. We mean something more specific: namely, that fundamental changes are needed in the economic and social power structure of the agricultural sector as a precondition of real economic and social improvement in most of the countries of the region. For this reason, it is necessary to define which groups should be benefited with what kinds of agricultural development programmes. Furthermore, the means used for mobilising financial resources for agricultural development are important elements of the agricultural development programme itself. It is quite possible to use the tax system either to complement or to frustrate the aims of the development programmes. In any case, it is essential that the two seemingly distinct policy and programme areas be considered in conjunction. Unfortunately this is seldom done.

In sum, then, we will be arguing in this chapter that the strategies for agricultural development and for resource mobilisation from agriculture are intimately interrelated and should be designed to complement one another. The 'best' strategies for each country depend mostly upon the existing agrarian structure, and upon the relative importance of agriculture in the economy.

There are at least three different ways in which these issues can be presented. We could try to analyse the situation country by country for the region; lack of space precludes this approach. We might, alternatively, conduct the argument at such a general level that it would apply, in some degree, to agricultural sectors of all the different countries; the results – even if rigorously correct – would tell us very little about on-going policies and desirable changes for the countries themselves.

The middle course we have chosen has some of the difficulties of each but, we believe, is still the best for present purposes. The countries of the region are grouped according to their agricultural development situations and their potential for resource mobilisation. For each group of countries those programmes that best foster and accelerate agricultural development are examined, and rough estimates made of investment needed. The nature and amounts of agricultural taxes are then reviewed to determine how well they fit agricultural development and reform needs. Desirable and feasible changes in agricultural tax burden and structure are suggested. The case of Peru is reviewed in some detail to illustrate a few of the strategic and operational issues that arise in this field.

(b) *Some Essential Definitions*

'Agricultural development strategy', as used here, describes the decision rules by which government officials select among relevant alternatives, when such choices are available. Such rules emerge from the governments' mediation of the clashes of interest among political-economic groups in a particular institutional setting. The rules, even when they are not explicit, guide official decisions about which sectors in the society receive priority investments, services, subsidies, protection and the like.[2] As a point of departure, therefore, we need to discuss the goals of the agricultural strategies and the instruments by which these goals are approached.

Public rhetoric in recent years – most notably the Punta del Este Charter of 1961 – has made it seem that there is a broad consensus concerning the objectives of agricultural development. None the less, it is important to recognise that 'development' will not necessarily be well received by everyone. As Heilbroner puts it: 'Development is much more than a matter of encouraging economic growth within a given social structure. It is rather the *modernization* of that structure, a process of ideational, social, economic and political change that requires the remaking of society in its more intimate as well as its most public attributes.'[3] 'Modernization' means moving away from the primordial human condition where the lives of most men are 'solitary, poor, nasty, brutish and short'. There will necessarily be change in the social and economic power structure as this kind of development occurs. There will be winners and losers, at least in relative terms. This is why a country's political power distribution and governing apparatus must be fully appreciated when pretending to prescribe economic policy.

But, returning to what constitutes 'development', at least three broad indices can be offered. We would emphasise, firstly, the amount of productive employment for the labour force in modern, capital-using sectors; secondly, the ease of access to opportunities for living longer and more satisfying lives, particularly through access to educational and health facilities; and finally, the possibilities for participation in effective political groups and institutions. For the agricultural sector, the goal of modernisation would require continuously rising productivity and *per capita* output, improved living levels and incomes for the mass of the rural population, greater 'social justice', plus a narrowing of the gap between incomes and opportunities of peasants and rural workers and those of the rural well-to-do and the urban employed. The remoteness from meeting these goals is the best measure of the seriousness of the 'agrarian problem' in each country.

The origins of this problem, however, lie not in the gap between goals and reality, but in the ways power is attained and held in the rural society. In the poorer societies, power is almost a simple function of how much land a family holds. In the more complex and urbanising societies in which most of the region's population now lives, control over land, as such, loses its overwhelming significance, but the narrowly based rural social and political structure is retained. The agrarian problem persists even though – and often because – agricultural production becomes mechanised and market-oriented. As Barrington Moore, Jr, amply documents,[4] the solution which each country is able to find to its agrarian problem determines not only the pace of its modernisation but also the political form it takes.

The achievement of economic modernisation, in these terms, requires an increase in labour utilisation, output and incomes by providing access to land for landless workers, and to additional land for the operators of 'sub-family sized' parcels (*minifundia*). Specific programmes would include redistribution of large holdings (land reform in its strict sense) and supporting activities such as linked credit and extension schemes, promotion of settlement of new lands, the massive use of rural labour in public works projects, and encouragement of handicrafts and small-scale industries. To be even more effective, such activities should be tied to expansion of urban employment opportunities.

The social and political parts of the modernisation process would require health and educational programmes directed primarily towards the rural areas, plus encouragement of political organisations. In spite of the importance of these measures and the obvious interaction with the economic measures (e.g. improved education makes workers more productive), we concentrate below on the economic activities.

(c) Priorities in Agricultural Development

Our first task is to provide a basis for classification which adequately distinguishes the countries of the region in two respects: what needs to be done in the agricultural sector (and to some extent in the other sectors as well) to achieve modernisation; and what are the fiscal means available to the government to achieve these goals. The nations in each of our groups are (or could be) pursuing similar agricultural reform and development strategies, and face similar problems in mobilising resources, particularly from the agricultural sector itself, to implement the strategies. We recognise that no grouping of countries according to development stages is fully satisfactory.[5] However, social analysts such as Horowitz, Germani and Lambert accept the notion that there is a sort of continuum of social structures among countries within the region.[6] Lambert, for example, ranges the countries on a scale from the 'archaic' to the 'integrated'. Most Latin American nations are in the middle of the range, that is, they are unevenly developed dualistic societies, in which both traditional and modern social structures exist in competition or conjunction.[7] The categories are based upon such measures as occupational structure, urbanisation and educational levels.

The process of modernisation has also been examined in terms of 'social mobilisation' theory. Karl Deutsch, for example, identifies eight variables which measure and correlate with the transition from traditional to modern society. His list includes exposure to modernity, shift into a mass media audience, change in the locality of residence, change from rural to urban residence, occupational shift out of agriculture, increase in literacy, income growth *per capita* and increase in voting participation.[8]

For our purposes the best starting point for a country typology according to strategic needs and resource potential is provided by Solon Barraclough.[9] The poorest, traditional agrarian countries are those whose agrarian structure is least apt for modernisation, and in which the resource base is also poorest. The dominant strategic need of these traditional agrarian countries is to reform the structure of landowning and power.

A second category includes the countries in which some modification has been made in the traditional agrarian structure, but in which reforms must still be completed or consolidated or both. For some of these countries the relative availability of resources for developing the agricultural sector is adequate, for others not. These countries need programmes leading to a restructured agriculture and economic consolidation of reform units, particularly for those regions and groups left out of the initial programmes. Finally, the richer countries of the region all have agricultural development problems but their relative significance is less, and the national resources are more ample. In these countries the restructuring of the agricultural sector, though less crucial as a precondition of development, still has great regional importance. Therefore in this study countries are grouped on the basis of (*a*) their agrarian structure and (*b*) the relative importance of the agricultural sector in the economy (see Table 1).

From the ample literature and studies now available on land tenure structure[10] there is sufficient information to indicate for each country the relative importance of modern and traditional patterns of landholding and the rural social-political structure. The tripartite grouping according to predominant agricultural strategy requirements follows the lines suggested by Barraclough, viz. those in which the traditional agricultural structure dominates the society and rural economy; those in which a significant part of the rural population participates in the commercial or reformed sectors of agriculture, but in which traditional forms are still common; and those in which commercial or reform agriculture is dominant nationally, even though important regional pockets of traditionalism and 'backwardness' continue to exist. There are, in brief, the poor agrarian countries, the mixed or dual traditional-commercial countries, and those with relatively modern agricultural sectors.[11]

A second basis for classification is the relative significance of the agricultural sector in the economy. This grouping is more amenable to direct numerical measurement, based upon both labour force participation and contribution to gross domestic product. The reason for insisting on both labour force and production measures needs to be made clear. Agriculture in Latin America is the residual occupation of the labour force.[12] It is still the major source of livelihood for the population where from 50 to 90 per cent of the rural population are engaged in low productivity or subsistence wage labour. Few can be said to be attracted into agriculture. The poor are held to the land by family and cultural ties, by lack of resources which would enable them to leave, by bonded servitude, by almost any reason except a belief that there are

Table 1. Classification of Latin American Countries according to Agrarian Structure and Importance of Agriculture in the Economy

| | *Importance of agriculture* | | |
Structure of agrarian sector	*Production a* More than 25% *Employment b* More than 55%	*Production a* 20–25% *Employment b* 40–55%	*Production a* Less than 20% *Employment b* Less than 40%
Traditional agrarian structure dominant	Haiti (46·3/77·4) Dominican Rep. (21·7*c*/69·7) Guatemala (30·0/64·7) Nicaragua (30·2/59·7) El Salvador (29·8/60·3) Ecuador (33·9/55·6) Honduras (21·7*c*/66·8)		
Transitional agrarian structure, with traditional dominant	Paraguay (33·5/52·2) Bolivia (26·3/63·3)	Peru (20·0/49·7) Colombia (32·0*c*/53·9) Brazil (21·4/51·6) Panama (20·2/46·2) Costa Rica (23·6/47·5) Mexico (16·9*c*/ 54·2)	
Mixed (dual) agrarian structure, with commercial dominant			Chile (10·1/27·7) Venezuela (7·2/32·1) Argentina (16·7/19·2) Uruguay (14·0/21·7) Cuba (15·2/38·0)*d*

a Ratio of agricultural product to gross domestic production, 1965–7 average. Source: Comité Interamericano de la Alianza para el Progreso (CIAP) (except Cuba).

b Ratio of agricultural to total employed labour force, mostly early 1960s. Sources: Economic Commission for Latin America (except Cuba); F.A.O. *Production Yearbook* (1958) for Haiti, Bolivia, Uruguay, Dominican Republic.

c Countries in which one characteristic is not consistent with its classification under the category 'Importance of Agriculture'.

d Sources for Cuba: *Estudio Económico de América Latina, 1963* (CEPAL, New York, 1965), p. 277 (production); (total excludes non-productive services, so that the ratio of agriculture to total output is greater in comparison to the other countries); Sergio Aranda, *La Revolución Agraria en Cuba* (Mexico, 1968), p. 11 (employment).

economic advantages of farm as compared to city employment. When the rural poor migrate to urban areas their employment opportunities and levels of living – even though wretched – often are improved, but they typically continue to be underemployed subsistence workers. In fact, economic development programmes which fail to recognise the continuity of rural and urban subsistence-type employment can lead to quite erroneous policy proposals. None the less, the proportion of the labour force still engaged in agriculture is an acceptable measure of the seriousness of the development problem.

The second index of agricultural dominance, viz. the sector's contribution to gross domestic production, indicates the possibility of providing resources from within or outside agriculture to fuel its development. Commercial agriculture, in particular, generates surpluses which could be mobilised for development, rather than, as is most common, being siphoned off into consumption or into international capital markets.[13] The domestic non-agricultural industries must supply specific 'packages' of goods needed for agricultural modernisation. In the poorest countries the surpluses from the non-agricultural sector must also be channelled for the development of agriculture.

Before summarising the elements of agricultural strategy which are most relevant to countries in each of the three groups, we emphasise what may be obvious: a development strategy for a specific country cannot be designed and analysed without attention to its political and historical context. Therefore, with respect to any one country, our generalisations must be understood as tentative and qualified, even when they are expressed in more affirmative terms.

(i) *The Poor Agrarian Countries*. The seven poor agrarian countries are all predominantly tropical: they include four of the six nations of the meso-American peninsula (Guatemala, Honduras, El Salvador and Nicaragua), Haiti and the Dominican Republic on Hispañola Island, and Ecuador on the South American continent.

They are all small. National population ranges from two to six million, with a total population of approximately twenty-five million, of whom eighteen million live in rural areas. Demographic growth rates are extremely rapid, going as high as 3·5 per cent per year. Domestic product ranges from $70 to about $300 *per capita* annually. Literacy is less than 50 per cent and as low as 5 per cent in some areas. Rural workers account for 55 to 80 per cent of the labour force, while only 5 to 10 per cent of the workers are employed in 'modern' industries including modern plantations. Technically and administratively the governments are inefficient, and there are few examples of competent public agencies.

Property, income and political power are narrowly held, and are, with minor exceptions, based upon agricultural enterprises. Only 3 to 10 per cent of the people are in middle or upper income brackets. With the exception of Haiti, plantations and traditional *latifundia* are the principal agricultural landholding systems. Foreign-controlled companies dominate the production and marketing of products significant in international trade (bananas, cotton, timber, sugar).

E

Attempts to bring about effective and durable changes in the land tenure systems and power structures either have been nominal or have been repressed. The Guatemala 1952–4 experience with massive and rapid reform was the most dramatic, and instructive, case in point.[14]

The most immediate need for the agrarian reform–development strategy in these countries is to create a new power structure based upon the *campesinos* and their allies, while at least maintaining levels of agricultural output. Priorities and techniques vary but these goals persist. The ways of achieving and consolidating political status for the *campesinos* include organisation of labour unions, co-operatives and credit associations, as well as working through pre-existing political organisations.

The techniques for increasing production, and for assuring wide distribution of the benefits, are relatively restricted, since there are relatively few resources in other sectors to draw upon, and few institutions and technicians. The initial emphasis, then, must be upon introducing technologies that are simple and require limited capital, such as fertilisers, improved seeds and improved irrigation systems, in combination with the construction and maintenance of public works.

(ii) *The Intermediate Group*. There are eight countries – Peru, Colombia, Brazil, Panama, Costa Rica, Mexico, Bolivia and Paraguay – which, though still basically traditional in most of their agricultural sector, have to one degree or another broken the traditional crust. Their strategic needs and possibilities are more complex than for the poorer countries. About half the regional population – more than 125 million persons – live in these intermediate countries. They range in size from one of the smallest (Panama) to the largest. Somewhat fewer than half the people are rural. *Per capita* national product is generally higher (from \$300 to \$500 except in Bolivia and Paraguay), but the distribution of income is extremely skewed in all the countries. Literacy levels run as high as 80 per cent in some countries, but of the total adult population only half can read. The availability of technicians, the quality of administrators and the stability of official government agencies are superior to those of the poorest agrarian countries, although Bolivia and Paraguay continue to suffer deficiencies in these respects.

In countries at this intermediate agricultural development level that have already become partially industrialised, the range of feasible production promotion techniques is wide. The opportunities for more rapid and effective programmes of reform are enhanced, since public administration generally is more effective and trained technicians and professionals are available. Achieving the economic aims of the reform–development strategy in a brief period is a genuine possibility.

Out of the reforms, new forms of landholding and cultivation are bound to emerge. Some combination of individual smallholdings, co-operatively managed estates or state farms will replace the traditional estates and commercial plantations. The means for assisting these reform units with technical advice, credit and other services will vary. Smallholders can be reached through co-operative marketing agencies and other organisations. Where the reforms result in large farm units, operated as co-operatives, group farming or state farms, it is easier and cheaper to reach the beneficiaries, but in some countries the political-administrative difficulties of adopting this course can be formidable.

As farming becomes more modernised, the farm organisation and work discipline become more exacting. The level of rural education will have to be raised rapidly. A growing supply of technicians and professionals will be required. Because underemployed agricultural labour will continue to be a serious problem in these countries, the development strategy requires numerous rural construction projects, in public works, infrastructure, community development activities and small rural industries. This policy, when well executed, leads to a rapid capitalisation of previously underutilised labour, and more rapid growth of production and marketing. In extreme circumstances it is possible to carry the policy too far and produce regional and seasonal manpower shortages, as seems to have occurred recently in Cuba.[15]

Since most of these countries are larger than the poor agrarian countries and have more sophisticated governmental structures and controls, the political and social transformation may be more difficult. Their size and economic organisation create a diversity in political alignments which tends to reduce the political importance of a peasant movement, particularly if it is built on a narrow regional base. None the less, without strong, politically effective organisations, and alliances with other groups, the possibilities of achieving effective reforms are limited. The Peruvian experience may prove to be the exception, in which a middle-class military government undertakes to reorganise the agricultural sector, even though *campesino* organisations are weak and fragmented. Historical precedents argue against such a reform, but at the moment it may be happening.

(iii) *The Relatively Developed Countries.* Five of the richer states of the region – Argentina, Uruguay, Chile, Venezuela and Cuba – have quite different agrarian problems and developmental alternatives from the others. *Per capita* income varies from about $600 to $900 (i.e. twice that of the poorer countries of the region but half that of the developed countries), literacy levels are 80–85 per cent, and agriculture absorbs 25–35 per cent of the labour force while producing generally 10 to 15 per cent of the G.D.P. Property and power are more widely diffused, there are trained government officials of reasonable ability, and there is stability in both public and private institutions. Strategic development needs and the power to mobilise resources are similar to those of the more developed countries. It is important to note, however, that there are localised agrarian problems which are as severe as those of the poorer neighbouring countries. It is arguable, for example, that the agrarian problems of Argentina's Northwest, where 3 million people live, are at least as serious as those of Peru or Bolivia. The mitigating circumstance in the richer countries has been the ability of the poor and landless to migrate to urban centres. There have been, at least historically, opportunities for the rural emigrants to find some employment in 'modern' industries. More recently, unfortunately, these opportunities have become relatively scarce.[16]

Rural poverty, which continues, can be remedied through modification of institutions and policies. The alternatives for attacking the problems of rural backwardness and poverty are numerous, and the economic difficulties of eliminating rural poverty are not formidable. But political obstacles may be as great as in the poorest developing countries.

This brief outline of alternative rural development strategies has concentrated on the technical and economic requirements for more rapid growth, but the complementary needs for political reorganisation are at least as fundamental. Without organisation, the *campesinos* cannot acquire power and maintain their gains. As we noted at the outset, the economic development 'strategy' that is followed by a government is a product of forces exerted through the political system. Economic policy is the output of the pressures which interested groups are able to exert, and *campesinos* without organisation have only marginal influence.

(d) Resource Requirements for Agricultural Development

The implementation of any development strategy for the rural sector – whether conceived in reform terms or otherwise – requires resources for infrastructure, services, facilities and farm inputs. Investment in new buildings, equipment and irrigation works is needed on the farms.

Techniques to increase production must be taught, learned and applied. Public roads, service centres and dams must be constructed and maintained. Production assistance and credit need to be made available. New and improved market facilities and organisations must be created.

Estimates of resource requirements for agricultural development – the capital and complementary inputs which would satisfy the agricultural reform and development needs of the countries of the region – should be based upon a comprehensive national and sectoral plan for each country. At present, such plans have not been completed; even the available basic data for most countries are rather unreliable. Therefore, the rough estimates of financial and resource needs offered here can only suggest the volume of public financing and private investment necessary for agricultural development.

In any case, these estimates will be more useful if we specify how the resources are to be used, and through what channels they will be made available. We must be concerned with (1) whether the resources are for new investment or for maintaining current operations, (2) whether they are for directly productive activities or for infrastructure, and (3) whether the requirements are financed with public, private or publicly assisted capital.

First, a distinction must be made between 'investment' and 'operating costs'. By convention we classify 'operating costs' as those expenditures incurred for items or activities which recur within a year. 'Investment' refers to those expenditures which recur less frequently.

A second distinction is made between costs which directly contribute to the output of the enterprise, viz. 'directly productive activities', and those which are external to it, viz. 'infrastructure'. Both investment and operation of the directly productive processes are, of course, essential for producing farm commodities, and are independent of how the farm units are managed, or the extent of public intervention in financing. Agricultural infrastructure, as Clifford Wharton defines it, is 'the physical capital and the institution or organizations, both public and private, which have a significant effect, directly or indirectly, upon the economic functioning of the individual farm firm, but which are external to the separate individual farm firm'.[17] He divides physical infrastructure into two categories: capital-intensive (that which is heavily dependent on reproducible capital for carrying out its functions), and capital-extensive, or service infrastructure. Each type requires construction and maintenance of facilities, as well as institutional implementation. Wharton considers the legal-institutional arrangements maintained by the government as a third type of infrastructure.

Finally, distinctions are needed regarding sources and control of financing of agricultural development activities. The alternatives can be grouped under three headings: private, public and publicly assisted. Public financing refers to activities funded by the government treasury (usually national) from its general revenues. Virtually all agricultural infrastructure (large dams, roads, educational and extension facilities) has been financed in this fashion. The operation of these infrastructural services has also been financed out of public revenues. There is no direct recuperation of costs of these facilities from beneficiaries, except in the form of increased taxes and fees.

Publicly assisted financing, as the term applies here, refers to government expenditures which are recovered directly from the beneficiaries. This technique is commonly used for establishing agricultural credit societies, as well as for land settlement and even land reform type projects. Subsidies and regulation of the private banking sector in order to increase credits to agriculture are special forms of public assistance.

Private financing comes from financial intermediaries, internal capital (that is, the farmers themselves) or private non-farm industry. The latter is particularly important in financing the marketing facilities and input supply industries, whereas internal capital and banking credits have been historically important for the directly productive investment and operating expenditures.

If sources of funds and control of their use could be separated, either public or private funds could be channelled to meet the needs for capital. But experience shows that the source and control of financing are inseparable. No easy generalisations can be offered about how best to channel private financial resources into agricultural development. Private capital cannot be counted upon to assure implementation of a programme whose purpose is to change the economic and social power structure of the sector. If bankers or landowners were asked to finance land redistribution activities, for example, the programme would almost certainly be frustrated. Where private capital (from banking institutions or from internal surpluses) can be channelled into activities that speed development, this should be encouraged.

In sum, to estimate financial and resource needs for sector development it will be necessary to distinguish four categories of costs: (1) infrastructure investment, (2) infrastructure operating (or service) costs, (3) directly productive investment, and (4) enterprise operating costs.

Estimates are also needed of the flows of public, private and assisted private capital for financing.

We shall attempt to estimate total resources required to carry out agricultural reform and development strategies, and having done so we will be able to judge the required changes in both expenditure levels and tax effort.[18] Although development planning is not sufficiently advanced in the region for such data to be available, estimates can be made which at least establish orders of magnitude. A brief look at the available projections will be helpful in this regard.

Yudelman developed a regional estimate of the requirements for directly productive investment based upon the assumption that the productive investment–output ratio will be in the range of 2·7 to 3·7.[19] To achieve a 5 per cent annual output increase, he calculates, would require progressively increasing investments during the decade, ranging from the 1 billion dollars now spent to $1·6 billion in 1980.

Table 2. Projected Agricultural Production and Investment Needs,
Ten Countries of Continental South America, 1965 and 1985

Year	Agricultural population (millions)	Agricultural product (million U.S.$)	Agricultural investment (million $)	Agricultural consumption (million $)	Agricultural investment as per cent of agricultural production
1965	70·6	14,750	1,475	13,275	10·0
1985					
Hypothesis *a*	98·1	29,928	3,771	26,157	12·6
Hypothesis *b*	98·1	33,586	3,771	29,815	11·2
Hypothesis *c*	104·9	33,586	3,771	29,815	11·2

a Assumes a 1·5 per cent yearly increase in agricultural population and agricultural production increases at 3·6 per cent a year.

b Assumes a 1·5 per cent yearly increase in agricultural population and agricultural production increases at 4·2 per cent a year.

c Assumes a 2 per cent yearly increase in agricultural population and agricultural production increases at 4·2 per cent a year.

Source: F.A.O./ECLA Joint Agricultural Division.

Another estimate of the directly productive investment required for continental South America was prepared by the F.A.O./ECLA Joint Agricultural Division. These projections assume there is a redistribution of land and other resources and a 3·6 to 4·2 per cent annual increase in output over a twenty-year period in the ten countries of South America. An estimated $55–60 billion in directly productive investment would be needed to sustain the output increase, and the related administrative and infrastructure costs would be additional (see Table 2).

A projection built upon country-level data of resource requirements for agricultural development in the countries of continental South America was prepared by the Food and Agriculture Organisation in its Indicative World Plan.[20] The assumptions underlying the projections are developed for each country, but they can be aggregated for the continent as a whole.

The central growth model is based on the assumption that the average rate of total investment rises to 24–25 per cent of gross domestic product (compared with an estimated 20–21 per cent in the early 1960s). The incremental capital–output ratio is assumed to be 4·2 by 1985 (compared with 5 in the 1955–64 period).[21] By 1985 these assumptions imply a G.D.P. growth rate of 5·8 per cent.

Average savings are assumed to be 22 per cent of G.D.P. in 1985 (compared to 18 per cent in the early 1960s). Both imports and exports are projected to rise at a rate of 5·8 per cent a year, the same as G.D.P. There is the projected possibility, given these import and export elasticities, of a trade gap of $2·6 billion by 1985, but this estimate is extremely sensitive to relatively small changes in external market conditions.

Table 3. Identified Agricultural Sector Investment Requirements, Ten
Countries Continental South America 1962–85
(millions of 1962 dollars)

| Type of Investment | Annual investment requirements | | Total |
	1962–75	1976–85	1962–85
Land improvement and development	320·3	408·8	8,572·8
Equipment, machines, etc.	447·1	747·7	13,737·0
Livestock inventory	284·4	456·0	8,542·1
Livestock buildings and plant	51·0	81·1	1,524·2
Fisheries	12·3	18·7	358·6
Forestry and logging	24·9	47·6	825·1
Total	1,140·0	1,759·9	33,559·8

Source: F.A.O., *Indicative World Plan for Agricultural Development to 1975 and 1985* (Provisional Regional Study no. 2, Rome, 1969), ii, 227.

The important projections of annual growth rates affecting development of the agricultural sector up to 1985 were the following: total population increases by 2·7 per cent; overall food demand *per capita* increases by 0·6 per cent; export sales increase by 2·9 per cent; expenditures for agricultural inputs increase by 4·4 per cent; G.D.P. from agriculture increases by 2·5 per cent up to 1975 and by 2·7 per cent thereafter; agricultural population and labour force increase by 1·6 per cent; agricultural productivity increases by 0·9 per cent up to 1975 and 1·1 per cent thereafter; growth rate for non-agricultural G.D.P. is 4·9 per cent up to 1975 and 6·2 per cent thereafter. Average income per person in agriculture in 1962 was $138; following the projected growth rates income would be increased to only $170 by 1985.

The same study offers an agricultural project and investment inventory in which on-farm and directly productive investments were identified. The inventory included more than $33 billion dollars' worth of projects which could be undertaken in the twenty-three years of the Plan (Table 3). However, this is less than 10 per cent of the capital formation necessary to achieve the projected rate of agricultural development.

Finally, we offer 'naïve' projections of agricultural investment requirements on a country by country basis on the following assumptions: a 4·2 per cent compound growth rate in agricultural production, and an incremental capital–output ratio of either 2:1 or 4:1. For the eighteen countries of the region for which data are available, these projections indicate that a total of 2·1 to 4·2 thousand million dollars' average investment per year would be needed, or about 13 to 25 per cent of base year (1965) production (see Table 4).

The required amounts of new on-farm directly productive investment probably would be less after a land reform than under the present system of large holdings. The reason for this is that efficiency increases when farm operators manage their own land and more thoroughly exploit their own and family labour.[22] On the other hand, there will almost certainly be more demand for publicly financed or publicly assisted investments and service infrastructure under reform-oriented strategies, at least in the early stages. This is particularly true when the post-reform landholdings are small and the farmers are not well organised in co-operatives. The demand for capital-extensive infrastructure – extension, credit, education – is a direct function of the strategy pursued.

It would be extremely adventurous to offer even illustrative projections of the financing required for infrastructure. There are huge variations among the countries of the region in public expenditures for this purpose. On a *per capita* rural resident basis, central government expenditures range from about $1·75 in Bolivia to $50·40 in Venezuela, with most countries in the range of $3·00 to $8·00. To the extent that these existing flows of government services and investments can be redirected towards the reform sector, the need for increasing overall spending under a reform strategy is less. But any detailed projection of needs and possibilities is impossible on the regional or sub-regional level without more information than is now available. None the less, substantial increases are certain to be needed in government expenditures – and revenues – for agricultural development.

Table 4. Agricultural Production, Investment Requirements, Government Expenditures and Tax Payments, Eighteen Latin American Countries (millions of U.S. $)

Country and group	Agricultural production 1965	Directly agricultural requirements Low (2:1)	Productive investment annually 1965–85: High (4:1)	Government expenditures on agriculture	Agricultural tax payments to central government (1966–8 average)
Poor agrarian					
Haiti	...	...	...	...	...
Dominican Republic	163	21·1	42·2	15·7	13·6
Guatemala	422	54·5	109·0	5·6	7·7
El Salvador	238	30·7	61·4	5·3	17·6
Honduras	195	25·2	50·4	5·2	2·3
Nicaragua	176	22·7	45·4	10·1	4·3
Ecuador	389	50·3	100·6	14·2	25·6
Mixed traditional					
Paraguay	147	19·0	38·0	6·5	6·0
Bolivia	158	20·4	40·4	3·6	0·5
Peru	861	111·2	222·4	32·4	52·1
Colombia	1,648	212·9	425·8	76·7	40·5
Brazil	4,686	605·4	1,210·8	113·3	378·9
Panama	124	16·0	32·0	5·1	2·1
Costa Rica	140	18·1	36·2	4·2	12·3
Mexico	3,301	426·8	853·6	174·6	73·8
Mixed commercial					
Chile	431	55·6	111·2	71·5	33·6
Venezuela	2,605	336·5	673·0	188·5	0·5
Argentina	218	28·2	56·4	35·0	237·6
Uruguay	554	71·6	143·2	8·7	26·5
Cuba	...	...	...	...	...
Region (18)	16,456	2,126·1	4,252·2	776·2	935·5

Sources:
Agricultural production: CIAP.
Investment requirements: Based upon projection of 4·2 per cent cumulative growth rate in agricultural product, and incremental capital–output ratios of 2:1 (low) and 4:1 (high).
Government expenditures: U.S. Agency for International Development, *Summary Economic and Social Indicators. 18 Latin American Countries 1961–1968* (Washington, D.C., 1969).
Agricultural tax payments: Own estimates, based on sources listed in Tables 5–10.

(e) Resource Mobilisation for Agricultural Development

We can now see that the resources needed to bring about a massive transformation and development of the agricultural sector are substantial, whether they are to be financed by public or private capital. The aim of the following discussion is to suggest how, and to what extent, these resources might be financed domestically, and – more specifically – from within the rural sector itself.

The classification of countries according to the existing agrarian structure enabled us to indicate the most appropriate development strategies for countries with different structural impediments to growth. In the same way, by grouping countries according to the relative importance of non-agricultural activities in the economy the problems of resource mobilisation – at least through the public sector – can be seen.

The overall development financing problem varies with the degree of modernisation and industrialisation in the economy as a whole. In the poorest traditional economies, growth is inhibited by the inadequate skills of most of the rural population and their lack of access to land and the simplest types of improved technologies. To overcome these deficiencies, some net transfer of resources from the rest of the society may be required, but the structural transformation is generally more important to future growth.

In the intermediate economies, where agriculture has been restructured, improvements in production and employment are likely to require substantial short- and medium-term net inflows of capital. Over the longer term it can be assumed that the capital required for both directly productive and infrastructure investment will be provided from the surpluses of the agricultural sector.[23] Where commercially oriented and traditional agricultural subsectors already exist side by side, it is possible to channel the surpluses formerly generated by the commercial subsector into improvements in the traditional subsistence subsector.[24] After an agrarian reform the management of some or all of the commercial subsector may be assumed by the state or by former workers. Thus, the apparent 'savings gap' problem becomes an intrasectoral transfer problem once agriculture enters the post-reform period of development.

In countries where there has been a programme of land distribution along with basic skill improvement and provision of minimum social services, the most serious restraints on development are likely to originate in the market, particularly for export commodities. The relative importance and potential of domestic and export markets is crucial at any stage of development, of course, but there is a tendency for countries in the immediate post-reform period to place first priority on production for internal markets. The reasons for this are numerous. The list includes the nationalistic desire to avoid foreign dependence, the foreign exchange saved by import substitution, and the rise in the demand for food as a result of the redistribution of income and wealth. Once the demand created by expanded domestic consumption has been satisfied, one would expect agriculture to continue to expand into export markets. Agricultural development problems at this stage in a country's development become more complex, at least in economic policy terms, and probably require a different set of analytical tools from those being applied here.[25]

(f) Techniques for Mobilising Resources

Latin American countries use a variety of instruments other than taxes to extract resources from the agricultural sector. Among them are fees, marketing boards, export monopolies, price controls, multiple exchange rates, and subsidies and taxes on imports of agricultural inputs and products. Although attention is concentrated here on tax measures in actual use by these countries, with an attempt to quantify their effects, a brief review of the other measures will put the taxation issue in perspective.[26]

Non-tax measures generally produce effects similar to those of specific taxes. If a marketing board or an export monopoly buys at a fixed price below the world market price and subsequently resells at the higher price, the government captures the difference; the effect is similar to an export tax. Where boards buy at fixed prices around which average world prices fluctuate, their net tax effect probably is zero, periodic subsidies offsetting taxes. Even so, a policy of stable prices probably will stimulate production.

Price controls over agricultural products, aimed at keeping food prices relatively low in order to limit wage demands – a policy often used to redistribute real income in favour of the urban groups – result in a net income transfer from agriculture to other sectors. Chile's controls over retail milk and bread prices have this effect. The public sector as such does not benefit from increased tax revenues but it may be relieved of pressures to undertake other expenditures.

Real income transfers from agriculture are also achieved through exchange controls. When the national currency is maintained above its equilibrium rate or when multiple rates of exchange discriminate against agricultural commodity exports, agricultural exports are taxed. In the first case the transfer will be in favour of importers, and in the latter the beneficiary will depend on whether the objective is to promote non-traditional exports or to permit the public sector to increase its income and foreign exchange holdings. The former will produce only a transfer among groups in the economy but the latter is similar in incidence to an export tax on agricultural products.

Licensing of imports at fixed prices, and tariffs on imports of non-agricultural products also produce a transfer of real income from agriculture. In the first case the transfer is to importers, and in the second to the public sector.

(g) *Tax Systems and Agricultural Development Strategies*

Let us now analyse how agricultural taxation is related to strategies for development and reform of the sector. The purposes of the reform can be encouraged, neutralised or even reversed by the tax programme. There is not as much information as one would like, but enough exists to suggest preliminary conclusions about the present situation and the priorities for future research and policy.

The present tax systems can be examined from two viewpoints. Examining the flows of taxes from agriculture and public expenditures into the agricultural sector enables us to judge the adequacy of these flows in terms of development needs. Secondly, by analysing the tax structures, and particularly the taxes on agricultural producers, resources and production, we will try to determine what contribution the tax system is making to reform and development of the sector.

There are numerous criteria by which tax structures and tax effort might be judged. R. A. Musgrave,[27] for example, lists such indicators of good tax structure as 'ability to give up', efficient resource use, ability to collect and comparison with 'average' performance. Although these all might be relevant on some occasion, we take the view that there should be a deliberate and continuing evaluation of the tax structure in terms of its impact on development, and specifically as it affects agriculture. Unfortunately, the authors of the numerous studies and consultant reports now available seldom attempt to justify their tax proposals in terms of anything but the amount and ease of revenue collection.[28]

As regards tax structure, for each of the groups of countries we consider the principal agricultural taxes (on land, exports and incomes, as well as some of those less commonly applied) from the point of view of their 'desirability' and their 'feasibility'. The gap between what actually occurs and what would best contribute to development indicates where improvement can be made in the tax structures.

The 'desirability' of an individual tax, in the sense used here, refers to how well its collection serves both to provide revenue and to promote the agricultural development strategy. Since the emphasis and effectiveness of agricultural programmes change in the process of development, the possibility and desirability of imposing various taxes change as a country develops. At each stage of development the agricultural tax instruments should be consistent with, and reinforce, changing agricultural development strategies.

Beyond these objectives, there are the normal feasibility criteria applicable to all taxes. The feasibility of a tax must be determined on both technical and administrative grounds. A systematically and equitably applied tax requires that the tax base be knowable, that the tax rates be calculable and that the taxes be collectable. There must, in brief, be a 'tax handle', and a staff able to assess and collect the taxes.

It is obvious that the feasibility of certain taxes – say, on net income or retail sales – is greater in an economy in which modern accounting procedures are followed and reliability in commercial transactions can be taken for granted. Other taxes, such as those on imports, exports or on land, can be enforced in poorer countries, although they may also be easier to apply in developed economies. In addition, the revenue from a tax should exceed its cost of collection. Unfortunately, this point seems to have been neglected in the case of some of the taxes applied to fixed value bases in countries which have passed through periods of prolonged inflation.

Finally, we must note the general difficulties in administering taxes. These problems fall under four headings: multiplicity of taxes, lack of codification, poor enforcement and weak administration.[29] The feasibility of any individual tax and of the overall structure of taxes is affected by the existing legal and administrative situation. The specific difficulties that arise in agricultural tax administration are discussed below.

(h) Agricultural Taxation in Poor Agrarian Countries

When judging the desirability of a tax policy to promote reform in the agricultural sector of the poorest countries, we should remember that the main obstacle to agricultural development lies in the structure rather than in the functioning of the system. For this reason tax policy can play only a marginal role; little can be done through taxation which promotes reform or affects the agrarian structure.

Effective tax systems designed to complement agrarian reform programmes in poor countries would have certain common characteristics. The tax burden would fall primarily on the traditional landowners and the commercial agricultural subsector. This should occur not just to penalise these groups, but because they are the ones who have taxable incomes and resources.

In poor agrarian countries overall tax effort, particularly in agriculture, is likely to be very low, since landowners have sufficient political power to prevent effective taxation and, in any case, the government's capacity to administer a tax system is very limited. The limitation on tax revenues in these countries, and specifically in the agricultural sector, are obvious: low income and inefficient administration. As a result the government is compelled to rely on those taxes which have simple handles, minimising administrative complexity. Export and land taxes meet this condition better than the alternatives, since the tax base and the taxpayer can easily be identified, and the tax application can be 'objective'.

As one would expect, the overall tax effort of the poorest countries is comparatively low, varying from 10 to 15 per cent of gross national product. The contribution of agriculture to total tax income varies from about 4 to 12 per cent, while the importance of the sector in the total economy ranges from 25 per cent (Dominican Republic) to 39 per cent (Honduras). (See Table 6.) If we were to use as a standard the value added by each economic sector, agriculture would seem to be under-taxed. However, the taxable surplus in these economies is generated in the commercial, export-oriented sector. It is the relative size of this sub-sector that determines the amount of revenue that can be extracted from agriculture. An extreme case is Bolivia, where agriculture contributes less than 1 per cent of total taxes. Although agricultural output accounts for more than 26 per cent of total output, only a fraction is exported and virtually none of these exports pass through a control point where taxes can be assessed.

Some system of land taxes is applied in all nine poor agrarian countries except Haiti and the Dominican Republic, but only in Paraguay and El Salvador are significant amounts of revenue collected from such taxes. Land taxes are desirable in poor economies not only for the revenue they can generate.[30] The theoretical advantages of the tax are that it can induce a more intensive use of land, it cannot be shifted either forwards or backwards, and it can be made to be progressive in its application. It has feasibility arguments favouring it as well. For instance the value of the tax base can be established in a number of ways (flat assessment, presumed value, self-reporting). Ideally, the tax would be based upon potential output of the land, although in practice the tax usually is based on the fiscal value of the land and the rate applied is proportional (see Table 5). Special taxes on land according to its use or according to size of holding are on the books in six countries. The administration of these taxes, however, is inherently difficult, requiring

Table 5. Agricultural Tax Structure in Poor Agrarian Countries

				Sources				
		Land:			Net income:		Gross income:	
Countries	Land base	Tax rate	Transfer tax	Tax on unused land	Income tax	Sales tax	Production tax	Export tax
Poor traditional agrarian countries								
Dominican Republic	—	—	—	—	×	—	—	×
Ecuador	Fiscal value	Progressive	×	—	×	×	×	×
El Salvador	Fiscal value	Proportional	—	×	×	×	—	×
Guatemala	Declared value	Proportional	×	×	×	—	—	×
Haiti	—	—	—	—	×	—	×	×
Honduras	Fiscal value	Proportional	—	×	×	×	—	×
Nicaragua	Declared value	Proportional	—	×	×	—	—	×
Mixed traditional–commercial agriculture but insignificant non-agricultural sectors								
Paraguay	Fiscal value	Proportional	—	—	—	×	×	×
Bolivia	Fiscal value	Proportional	—	×	× *a*	×	—	—

a Tax on potential income with progressive rate.
A dash (—) means that no tax is applied; an × means that a tax is applied.

Sources: *Statements of Laws* of each country published by Pan-American Union, Washington, D.C. Also *Sistemas Tributarios de America Latina*, several countries, published by Programa Conjunto de Tributación O.E.A./B.I.D., Pan-American Union, Washington, D.C.

either regular field examination of the plots or more detailed ownership information than is generally available. In Guatemala and Nicaragua, for instance, the tax is based on the value of the land as declared by the owner; no effective check is made by the fiscal authorities.

In all the poor agrarian countries except Bolivia export taxes on agricultural products are the most important single tax on the sector. In general they produce more than half the revenue collected from the sector. Bolivia stands as an exception because agricultural exports account for only 5 per cent of Bolivia's exports. In Nicaragua and Paraguay export taxes contribute less than 50 per cent of agricultural revenue; in the other six countries the proportion is greater than 50 per cent. In Paraguay, however, in addition to the 43 per cent of revenue obtained from the export tax, one must include part of the tax on the production and sale of leather and meat, since this also affects exports and accounts for 37 per cent of the agricultural taxes of Paraguay.

Table 6. Agricultural Tax Burden in Poor Agrarian Countries

Countries	Land taxes	Agricultural taxes:[a] Income taxes	Export taxes	Others	Total	Importance of the agricultural sector[b]	Total tax burden[c]
Poor traditional agrarian countries							
Dominican Republic	—	3·3	5·5	0·2	9·0	16·2	14·4
Ecuador	0·8	—	9·2	2·2	12·2	33·9	15·6
El Salvador	2·5	1·9	16·1	—	20·5	29·8	10·6
Guatemala	0·6		6·0	0·2	6·8	30·0	9·6
Haiti	—	4·3	11·0	5·0	20·3	46·3	7·8
Honduras	0·3	0·5	3·2	0·2	4·2	38·7	10·4
Nicaragua	4·4		2·4	—	6·8	30·2	12·0
Mixed traditional–commercial agriculture but insignificant non-agricultural sectors							
Paraguay	2·4	—	5·3	4·6	12·3	33·5	13·6
Bolivia	0·1	0·6	—	—	0·7	26·3	12·2

[a] As percentages of total taxes.
[b] Agricultural output as percentage of total output, average 1965–7.
[c] Total taxes as percentage of gross national product, average 1965–7.

Sources:
Bolivia: Year 1967, unpublished estimates of the Joint Tax Programme of the Organisation of American States (O.A.S.) and the Inter-American Development Bank (I.D.B.), Washington, D.C.
Dominican Republic: Year 1967, estimates.
Ecuador: Average 1964–6, estimates based on Inter-American Committee of Agricultural Development, *Inventario sobre Información para la Reforma Agraria* (Washington, D.C.), also G. N. Nunn, *La Tributación en Relación con el Desarrollo de Ecuador* (Quito, 1961), also D. Baerresen, *An Analysis of Tax Policy of the Ecuadorian Central Government* (Quito, 1965).
El Salvador: Average 1965–7, estimates based on official figures.
Guatemala: L. Fletcher, E. Graber, W. C. Merrill and E. Thorbecke, *Agricultural Development and Policy in Guatemala* (Iowa State University, April 1969, Ames, Iowa).
Haiti: Year 1967, estimates based on official figures.
Honduras: Year 1967, estimates made by the Joint Tax Programme O.A.S./I.D.B.
Nicaragua: Average 1965–7, estimates based on official figures.
Paraguay: Average 1964–7, data from Ministerio de Hacienda, published by J. I. Arriola, 'La Tributación y el Desarrollo Económico. El sistema Impositivo Paraguayo', in *El Economista Paraguayo* (Asunción, May 1969); also O.E.A./B.I.D., *Reforma Tributaria en Paraguay* Washington, D.C., June 1966).

By comparing the present tax effort and structure prevailing in these countries with what would be desirable and feasible from a theoretical point of view, we can draw some general guidelines for policy-making. First, it must be re-emphasised that direct reform programmes are essential to development and that tax policy can only be a complement to these direct reforms.

In a sense, Bolivia constitutes an exception to this rule, for there a profound agrarian reform already has taken place, and the problem is primarily one of widespread poverty and the consequently low taxable capacity of the agricultural sector. In cases such as this one could use tax policy to help solve institutional problems. However, the large-scale commercial producers of sugar-cane and livestock in the tropical lowlands escape virtually untaxed. Various reforms of Bolivia's agricultural tax system have been seriously considered, including a proposal that there be a 'unified agricultural tax' based on land, and that the revenues be used primarily for programmes directed towards beneficiaries of the reform.[31]

Since land taxes do not produce significant revenue, agricultural tax structures in these countries rely heavily on export taxes. One is tempted to suggest that efforts be increased to make the present land taxes more effective, but such a recommendation is mainly of theoretical interest, since the political constraint is so strong that such a policy could not be implemented. Political power in almost all the poor agrarian countries is still concentrated in the hands of the wealthy. Their opposition to increased taxation takes different forms, but they have generally sought to identify any tax reform as 'left-wing' and foreign-inspired. In El Salvador a 'National Council for the Protection of National Dignity' published full-page newspaper advertisements condemning the 'International Mafia of the United States – the State Department, the World Bank and the International Monetary Fund' for putting pressure on the government to levy and collect taxes. The Council fought the taxes, according to newspaper reports,[32] because they 'would end capital accumulation and open the country to Communism'.

(i) Agricultural Taxation in Urbanising Countries

The countries less dependent on agriculture have greater opportunities to combine agrarian reform and development strategies with a more effective agricultural tax system. This does not mean that tax policy can be a substitute for agrarian reforms, but rather that tax measures can effectively complement the reforms.

The desirable incidence of taxation is similar to that identified for the poorer agrarian economies, that is, taxes should fall on the traditional large landowners and the commercial agricultural subsector. In addition to promoting redistribution and subdivision of large estates, the tax system should give incentives to use land and labour more intensively, rather than to mechanise agriculture. Of course, it is essential to introduce more capital and improved technology into farm operations in order to increase production and productivity, but the tax structure should not give incentives to achieve these ends by displacing rural labour.

Tax effort on the part of the agricultural sector should be greater than in the poorest countries of the region, since both taxable surpluses and administrative capacity are greater. Net revenue flows to and from agriculture probably should be approximately equal, that is, income collected from the sector should be at least enough to finance public expenditure on agriculture. However, the tax system should permit intra-sectoral transfers from the large commercial farms to the small traditional farms. This implies greater taxation of commercial agriculture, and relatively more expenditure in the backward subsectors.

The need for a simple tax base combined with ease of administration should bias the agricultural tax structure in favour of export and land taxes. However, as the administrative capacity is greater in these countries than in the poorer countries, an agricultural income tax can play a more prominent role.

Table 7. Agricultural Tax Structure in Urbanising Countries

	Land:			Sources Tax on unused land	Net income: Income tax	Sales tax	Gross income: Production tax	Export tax
Countries	Land base	Tax rate	Transfer tax					
Brazil	Fiscal value	Progressive	—	—	×	×	—	—
Colombia	Fiscal value according to potential capacity	Proportional	×	×	×	—	—	×
Peru	Gross income minus 10%	Proportional	×	×	×	—	—	×
Panama	Declared value	Proportional	—	×	×	—	—	×
Costa Rica	Fiscal value	Proportional	—	×	×	×	—	×
Mexico	Fiscal value	Proportional	—	—	×	—	×	×

Note: A dash (—) means that no tax is applied; an × means that a tax is applied.

Sources: *Statements of Laws* of each country published by Pan-American Union, Washington, D.C. Also *Sistemas Tributarios de América Latina*, several countries, published by Programa Conjunto de Tributación O.E.A./B.I.D., Pan-American Union, Washington, D.C.

In these six countries the total tax burden varies from 10 per cent in Colombia, among the lowest in the region, to 28 per cent in Brazil, where the tax ratio is not only the highest in the region but also similar to that found in the most developed countries of the world.[33] The contribution of agricultural taxes to total taxes, however, is more or less comparable among the countries. Around 8·5 per cent of total taxes are collected from the agricultural sector. At the extremes are Costa Rica and Panama: the agricultural tax burden in the former is more than 14 per cent, and in the latter only 2 per cent. Comparing agriculture's share in total tax revenue with its share in total product, it is clear that the sector is undertaxed.

The legal agricultural tax systems, following the pattern found in all countries of the region, contain a multiplicity of taxes. All countries have direct taxes on exports, with the exception of Brazil. However, in Brazil a tax applied to commodity sales (*imposto sobre circulacão de mercaderias*) affects exports. Income taxes are on the statute-books of all these countries, as are land taxes, although the land tax base differs from one nation to another. Brazil, Costa Rica and Mexico tax the fiscal value of the land, while Panama uses the value declared by the taxpayer. Colombia, which along with Chile has the best data on soil quality and capacity in the region, takes account of the potential capacity of the land (see Table 7).

The effective agricultural tax structures of these countries are different from those of the traditional agrarian countries in several respects. Export taxes are less important as a source of revenue, while income taxes are relatively more important, although in Mexico and Panama income taxes are not significant. Land taxes also are relatively more important, with the exception of Brazil, where, according to the most recent data, revenues from this tax account for only 2 per cent of agricultural taxes (see Table 8).

Table 8. Agricultural Tax Burden in Urbanising Countries

| | | Agricultural taxes: [a] | | Sources | | Importance of the agricultural | Total tax |
Countries	Land taxes	Income taxes	Export taxes	Others	Total	sector [b]	burden [c]
Brazil	0·2	2·4	—	6·0	8·6	21·4	27·6
Colombia	1·8	6·3	0·1	—	8·2	32·0	10·4
Peru	1·7	4·5	3·3	—	9·5	20·0	14·9
Panama	0·5	1·5	0·3	—	2·3	20·2	13·7
Costa Rica	1·0	4·2	1·8	7·2	14·2	23·6	13·4
Mexico	0·7	0·4	3·3	0·2	4·6	16·9	11·6

[a] As percentage of total taxes.
[b] Agricultural output as percentage of total output, average 1965–7.
[c] Total taxes as percentage of gross national product, average 1965–7.

Sources:
Brazil: Average 1964–6, estimates of the Joint Tax Programme O.A.S./I.D.B., Washington, D.C.
Colombia: Average 1961–3, figures from *Anuario General de Estadística*, 1963 (Colombia, 1965), and O.E.A./B.I.D., *Estudio Fiscal de Colombia* (Washington, D.C., 1967).
Peru: Year 1968, estimates of the Joint Tax Programme O.A.S./I.D.B., Washington, D.C., and also A. J. Aizenstat, 'Structure of Taxation of Agriculture in Peru', in *Conference on Agricultural Taxation and Economic Development* (Cambridge, 1954).
Costa Rica: Average 1965–7, estimates based on official figures.
Mexico: Average 1965–7, estimates based on official figures.
Panama: Estimates based on official figures.

It is obvious that tax policy should be moving towards increased reliance on direct taxes in agriculture, with both land and income taxes used to promote a redistribution of land and a better utilisation of resources. Administrative capacity of the government still constitutes the major 'feasibility' constraint. Simplicity should continue to be emphasised when designing the tax structure.

Unquestionably, the effective use of taxation to achieve non-fiscal objectives must be further investigated. For example, it is commonly argued that higher tax rates on land will lead landowners to sell idle or underutilised land to others who are more interested in intensive farming. Recent investigations of Chilean agriculture (generally more commercial than that of the countries in this group) fail to support this view. Surveys were conducted on 118 parcels which resulted from private subdivision of 10 large farms that were sold because the original owners ran into financial difficulties and needed liquid capital. The new owners failed to increase either production or the amount of capital used. The reason for this, the survey indicated, was that they had committed all their present and potential savings to the purchase of the land and had no resources available to finance needed improvements. In fact, people willing to rent could no longer be found for most of the farms in the sample because of their poor state of maintenance. Only 14 out of the 118 parcels were bought by former farm workers; the other 104 buyers had had no previous experience in agriculture. It seems likely that motives other than the desire to create productive enterprises (e.g. to hedge against inflation) played an important part in the decisions to buy.[34]

(j) Tax Policies in the Relatively Urbanised Countries

In the five richest countries of the region (Venezuela, Argentina, Chile, Uruguay and Cuba), agriculture provides a relatively small part of the total economic product (less than 20 per cent), and employs less than 40 per cent of the labour force. However, there are important differences among the countries in terms of present and future sources of taxation. Chile and Venezuela, where mineral exports are substantial,[35] form one subgroup. In both, agriculture accounts for less than 10 per cent of gross national product and exports of agricultural goods are negligible. Argentina, Uruguay and Cuba form a subgroup where agricultural exports are important. Agricultural production in the first two countries accounts for about 15 per cent of G.N.P., and for most of the income from exports.[36] As might be expected, the objectives and possibilities of tax policy are different for each subgroup.[37]

Although some non-fiscal objectives can be attained through taxation in Chile and Venezuela, the problems of the agricultural sector in these countries are largely related to the internal structure of the sector and, hence, the need for direct structural reforms limits the possibilities of relying heavily on tax instruments. Agriculture in these two non-agricultural-exporting countries is quite similar to that of urbanising

Table 9. Agricultural Tax Structure in Urbanised Countries

| | Land: | | | Sources | | | | |
| | | | Trans- | Tax on | Net income: | | Gross income: | |
Countries	Land base	Tax rate	ference tax	unused land	Income tax	Sales tax	Production tax	Export tax
Argentina	Fiscal value	Proportional or progressive *a*	×	—	×	×	×	×
Chile	Fiscal value according to potential capacity	Proportional	×	—	×	×	—	—
Uruguay	Fiscal value	Proportional or progressive	×	—	× *b*	×	—	×
Venezuela	--	—	—	—	×	—	—	—

a Since land taxes are not the responsibility of the central government but are determined locally, both proportional and progressive rates are found, depending on the state.

b Tax on potential income with proportional rate.

Sources: *Statements of Laws* of each country published by Pan-American Union, Washington, D.C. Also *Sistemas Tributarios de América Latina*, several countries, published by Programa Conjunto de Tributación O.E.A./B.I.D., Pan-American Union, Washington, D.C.

countries where traditional agriculture is dominant. Therefore, the prescription is the same: tax income should come from the traditional large landowners and the commercial farms. Similarly, taxes should heavily penalise idle or underutilised farm land, since very little can be expected from export taxes. The agricultural tax structure should rely mainly on direct taxes, i.e. land and income taxes. The overall tax effort of Chile and Venezuela should be greater than that of the countries of the previous group, however, since their administrative capacity already is well developed.

Argentina and Uruguay, in contrast, could enforce tax policies which combine both fiscal and non-fiscal objectives. In spite of some large intrasectoral and regional differences, taxable income is high throughout the sector, since commercial agriculture is dominant. Apart from the revenue-raising aims which exist under any tax policy, non-fiscal objectives should promote land subdivision and more intensive cultivation. As rural labour becomes less abundant in these two countries, some substitution of capital for labour can be encouraged and labour-saving technologies can be introduced.

The availability of tax 'handles', plus the well-developed administrative capacity in Argentina and Uruguay suggest that the tax effort in the economy as a whole and in the agricultural sector in particular should be large in comparison with the other countries of the region. Given the relative level of development, the agricultural sector could be expected to contribute in net terms to the development of the other sectors of the economy – that is, agricultural taxes should exceed public expenditure directed towards the sector. The agricultural tax structure should be based on both direct and indirect taxes, giving more emphasis to the former since non-fiscal objectives can be more easily achieved through them.

Table 10. Agricultural Tax Burden in Urbanised Countries

				Sources			
		Agricultural taxes:[a]				Importance of	Total
	Land	Income	Export			the agricultural	tax
Countries	taxes	taxes	taxes	Others	Total	sector[b]	burden[c]
Argentina	2·3	1·4	4·7	4·0	12·4	16·7	22·1
Chile	2·3	0·4	—	0·4	3·1	10·1	26·6
Uruguay	2·2	0·1	9·7	1·8	13·8	14·0	27·2
Venezuela	—	0·03	—	—	0·03	7·2	19·6

[a] As percentage of total taxes.
[b] Agricultural output as percentage of total output, average 1965–7.
[c] Total taxes as percentages of gross national product, average 1965–7.

Sources:
Argentina: Year 1961, Stanford Research Institute, *The Economic Impact of Taxes on Argentina's Industrial and Resource Developments*, i (Menlo Park, May 1963).
Chile: Average 1965–6, Ministerio de Agricultura, Oficina de Planificación Agrícola, *Plan de Desarrollo Agropecuario, 1965–80*, iii (Santiago, 1968).
Uruguay: Average 1963–4, Ministerio de Ganadería y Agricultura, Oficina de Programación y Política Agropecuaria, *Estudio Económico y Social de la Agricultura en el Uruguay*, i (Montevideo, 1967).
Venezuela: Average 1965–7, estimates based on figures from G. Pinto Cohen, *Agricultura y Desarrollo. El Caso Venezolano* (Maracaibo, 1966), and C. S. Shoup *et al.*, *The Fiscal System of Venezuela. A Report* (Johns Hopkins Press, Baltimore, 1959).

In the four countries analysed the overall tax effort is above 20 per cent – a level similar to some developed countries. However, as a consequence of the relatively small size of the agricultural sector in Chile and Venezuela, revenues collected there are very low, viz. around 3 per cent of total taxes in Chile and almost nothing in Venezuela. Agricultural taxes in Venezuela are insignificant, while land taxes are the most important source of revenue from agriculture in Chile.[38] In contrast, agricultural taxes account for 13 per cent of total taxes in Argentina and Uruguay, a share approximating the ratio of agricultural output to total output. These two countries seem to be an exception to the general rule of undertaxation of agriculture which prevails in the region. Indirect taxes contribute the largest part of tax revenues from agriculture in Argentina and Uruguay; direct taxes yield more in Argentina than in Uruguay. In both cases export taxes are important, although in Argentina their importance is no greater than that of sales and production taxes (see Table 10).

One can see the direction in which policies should move by comparing the present situation with the general principles mentioned earlier. When Chile and Venezuela, for example, accelerate their agrarian reforms, more rapid improvement also could be made in the tax system. In Venezuela, where virtually no taxes are applied to agriculture, tax policy must start from scratch. Chile already has a legal framework for applying an effective tax policy. The land tax is important because it is high enough to affect the production plans of landowners. The rate in Chile is 2 per cent on assessed value; this value, according to studies conducted in 1966–7, is about half the going market value.

Argentina and Uruguay should strive to change the structure of agricultural taxation, giving more importance to land and income taxes.[39] Both are federally organised countries where local governments can impose their own taxes; this results in a great variety of land taxes in the same country. An obvious improvement would be to co-ordinate, or even administer, land taxes at the national rather than the local level. More importance also should be attached to taxing agricultural incomes. Uruguay's recently established income tax based on potential farm income possesses the theoretical advantage of providing incentives for efficient producers while penalising the inefficient. The results of this departure from the conventional income tax may be significant.

(k) Peru: A Case Study in Financing Agrarian Reform

In June 1969 the Peruvian government proclaimed a new agrarian reform law. The same day, the government expropriated the largest sugar plantations on the coast and began the process of converting the plantations into enterprises managed co-operatively by workers and the state. In October 1969 the government announced its intention to benefit half a million families through the agrarian reform programme by 1975. This implies that about 85,000 to 100,000 families will benefit each year, easily the most ambitious 'gradualist' reform programme ever attempted in Latin America.

Peru is similar to the other countries of the region in which industrialisation and modernisation are just beginning. The great mass of the population (about 75 per cent in Peru) are poor, unskilled, unschooled and politically powerless. Most of the population of about 12·5 million still live in rural poverty, or in the *barriadas* surrounding Lima, Arequipa, Piura and the other provincial cities.[40] According to a 1961 census, out of the active work force of 3·1 million, half were directly employed in agriculture.[41] Another 900,000 – although listed as working in commerce, services and unspecified activities – were underemployed, and up to 700,000 others would be listed as unemployed in a full census of the work force.

Within the rural society, productive land and political power have been concentrated in the hands of perhaps a thousand families. In the highlands, the land and people are exploited in holdings ranging up to 1·5 million hectares. Although virtually all these *haciendas* are 'traditional' in management, some have been sufficiently remunerative to attract and retain foreign investors. For the most part, however, they were operated virtually as rural fiefdoms. The Indian population, which provides the labour force, is kept tied to the *latifundia* system in one fashion or another. Gross family incomes of farm workers in the Sierra average U.S. $150 per year, compared to net incomes of U.S. $20,000 for the families of the large landowners in the same area.[42]

In the coastal areas, land is more intensively worked, especially on commercially oriented plantations, and there are at least some alternative sources of employment outside agriculture for the work force. Agriculture has been a good investment and landowners have been powerful and politically sophisticated. Until the sugar-cane plantations of the north coast were expropriated in 1969, most were controlled by non-Peruvian capital. The high earnings of these enterprises (which depend on the United States sugar quotas and subsidies) were lightly taxed, and most of the income leaked abroad. Moreover, since these rich lands were not dedicated to food crops, Peru was obliged to import 135 million dollars' worth of food supplies annually.

After most of the violent peasant uprisings of the early 1960s had been suppressed, the government enacted agrarian reform legislation. During the years 1964 to 1968, however, no significant changes were brought about in land distribution or rural social structure. Beneficiaries of the reform programme in the period were fewer than the number of new rural families established annually. In 1969, it is estimated, there remained about one million families, constituting some 88 per cent of the rural population, as potential agrarian reform beneficiaries, that is, landless farm labourers, *minifundistas*, *feudatarios* and others of dependent status. In these circumstances, then, the announced reform goal of half a million families in six years cannot be considered overambitious.

The reform, to be carried out 'gradually', legally and with attention to maintaining the level of production, will require planning and personnel. If legal and administrative difficulties can be overcome, the government still faces the problems of mobilising financial resources. Planning has gone far enough to suggest the magnitude of the needs, based in part on the experience with reform projects instituted in 1965 and 1966,[43] and the budget for 1970. Some ideas on possible financing strategies, including taxes, can also be indicated.

In order to estimate programme requirements, it is useful to recognise five classes of activities related to the reform. In Peru these activities are being carried out by separate agencies, and there will be different alternative sources of finance for each. The classes are: (1) reform administration (acquisition and distribution of land, selection of beneficiaries); (2) organisation and training of *campesinos*; (3) agricultural services (extension, marketing and other 'capital-extensive' infrastructure); (4) production and marketing credits (essentially short- and medium-term); and (5) investments in 'capital-intensive' infrastructure, including on-farm, directly productive activities.

Reform administration costs include the transfer payments to ex-landowners, and the technical and administrative costs of the reform proper. The latter items are relatively insignificant, averaging perhaps U.S. $2 million a year. However, the obligation to pay compensation for the land can have important budgetary consequences, and is a highly 'political' item in any reform budget. Rationales have been advanced to justify paying landowners anything from nothing to a premium over full, *status quo ante* market value.[44] Whatever rationale is eventually offered will necessarily reflect the relative political power of the landowners and of those interested in changing the agrarian system. Valuation of land and capital, and the terms of payment are the two instruments for legitimising the transfers. Under the 1969 law the expropriated land is valued at declared fiscal value,[45] and paid for largely in bonds of up to thirty years' duration and 4 to 6 per cent interest. The bonds do not provide for adjustment for inflation. However, two concessions to the landed interest were made. The bonds, although not marketable even for tax payments, are not themselves taxable (nor is the interest); further, they can be used for industrial investments if the bondholder puts up the equivalent in cash for the same purpose. The intention of this last clause is to capture some of these payments, which are by their nature unproductive and regressive, for real investment.

The total financial requirements for the reform, including land acquisition under the above terms, have not been determined. Bonding authority for 15,000 million soles (U.S. $380 million) has been created. About 90 per cent of the 1970 expropriations are being compensated in bonds. Amortisation and interest payments for the 1969–75 period, the government estimates, will be equivalent to U.S. $160 million. On a cash-flow basis, then, the government will need to find more than U.S. $20 million per year during the period crucial to the success of the reform. One of the more obvious and immediate means for increasing general revenues to recover these costs is through higher levies on land retained by the large landowners (up to 200 hectates of irrigated land), and through charges for irrigation water and system maintenance. The new water law permits the government to exercise real control in this area.

Programmes promoting the organisation of the *campesinos* and training of both the technicians and *campesino* leaders, although not costly, are central to the entire reform process. The goal of 500,000 beneficiaries in six years implies the training of about 5,000 technicians, and up to 50,000 *campesino* leaders. The direct financial requirements for the organising and training activities are relatively small, reaching a total of around $10 million for training centres and personnel. The organisational work with *campesinos* is more costly, but only a small portion of these costs is likely to be assumed directly by the government; many outside agencies, including the Catholic church, the United Nations and bilateral programmes, have entered the field. The *campesino* unions and co-operatives will take over, it is hoped, after the initial organisational work is completed.

The costs of extension activities have not been carefully estimated. If 5000 field agents are to be provided with adequate support, an annual budget of 1200 to 1500 million soles (U.S. $30–40 million) would be needed. This would require that current expenditures be at least tripled.

Production credits for the beneficiaries of the reform will constitute the largest single financial obligation in the programme. If the experience of earlier reform projects is followed, the requirements per family would average about $1800, without including associated credits for co-operative marketing agencies. If only half the amount is provided, the new credit needed will average $100 million per year by the second year of the programme.[46] The total bank credit outstanding in mid-1968 was 20,000 million soles, or approximately $1000 million at the then prevailing exchange rate. A large but undetermined part of this amount was for the commercial agricultural sector. Total credits for the reform sector could probably reach $500 million by the end of 1975, but there is room for a great increase in internal financing, especially if production and marketing co-operatives are strongly supported. The expropriated sugar industry, for example, had about 200 million soles on commercial deposit which could be used to create the beginning of an independent co-operative credit system. Other sources of capitalisation – such as supplier credits for *campesinos*' machinery pools and advance credits from buyers for plantings – deserve exploration as supplements to official credit sources.

Finally, the investment programmes associated with the reform could absorb substantial capital. Our 'naïve' estimates of total investment needs, maintaining a 4·2 per cent cumulative increase until 1985 in agricultural product (Table 4 above), suggest a need for U.S. $111–222 million annually. On-farm production investments in the 1960–6 period – when an annual G.D.P. growth rate of about 8 per cent was reported – were almost U.S. $70 million.[47] The large amount of investment in slow-maturing irrigation systems in this period (about half of total agricultural investment) makes direct comparison of investment and production increments misleading. However, the projected level of agricultural investments, which might be either publicly or privately financed, is not too far from our 'naïve' projections.

If total agricultural investments in the 1970–5 period average U.S. $100 million, new capital requirements will, of course, be substantial. However, these needs, like those for operating capital, would have been at least as great without reform, if output were to be increased.

Rough overall estimates of financial needs for carrying out the six-year 500,000 family agrarian reform cum development strategy can be offered. The reform proper would require only U.S. $20–25 million in the six years, including promotion of co-operatives and training of *campesinos*. Land compensation during this period will cost about U.S. $160 million, an amount, as we have seen, which is determined politically and is not properly a charge to the reform programme as such.

The rest of the financial requirements of the programme could amount to U.S. $800 million in the 1970–5 period. However, nearly half this sum will be used for creating revolving funds for short- and medium-term credits. Only a small fraction (perhaps a quarter) is likely to be needed from official sources. If the government begins to exercise greater control over financial institutions – as was under consideration in early 1970 – it is probable that all these credit needs could be met without new funds being provided by the government.

Productive investment on reform units will require U.S. $250 million over the six-year period, a large portion of which would be publicly assisted capital. The public service infrastructure, by which most of these credits would be planned and supervised, will require perhaps U.S. $3·5 million annually by the end of the period.

The total amount of financing which will be provided by government or official sources, according to these unquestionably rough projections, will be in the range of U.S. $120–U.S. $160 million by 1975. However, the production and investment costs, and most of the land compensation payments, will be recovered from the reform beneficiaries directly in fees and charges and indirectly as taxes.

In order to assure greater fiscal revenues from both the agricultural and other sectors, some tax reforms were recently instituted, and more are contemplated. The government undertook a thorough review of its tax structure in 1970, but neither the nature of the new measures nor the probable revenue and incidence are predictable. Peru's administrative capacity would permit a sophisticated tax programme to be developed and enforced.

In June 1968 Congress authorised the Executive to decree changes in income tax and in the taxes on real estate, corporations, petrol and other lesser items. The overall effect of these measures on fiscal revenue has not yet been determined, but an increase of 2000 million soles (about U.S. $50 million) was anticipated when the measures were approved. These reforms should at least reduce the fiscal deficits which limited public expenditure in general and particularly that directed towards land reform programmes.

The chances for internally financing the reform would be strengthened by improvements in the land tax structures. For instance, the level of exemptions under the new real estate tax law – 300,000 soles for urban property and 500,000 soles for rural property, i.e. roughly U.S. $8000 and U.S. $12,000 – is not justified. The land reform beneficiaries should not be exempted automatically from land taxes; and if *they* are required to pay, there is even less reason why other landowners should not be taxed. The present exemptions should be abolished, and a tax should be levied on all holdings in excess of a minimum family scale unit.

NOTES

1. The views expressed in this chapter are those of the authors and do not necessarily reflect the opinions of the United Nations or the Organisation of American States. The authors are indebted to Solon Barraclough, John Strasma and Jacobo Schatan for helpful comments.

2. Agricultural development strategy, as the expression is used by the strict constructionists, implies that there is a national development plan by which public (and some private) investment priorities are set, and policy decisions are made which take account of all important contingencies. Targets are set for production, for investment, for prices, etc. Official decision-makers then manipulate policy instruments for controlling resource allocation. When the term is used in this fashion it has the deceptively authoritative sound for economists that 'perfect competition' did in older, simpler times. For instance, W. Arthur Lewis (*Development Planning*) gives a matter of fact and informed view of the planning process. But his approach leaves the reader ignorant of the impediments to plan implementation which conservative groups with economic interests and political power represent.

3. R. L. Heilbroner, 'Counterrevolutionary America', in *Commentary* (April 1967), 32.

4. *Social Origins of Dictatorship and Democracy: Lord and Peasant in the Making of the Modern World* (Beacon Press, Boston, 1966). His hypothesis is that 'The ways in which the landed upper classes and peasants reacted to the challenge of commercial agriculture were decisive factors in determining the political outcome' (p. xvii).

5. For a discussion of the problems of employing typologies of this sort, see Phillipe Smitter, 'New Strategies for the Comparative Analysis of Latin American Politics', in *Latin American Research Review*, iv, 2 (summer 1969), 83–110.

6. I. L. Horowitz, 'Electoral Politics, Urbanization and Social Development in Latin America', in I. L. Horowitz, J. de Castro and J. Gerassi (eds), *Latin American Radicalism* (Random House, New York, 1969), pp. 140–77; Gino Germani, 'Estrategia para estimular la movilidad social', in J. P. Kohl (ed.), *La Industrialización en América Latina* (Fondo de Cultura Economica, Mexico, 1965), pp. 294–5; Jacques Lambert, *Latin America: Social Structure and Political Institutions* (University of California Press, Berkeley, 1967), pp. 21–48.

7. André Gunder Frank argues that the apparent dualism is better described as a symbiotic dependence on and exploitation by the developed capitalist sector of the underdeveloped traditional sector. See his *Capitalism and Underdevelopment in Latin America*, rev. ed. (New York, 1969).

8. 'Social Mobilization and Political Development', in *American Political Science Review* (Sept 1961), 494–5.

9. 'Employment Problems Affecting Latin American Agricultural Development', in *Monthly Bulletin of Agricultural Economics and Statistics* (F.A.O., July 1969). Also, Samuel P. Huntington, in his *Political Order in Changing*

Societies (New Haven, 1968), offers a similar country classification according to 'vulnerability to agrarian unrest' (p. 382).

10. See particularly S. L. Barraclough and A. L. Domike, 'Agrarian Structure in Seven Latin American Countries', in *Land Economics* (Nov 1966), 391–424, and the specific studies for Argentina, Brazil, Chile, Colombia, Ecuador, Guatemala and Peru published by the Inter-American Committee for Agricultural Development (CIDA), each under the title: *Land Tenure Conditions and Socio-Economic Development of the Agricultural Sector* (1965 and 1966).

For Bolivia, Venezuela, Mexico and the Central American countries preliminary reports have also been issued by CIDA. An extensive bibliography of studies of agrarian structure has been prepared by the director of the latter studies, Thomas F. Carroll, in *Land Tenure and Land Reform in Latin America* (Inter-American Development Bank, Washington, D.C.), 1965.

11. This classification, which is for the purpose of examining agricultural development needs, differs from the grouping according to resource mobilization possibilities used in the second portion of the paper.

12. Folke Dovring, 'Underdevelopment in Traditional Agriculture', in *Economic Development and Cultural Change*, xv, 2 (Jan 1967), 163–73.

13. See, for example, Marvin L. Sternberg, 'The Latifundista. The Impact of his Income and Expenditure Patterns on Investment and Consumption in Latin America' (State University of New York at Albany, 1969, mineograph version). Also see Barraclough and Domike, op. cit.

14. The definitive history of the reforms in this period have yet to be written; virtually all official records were destroyed by the military junta that removed President Jacobo Arbenz Guzmán from office. See, however, *Tenencia de la Tierra y Desarrollo Socio-Económico en Guatemala* (CIDA, Washington, 1966).

15. See Erich Jacoby, 'Cuba: The Real Winner is the Agricultural Worker', in *Ceres*, ii, 4 (July–Aug 1969), 29–33.

16. A reorientation of development priorities seems to be occurring, with substantially greater priority now being given to employment goals as compared to G.N.P. goals. See 'Report of the Director General to the International Labour Conference: The World Employment Programme' (ILO, Geneva, 1969), particularly pp. 55–100.

17. 'The Infrastructure for Agricultural Growth', in H. M. Southworth and B. F. Johnston, *Agricultural Development and Economic Growth* (Cornell, 1967), p. 108.

18. In a broader planning context, of course, the benefits and costs of carrying out the agricultural development strategy presumably must be compared with those in other sectors.

19. 'Agricultural Development in Latin America, Current Status and Prospects' (Inter-American Development Bank, Washington, Oct 1966), pp. 76–8.

20. F.A.O., *Indicative World Plan for Agricultural Development* (Provisional Regional Study no. 2: South America, Rome, 1968). The programme refers to the period 1962–85.

21. Serious estimates of I.C.O.R.s for the economy as a whole, of the ten South American countries, prepared by ECLA (document E/CN. 12/831, 1969) (at market prices), vary from 2·77 for Ecuador to 4·81 for Paraguay. The G.D.P. weighted average I.C.O.R. value (at factor cost) for nine countries (excluding Venezuela) is 3·62. If this lower I.C.O.R. value is in fact the appropriate one, then the G.N.P. growth rate would be 5·5 per cent by 1985 and total investment only 20·7 per cent of G.D.P. (See 'Comentarios Preliminares Sobre el Modelo Global Empleado en el Plan Indicativo Mundial de la FAO', document no. E/CN. 12/L. 39, 23/6/69, mimeo.)

22. Philip M. Raup, 'Land Reform and Agricultural Development', in Southworth and Johnston, op. cit. pp. 267–314.

23. This is not intended to be a normative judgement, but rather a neutral working hypothesis, the validity of which will vary from one country to another.

24. Study of this issue has been limited, but see G. Carrasco, J. Kozub, J. Strasma and A. L. Domike, *Movilización de Recursos Económicos y Financieros para la Reforma Agraria Peruana* (Washington, D.C., 1969).

25. The changes in the main constraints on agricultural development recognised here are similar to those identified by Chenery and Strout in their 'gap analysis'. Their model assumes that the rate of economic growth in the poorest countries is limited by a deficiency in the skills of the people. As these deficiencies are overcome the needs for internal capital accumulation increase. In this second phase the economy is likely to encounter a savings gap which inhibits more rapid growth. As the process of growth continues, the economy is likely to face an exchange gap in which a lack of adequate foreign reserves causes dislocations and difficulties in growth. See H. Chenery and A. Strout, 'Foreign Assistance and Economic Development', in *American Economic Review*, lvi (Sept 1966).

26. For a catalogue of the available techniques for resource mobilisation, see S. Smith, 'Agricultural Taxation in a Developing Country', in *Agricultural Development and Economic Growth*, ed. Johnston and Southworth. This work includes a selected bibliography of specialised literature on marketing boards export controls, import taxes and the like.

27. *Fiscal Systems* (New Haven, 1969), pp. 158–63.

28. See R. M. Bird and O. Oldman, 'Tax Research and Tax Reform in Latin America. A Survey and a Commentary', in *Latin American Research Review*, iii, 3 (summer 1968), 5–23.

29. For a recital of the typical problems of this sort, see Joint Tax Programme O.A.S./I.D.B., *Problems of Tax Administration in Latin America* (Papers and Proceedings of a Conference held in Buenos Aires, Argentina, 1961, Johns Hopkins Press, Baltimore).

30. The bibliography on land taxes for developing countries is large and growing. The basic work is Haskell Wald, *Taxation of Agricultural Land in Underdeveloped Economics* (Harvard University Press, Cambridge, 1959).

31. Cf. 'Impuesto Unificado al Sector Agropecuario' (La Paz, 1967), prepared by an interministerial committee. The proposal was still under consideration in 1970.

32. 'El Salvador Threatens to Keep Troops in Honduras', *New York Times*, 22 July 1969, p. 3. Other illuminating examples are given by A. O. Hirschman, 'Land Taxes and Land Reform in Colombia', in *Readings on Taxation in Developing Countries*, ed. R. Bird and O. Oldman (Johns Hopkins Press, Baltimore, 1964).

33. See H. H. Hinrichs, *A General Theory of Tax Structure Change during Economic Development* (Harvard Law School, Cambridge, 1966), p. 65. A comparison of the tax burden of each Latin American country with fifty-three other countries, considering differences in *per capita* incomes and in the degree of openness of the economy, is made by J. R. Lotz and E. R. Morss, 'Measuring Tax Effort in Developing Countries', in *I.M.F. Staff Papers* (Nov 1967), 478–99.

34. A. Idiaquez, *Private Subdivision of Land in Chile* (Land Tenure Centre, Newsletter no. 22, Nov 1965–Feb 1966, University of Wisconsin, Madison), pp. 15–20. While the sales were probably induced more by fear of land reform than by tax pressure, they suggest that tax-induced sales would be to buyers

who would do little to intensify output or conserve the soil. The problem originates in the high down payments and short repayment terms typical of private land sales in less developed countries.

35. Petroleum and mineral exports account for nearly 90 per cent of total exports in Chile and 95 per cent of total exports in Venezuela.

36. Around 90 per cent of total exports in Argentina and Uruguay are agricultural and livestock products. In Cuba the percentage is even higher.

37. Cuba has not been analysed because very little information on taxes and resource mobilisation is available. The importance of agricultural production and exports would place Cuba in the same class as Argentina and Uruguay.

38. See John Strasma, 'Property Taxation in Chile', in Arthur Becker (ed.), *Land and Building Taxes, their Effect on Economic Development* (University of Wisconsin Press, Madison, 1969), pp. 187–200.

39. See A. L. Domike, 'Tax Policy and Land Tenure in Argentina', in *Land Reform, Land Settlement and Cooperatives* (F.A.O., Rome, 1964), and V. E. Tokman, 'Land Tenure and Socio-Economic Development of the Agricultural Sector in Argentina in the Post-War Period' (D.Phil. thesis, Oxford University, 1969, mimeographed), pp. 263–310.

40. In the early 1960s, according to one reliable estimate, there were 271 *barriadas* in the country, of which half were in Lima and Callao; about 1·3 million out of an urban population of 2·4 million people were living in these conditions: *Tenencia de la Tierra y Desarrollo Económico de Perú* (CIDA, 1966), pp. 255 and 260.

41. See E. Watson Cisneros, 'Población e Ingreso Nacional' (Universidad Agraria y Ministerio de Agricultura, Lima, Dec 1964), cuadro 8.

42. *Tenencia de la Tierra y Desarrollo Económico de Perú*, pp. 266–9.

43. Gamaliel Carrasco, 'Algolán' (CIDA, Washington, 1968) and 'La Convención y Lares' (F.A.O./I.D.B., Washington, 1968). These and other project data are summarised in *Movilización de Recursos Financieros y Económicos para la Reforma Agraria Peruana*, ed. Carrasco *et al*. Estimates here are expressed in U.S. dollars.

44. In all other Latin American reforms, the laws provided for compensation to ex-owners. However, effective payments were never made in the Mexican, Bolivian or Cuban reforms. (See United Nations, *Fourth Report on Progress in Land Reform* (New York, 1966), ch. 2.)

45. *The Economist for Latin America*, 6 Aug 1969, p. 40, in its commentary on the new law, called this provision 'un poco impertinente en un país donde existe tanta evasión fiscal'. However, the evidence on tax compliance which is available tends towards the conclusion that land taxes were reasonably well enforced.

46. The experience in recovering credit from smallholders has been substantially better than for large farmers. The latter group, for example, was able to secure approval from 1964 to 1966 of seventeen different laws and decrees abolishing or postponing repayment obligations for up to twenty years. In some areas under the earlier programmes smallholders had repaid 87·5 per cent of their loans after three years. (See Carrasco *et al.*, op. cit. pp. 156–61.)

47. Instituto de Planificación (Peru) and Inter-American Development Bank estimates.

F

5. Private Savings

TIMOTHY KING

(a) Introduction

PERHAPS no other characteristic of an economy is at the same time so important, so elusive of precise measurement and so difficult to explain as the private savings rate. Its importance in the context of Latin American development is obvious. All Latin American economies except Cuba have mixed economies. Governments play an important role in capital accumulation, but the bulk of investment is carried on and financed by the private sector. The proportion of the national income taken as tax varies a great deal within Latin America and while it is likely that some governments – for example, Mexico – could raise more revenue if it was felt to be essential, this is not a general position. Within the constraints imposed by their institutional structure and ideological outlook, it is safe to say that most governments could not substitute tax revenue for private savings and maintain existing savings levels.

Private savings in this context must be domestic savings. Though private foreign investment can be a useful addition to domestic investment, it is probable that it will be politically unthinkable in future for most Latin American governments to allow foreign investors to acquire or provide a really substantial proportion of a country's capital stock. (It is not possible, however, to define what 'really substantial' means in this context; diffused among a very wide range of manufacturing industries the proportion is probably higher than where a major primary-exporting industry is dominated by foreigners. In recent years governments appear to have been more ready than previously to take steps to reduce this sort of domination, either by nationalisation or by various partnership arrangements.)

Reliance on voluntary private savings to finance development means that the makers of economic policies have always had to consider the effects on private savings of policies designed to do other things. Unfortunately very little empirical information about the effects of different economic policies on savings exists, and our understanding of savings behaviour is still very limited. In these circumstances, economists have tended to draw instead on plausible but unproven theories about the way that people behave. The view usually taken is that savings out of profits will be much greater than those out of wages and salaries, and that people with higher incomes will tend to save a higher proportion of them than those with lower ones. These *a priori* theories are often used to support fairly harsh judgements. For example, it is sometimes argued that measures to reduce the cost of labour to an employer relative to that of capital – thus more accurately reflecting their relative opportunity costs to the economy and leading to larger total output, greater employment and a more equal distribution of income – may be undesirable because this may lead to lower savings and investment, a slower growth of output and ultimately lower incomes for all. Similar arguments can be used to oppose any measure that offers the opportunity of achieving a more equal distribution of income. In some Latin American countries (for example in Mexico) a very light taxation of profits is also often justified on the ground that it encourages saving. There is probably a great deal of truth in these arguments in very many circumstances. Nevertheless, without a great deal of information on the savings propensities of different groups, and on the possibilities of using tax policies to offset unfavourable savings effects of other policies or to increase government revenue without reducing savings, it is impossible to calculate what is the trade-off between greater output and employment now and economic growth, or between a more equal distribution of income and other socially desirable objectives. It is then extremely easy to appear to justify on economic grounds great and growing economic inequality, which any criterion of social justice, no matter how defined, would lead one to condemn.

An understanding of private consumption and savings behaviour is also of the utmost importance in preparing month-to-month economic forecasts and in planning growth over several years. These variables are at the centre of all macroeconomic models, both short-term and long-term. Nevertheless, knowledge is meagre. The purpose of this essay is to survey the few, and on the whole rather unsuccessful, attempts to try to explain savings behaviour both across the whole of Latin America and in individual countries. Most of these attempts have involved the use of statistical techniques and the problems that they have encountered either have been inherent in the techniques adopted or have arisen from limitations of data.

This chapter is not, of course, directed to professional econometricians or statisticians who would need a quite different sort of survey.

On the other hand, it did not seem sensible to try to explain from first principles every statistical term used. I have left some of these unexplained, on the grounds that the information they convey will be useful to those who understand it but is not essential for the general sense of the argument.

This essay is concerned with the problem of explaining savings behaviour – the amount that will be saved in differing circumstances, for example at different income levels and different interest rates. The most important thing about savings from the economic point of view is that they represent an opportunity to consume that has been foregone, so that resources that might otherwise have been used to supply consumption goods are now available for capital formation. In most economies, savers and investors are quite different people, and the act of saving is quite different from the act of investment. Even firms, which save by retaining profits in order subsequently to reinvest them, will normally save and invest at different times, and from the economy's point of view these are quite separate acts; saving in 1970 means that resources are available in 1970 for capital formation; the firm's investment in 1971 has to be matched by somebody else's saving. This essay is not concerned with the mechanism by which saving and investment are made equal to one another, as we know from elementary macroeconomic theory that they have to be. Nor is it concerned with how the savings that are made get allocated to their most productive use, which would involve a discussion of the various institutions which provide credit, or bring investors into direct contact with savers and so on. This is greatly affected by the form in which people wish to hold their assets, and this is another complex question that this chapter does not go into. It is possible that the existence or non-existence of certain types of institution (as opposed to the return that they offer) may affect people's propensity to save – for example, patriotism in wartime may lead people to lend to the government on conditions which would have stopped them saving at all in time of peace. Such institutional questions are not examined here. These are all highly important issues, worthy of anybody's attention, but one short chapter cannot hope to cover everything.[1]

(b) Data Problems

Why has it been so difficult to obtain the information needed, given that it might have such a high return in improving economic and social policies? First, there is a very great shortage of any information at all;

second, there is the lack of accuracy of this information; and third, there is the problem of interpreting even the information that is considered accurate.

Information about savings is usually supplied by national income statistics, although sometimes sample surveys have also provided information. Table 1 summarises the savings picture in recent years in fourteen Latin American countries. No attempt was made to include recently independent countries in the Caribbean, which now feature more often in Latin American statistics; the absence of other countries reflects the absence of comparative data. The most conspicious absentee is Mexico, which has no national income statistics collected on an income basis, and whose capital formation statistics have recently been undergoing major revision. In a number of other countries recent statistical revisions have limited the period over which the contribution of the different components of savings can be averaged; several others have published information for a period and then apparently gave up. It can also be seen that those countries which do publish savings information publish it in varying degrees of detail and in varying formats. Sometimes publicly owned corporations are grouped with the government, sometimes with private corporations. This reduces the opportunity to make international comparisons about the structure of saving. The table demonstrates what little data national income statistics offer for making saving comparisons.

The second problem concerns the accuracy of this information. The act of saving is not an act that can be observed and counted by anybody. It does not have to be marked by any transaction such as a deposit in a bank or the purchase of a bond. Instead measures of saving are derived in national income statistics as a residual. The measure of capital formation in Table 1 is gross capital formation, sometimes called gross domestic capital formation; another measure sometimes used is gross national capital formation, and the distinction between them parallels the one between gross domestic and gross national product. That is to say, gross domestic capital formation includes all the capital formation that takes place in the country whether financed by the savings of the residents of that country or by an inflow of resources from abroad; gross national capital formation is all the capital formation financed with the savings of the residents of the nation, whether taking place there or, via a net outflow of resources, abroad. On balance, almost all the countries in Table 1 experienced a net inflow of resources over the period in question. It is worth noting that in developing countries where a sizeable amount of agricultural investment is made by farmers contributing their own labour, all these measures are apt to underestimate the total amount of investment, and hence of savings, but in the relatively urban and industrialised countries of Latin America this phenomenon is probably less important than in Africa or Asia, though it may contribute to inter-country differences.

Table 1. Sources of Saving for the Financing of Capital Formation in Fourteen Latin American Countries, average percentages of G.N.P. (at market prices)[a]

		Gross capital formation	Depreci-ation	Govern-ment savings[b]	Public Corpor-ations[b]	Private Corpor-ations[b]	Households and private non-profit Institu-tions[b]	Deficit on current account of balance of payments
Argentina	(1955–63)	19·9	4·0	1·4	−0·5	2·5	11·0	1·5
Bolivia	(1958–67)	15·2	7·1	0·4	0·7	0·5	1·4	5·4
Brazil	(1957–63)	16·9	5·0	3·5		7·4		1·8
Chile	(1960–7)	17·7	10·6	4·6	3·2		−4·2	3·2
Colombia	(1957–67)	19·2	9·4	3·9	2·5		2·0	1·4
Costa Rica	(1957–67)	21·7	5·4	1·7	0·4		8·5	5·6
Ecuador	(1960–6)	14·5	5·1	4·8			3·1	1·6
Guatemala	(1957–66)	12·9	4·6	2·1		2·8[c]		3·3
Honduras	(1957–67)	14·8	4·9	0·3	—	2·7	4·5	2·4
Nicaragua	(1965–7)	20·7	3·5	4·1	6·8		0·8	7·1
Panama	(1960–7)	19·5	8·6	4·1	0·3	8·0	−6·3	4·9
Peru	(1957–66)	22·1	5·5	0·9	5·7		7·2	2·7
Uruguay	(1957–63)	14·9	3·9	0·1	1·7		6·4	3·1
Venezuela	(1960–7)	20·9	10·0	7·9	1·6		4·3	−1·6

[a] The figures are averages of the annual percentages for the year stated. For this reason the component percentage figures do not necessarily add up to the figure in column 1.
   [b] Figures placed in between columns are the sum of both adjoining columns.
   [c] Both public and private corporations and household sector.

Sources:
Argentina and Brazil: O.E.C.D. Development Centre, *National Accounts of Less Developed Countries* (1950–66).
Other countries: U.N., *Yearbook of National Account Statistics*, supplemented by UNECLA. *Statistical Bulletin for Latin America*.

Because savings are derived as a residual, estimate of them will never be any better than the estimates of income and expenditures which underlie them. In the case of several countries it has been (independently) suggested that the national accounts significantly underestimate the proportion of output devoted to capital formation.[2] Because we are interested in the determinants of national saving and not of domestic investment, the figures are compared with gross national product and not gross domestic product. Capital formation itself can be measured from information on expenditure on capital equipment and construction, and from parallel information on consumption expenditure and the domestic production and import of consumer goods – the difference between these gives a measure of net stock accumulation. This means that the figures are derived primarily from the expenditure side of the national accounts, and to some extent from the product side, rather than from the income side. We therefore use gross national product at market prices, which is the appropriate expenditure measure. This is the measure very commonly used in analysing savings. Conceptually this is not very satisfactory, however, since one would prefer to relate savings to an income measure – the equivalent would be gross national product at factor cost (i.e. subtracting indirect taxes less subsidies from G.N.P. at market prices) – and to subtract from capital formation expenditure the indirect taxes paid on capital goods. Unfortunately the data do not make this possible. In practice this may not make much difference for international comparisons; in Latin American countries indirect taxes less subsidies are in most cases between 7 per cent and 10 per cent of G.N.P., so that differences in the burden of indirect taxes are not usually important in explaining differences in the proportion of G.N.P. devoted to capital formation. Nevertheless, it is worth remembering that the level of indirect taxes, and also the question of whether they are borne by consumption expenditure alone, or by capital goods expenditure as well, will affect the proportion of G.N.P. saved.

A related point that is often made is that there may be big differences in the relative prices of consumption and capital goods and that this will affect the proportion of income saved. For example, if a country protects domestic capital goods heavily so that prices in its capital goods industry are high relative to those in its consumer goods industry, this will affect the volume of investment goods that a given amount of saving will purchase. Luis Landau has examined the effect of this for Latin America.[3] He finds that the difference in relative prices of capital goods in different countries do indeed have a statistically significant effect on the proportion of income saved.[4] Landau's findings accord well with intuition. Countries where the prices of capital goods are relatively high – a common example is Argentina – tend to save more of their income measured in current prices than they would with a more usual price structure, but to invest less in real terms at international prices.

Not only would it be preferable conceptually to relate savings to an income rather than to an expenditure measure, but one would also prefer to use a net income measure rather than a gross one – that is, to measure income after depreciation has been subtracted from it rather than before. In other words, the most desirable comparison on theoretical ground would be of net saving out of net national product at factor cost (national income). Unfortunately measures of depreciation are inevitably arbitrary and by no means always comparable internationally. The second column of Table 1 shows how depreciation as a proportion of G.N.P. varies greatly between countries for no apparent reason. Why, for example, should depreciation be about 4 per cent of G.N.P. in Argentina and Uruguay but over 10 per cent in Chile? In measures of depreciation, by convention, foreseen obsolescence is allowed for in addition to wear and tear, though it might be argued that strictly speaking only the latter represented the actual capital stock used up during the year and the only reason why this year's capital stock could not go on producing the same output next year. The rate at which firms depreciate equipment is likely to be affected more by tax allowances than by the rate at which the equipment is wearing out or by its second-hand value. Information on actual depreciation is almost certainly not very good, and national income accountants are likely to resort to guesswork. In any case, the actual replacement of capital goods will usually bring with it technical improvements, so the rate of gross saving may have a greater effect on economic growth, and is certainly a less arbitrary figure, than the rate of net saving. Unfortunately the national accounts of most Latin American countries do not let one distinguish between depreciation financed by private savings and that financed by government savings so that we cannot measure gross private savings.

To calculate net private savings from the figures of net national savings one must deduct the savings by the government and by public corporations. In some countries these two are lumped together. In some others, however, savings by public corporations are combined with those by private corporations, which makes it impossible to separate completely public savings from private ones. Government savings are defined in a conventional way as the difference between the government's income and its current expenditure. Here there are some arbitrary distinctions that have little basis in logic – the building of the school is regarded as an investment whereas the training of the schoolmaster, who may serve the community equally as long, is current expenditure – but this arbitrariness does not affect the ability to make international comparisons.

What remains is the (net) private savings. In principle, one ought to be able to cross-check this from the income side of the national accounts – subtracting estimated private sector consumption expenditure from private sector income. Unfortunately this is often impossible.

Because income tax coverage is rather incomplete and evasion is known to be high, it may be difficult to get good information on both business and personal incomes. This then leaves private savings as the residual after a process of deducting a series of almost arbitrary magnitudes from a total which is itself subject to a considerable margin of error, as are most national income components in developing countries. It is not at all clear how far the rather striking differences between countries represent a difference in the guesses of their national income statisticians or differences in definition, and how far real international differences in behaviour. It is hard to believe some of the figures. It is difficult to believe, for example, that Chile could have negative savings in its household sector in every year since 1951, except 1953, as the data suggest. These apparently negative household savings of Chile will be discussed later in this chapter when we consider the determination of household savings.

The third set of problems are those of interpreting the data that do exist. Usually this has involved trying to run regressions (i.e. to test whether relative movements of different variables appear to be random or to be related in some way) on internationally comparative data. Usually these have not been confined to Latin America but have taken their data from a much wider range of countries, both developed and underdeveloped. National income statistics lend themselves to two types of approach. First there are time-series studies – these examine the causes of changes in the quantity of savings within a country. The second approach is a cross-section one – making international comparisons of the determinants of saving in various countries in a particular year. For the purpose of making such international comparisons, time-series and cross-section data are sometimes combined.

Which approach a researcher takes depends on what data are available, and the hypotheses that he wants to test. Most research has concentrated on the relationship between savings and income, since most macroeconomic theories would lead one to expect the two to be closely related. The use of national savings data on a time-series basis would imply, in this case, the hypothesis that there was a stable relationship between savings and income persisting nationally over a long period. A practical difficulty is that in many developing countries the necessary information is available for only a few years, but as time passes this is becoming less of an obstacle. A problem that confronts all time-series, however, particularly where one or more of the variables change in only one direction through time, is that a high correlation may be observed between variables that are not in any way causally related – merely that both have moved steadily through time. Thus, over a number of years one might find, say, movements in a country's birth rates closely correlated with the length of hemlines. If the correlation between the two variables is very close, and one is only interested in forecasting how one will move when the other moves, possible spuriousness of the correlation may not matter, but in that case we might just as well make a straightforward projection through time. In any case, in savings regressions, we are not usually dealing with very closely correlated variables – the determination of savings behaviour is evidently extremely complex and possibly influenced by a large number of variables – and low correlations observed in time-series could easily indicate parallel but causally unrelated movements over time.

A related problem is that of 'multicollinearity', which arises when one is trying to measure how much of the observed movements of one variable (e.g. savings) can be explained by movements in each of several other variables (e.g. income and interest rates). If in this example income and interest rates always move very closely together, then it is not possible to separate their individual effects on savings. This is a particular problem of international cross-section savings studies, though of course it can arise just as easily in national time-series studies as well. An international cross-section study of saving and income implies the hypothesis that there is a stable international relationship between savings and income – that a part of the differences between countries in the amount saved can be explained by differences in income. (As with all regression analysis, the words 'explained by' in this context do not necessarily mean 'caused by'.) It is quite clear that differences in levels of *per capita* income are very often accompanied by parallel differences in other indicators of the degree of development, such as urbanisation levels, the amount of industrialisation, educational indicators, etc. Because many such variables move so closely with income and consequently with each other, it is often impossible to sort out the effect of each on variables, such as savings rates, that may be correlated with income. Again, if certain variables are always associated this may not matter for forecasting purposes. If we know that, say, increases in income, urbanisation and private savings are always highly correlated, it may not matter that we predict that a certain change in savings will follow a rise in income, even if in fact the cause of the savings change has not been income at all but the increases in urbanisation. Supposing, however, we are anxious to predict what will happen to private savings in future if incomes rise but deliberate policies are adopted to restrain urban growth, then it matters very much indeed which has been the cause of the previously observed changes in saving.

In cases where data is scarce – as it obviously is in the Latin American case – combining cross-section and time-series data has the advantage that it provides a large number of observations – that is to say, of instances in which the hypothetical relationship under consideration can be observed. In the savings–income case, the hypothesis underlying this approach is that not only is there a stable relationship between income and savings existing internationally at any one time, but that it has remained stable over time. In other words, the assumption underlying the hypothesis is that the same relationship between savings and income that hold for, say, Mexico at a time when *per capita* income was $300 would hold for Brazil ten years later when its income reached the same level. This is clearly a much stronger assumption than the others.

(c) Studies of Aggregate National Savings

The purpose of the rather arid preceding discussion has been to explain why the harvest from several attempts to use national income statistics in order to understand savings behaviour has so far been rather limited. The most straightforward relationship that can be tested is that between aggregate savings and aggregate incomes. For example, one may be interested to know whether in fact wealthier countries do devote more of their resources to capital formation than poorer ones, since clearly they have a larger potential ability to do so, because they have a larger surplus of resources over the minimum needed to provide their population with a subsistence standard of living (or any other given standard). The relation between income levels and savings can then be held to be an indicator of the degree of development effort that the country is making, and it has sometimes been suggested that aid donors should take the degree of effort into account in their criteria for allocating aid. One can test whether wealthier countries save relatively more by comparing the savings rate of different countries, averaged over several years. The general conclusion to emerge from such studies is that there is a tendency for wealthier countries to save a larger share of their income, but that it is not strong.[5] Such studies have usually included a number of Latin American countries in their sample, but they cover a much wider selection of countries, including a number of developed ones.

The most thorough statistical comparative studies of aggregate national savings in Latin America have been made by Luis Landau.[6] Landau has carried out a large number of regressions, some on a cross-section basis, both for individual years and for averages over a series of years, others examining the pattern of savings for particular countries over time, and still others which have pooled cross-section and time-series data. For the most part these have examined the relationships both between *per capita* savings and *per capita* income, and between the share of income saved and *per capita* income. As is the case with other international comparisons, nothing very startling or very definite emerges. Differences in the absolute value of savings per head are much more closely correlated with differences in *per capita* incomes than is the share of income saved.

Any other finding would have been astonishing. Nations, as individuals, with large incomes would always be expected to save more in absolute terms if not always in proportionate terms. A simple linear regression of the absolute value of savings per head on income per head showed that for a number of separate years and groups of years about 85 per cent of the differences in savings per head between Latin American countries could be explained by *per capita* income differences (i.e. $r^2 = 0.85$). The intercepts of these linear equations (i.e. the implied saving when income was zero) were significantly negative, which implies that marginal propensities to save were in general greater than average propensities. The marginal propensities and the absolute value of the intercept both tended to fall slightly through time – from about 25 per cent in the early 1950s to about 20 per cent in 1967.

Per capita income differences explain only about 30 per cent of differences in the share in income saved when a simple linear regression is adopted. When a non-linear semi-logarithmic formulation is adopted and the share of income saved is correlated with the logarithm of *per capita* income, the explanatory power of the equation is increased slightly. (The implication of using logs in this case is that one is examining the relationship between movements in the share of income saved and proportionate rather than absolute movements in *per capita* income.) For twenty Latin American countries in 1963 Landau found that

$$\frac{S}{Y} = -0.1893 + 0.055018 \log\left(\frac{Y}{P}\right) \qquad r^2 = 0.410$$
$$(3.5)$$

where S is gross national savings, Y is income and P is population. (The figure in parentheses is the t-ratio, implying that the coefficient of log $\left(\dfrac{Y}{P}\right)$ is significantly different from zero.) A similar analysis was carried out pooling time-series information from all available countries. Instead of trying to fit one regression line to all the data, the statistical method used allowed Landau to alter the constant term of the equation for each country while keeping the slope (i.e. the marginal relationship between the share of savings and income per head) the same. The result was to increase the explanatory power of the savings equation, which became

$$\frac{S}{Y} = \text{constant} + 0\cdot05065 \, \log \left(\frac{Y}{P}\right) \qquad r^2 = 0\cdot703$$

A logarithmic or semi-logarithmic equation will give more weight to any absolute value of a change in income the lower the level of income at which it occurs. In this case, the reason why a non-linear formulation tends to fit the data better than a linear one is that, on the whole, differences in the share of income saved appear better explained by the level of income for the poorer countries than for the richer ones. Landau suggests that in 1963 the dividing line between richer and poorer in this case was about \$400 *per capita*. Above that point, additions to income appeared to make little difference to the proportion of income saved.

Other possible explanatory variables – including the growth rate of population, the proportion of the population that is dependent (i.e. not in the labour force), the structure of foreign trade, the level of urbanisation, financial assets, the growth rate of income and the rate of inflation and the burden of taxation – are introduced by Landau into his analysis. Several that were statistically insignificant when tested in the same equation as several other variables, because of the general problem of multicollinearity, became of greater significance when tested alone or in time-series or for smaller groups of countries. In particular, the ratio of exports to G.N.P. $\left(\dfrac{X}{Y}\right)$ appears to be an important determinant of saving. A pooling of time-series for eighteen Latin American countries for the period 1950–66 gave the following result (the constant term was again allowed to vary between countries):

$$\frac{S}{Y} = \text{constant} + 0\cdot02826 \, \log \left(\frac{Y}{P}\right) + 0\cdot00396 \left(\frac{X}{Y}\right) \qquad r^2 = 0\cdot739$$
$$(6\cdot3)$$

The importance of the degree of 'openness' of the economy probably reflects the fact that the proportion of income taken in tax and hence the potential for government saving is usually higher in more open economies.

Apart from the attempts at international comparisons of savings rates, some writers have examined the behaviour over time of savings rates in individual countries. Among these is a study by Leff.[7] Leff claims that over the period 1940–60 the Brazilian savings rate failed to increase in spite of many circumstances which might ordinarily have been expected to raise her marginal savings rates above her average rates. This was a period of rapid growth and buoyant profits, and the shares of both the corporate and the public sector in G.N.P. tended to increase. A domestic capital goods industry existed, and this should have prevented any inability to import goods from being a constraint on the level of investment. In short, there was every reason to expect both the demand for investment and the supply of savings to be high. Leff makes the point that there was also a good reason to expect consumption to rise vigorously too, at a time of rapid social change which may have improved the distribution of income, and at a time when new consumer goods were being introduced. There was no tendency for the marginal capital–output ratio to rise and therefore no tendency for this particular steady rate of growth of output to require higher investment rates. Leff's results have been challenged by Landau on the grounds that there was in fact a tendency for savings, and particularly for private savings, to rise.[8] Part of the trouble is that different sources were used for the periods before and after 1947 and this reduces the value of conclusions drawn about the pre-1947 period. If the period 1947–60 is taken and a three-year moving average is used, then there is a tendency for the share of savings to rise over this period; though for most of the 1950s this tendency was very slight. Private savings did certainly rise as a proportion of G.N.P., whereas the movement of public sector savings was much less steady. This can be seen from Table 2.

Table 2. Saving at Current Prices in Brazil as percentages of G.D.P.

	1947–49	1950–52	1953–55	1956–58	1959–61	1962–64
Private sector	4·5	5·8	8·8	6·0	7·5	11·0
Public sector	4·1	3·7	2·2	2·5	3·5	0·5
Net saving	8·6	9·6	11·0	8·5	10·9	11·4
Capital consumption	5·0	5·0	5·0	5·0	5·0	5·0
Foreign saving	1·1	2·2	0·4	1·0	1·8	0·6
Gross domestic capital formation	14·7	16·8	16·4	14·5	17·7	17·0

Source: L. Landau, 'Brazilian Saving: A Note' (Harvard University Project for Quantitative Research in Economic Development, Report no. 137, 1969).

PRIVATE SAVINGS

(d) Private Savings

To break down aggregate savings into their private and public components is potentially extremely interesting. Many of the most important economic questions about saving are not so much about the amount that a country has saved and invested, but how the individual components of saving have been determined. Most theories about saving result from a concern with the consumption function of individuals and are really dealing with personal saving – rather than with the savings of corporations or governments. Unfortunately it is not always possible to separate business and personal savings completely, as household sector saving usually includes saving by unincorporated enterprises. In most Latin American countries the proportion of the labour force engaged in agriculture still exceeds 50 per cent and a high (unusually high, by the national standards of those countries which are now developed) proportion of the remainder is engaged in urban services. The savings of all of these will be included in the savings of the household sector. In addition, as is apparent from Table 3, not all countries separate household from corporate savings in their statistics.

Table 3. Relative Importance of Alternative Sources of Saving, percentage 'structure' of gross domestic savings[a]

		Depreciation	Government savings	Public corporations	Private corporations	Households and private non-profit institutions	Deficit on current account of balance of payments
Argentina	(1955–63)	20·1	7·0	−2·5	12·6	55·2	7·5
Bolivia	(1958–67)	45·8	12·6	4·5	3·2	9·0	3·5
Brazil	(1957–63)	28·3	41·9			19·5	10·3
Chile	(1960–7)	60·9	26·4		18·4	−24·1	18·4
Colombia	(1957–67)	49·0	20·3		13·0	10·4	7·2
Costa Rica	(1957–67)	25·0	7·9	1·9		39·4	25·9
Ecuador	(1960–6)	35·0	33·0		33·0	21·2	1·6
Guatemala	(1957–66)	35·9	16·4	....	21·9	....	25·8
Honduras	(1957–67)	33·4	2·0	—	18·1	30·4	16·2
Nicaragua	(1965–7)	16·7	20·0		32·8	−3·9	34·3
Panama	(1960–7)	43·9	20·9	1·5	40·8	−32·1	25·0
Peru	(1957–66)	25·0	4·1		25·9	32·7	12·3
Uruguay	(1957–63)	25·8	0·9		11·1	41·9	20·2
Venezuela	(1960–7)	45·0	35·4		7·2	19·3	−7·2

[a] For an explanation of how these figures were derived, see text.

Source: Table 1.

Table 3 needs a word of explanation. It is entirely derived from Table 1, but the relative contribution of the different sources of saving are expressed as a percentage of gross capital formation rather than of G.N.P. (To avoid the labour of computing a percentage figure for each country in each category every year and then averaging them by category (which was the procedure used to obtain Table 1), I took the short-cut of using the average annual percentages of G.N.P. for each category, as derived for Table 1, and expressing these as a percentage of gross capital formation. The annual averages of the components of saving do not, however, necessarily add up to the annual average of total saving. But in Table 3 I have constrained the proportions of the components of saving to add up to 100 per cent, while keeping their same relative importance as in Table 1, in order to facilitate comparisons. The result is that the figures are something of a hybrid, but they serve their purpose of demonstrating relative orders of magnitude.) Unfortunately Table 3 makes it clear that the pattern of savings behaviour is very diverse. A very quick glance at the table to compare countries that might have been expected to have fairly similar structures of capital formation – for example, the Central American countries – makes it plain that the great variation in country behaviour – as well as the paucity and non-uniformity of the data inhibits any attempt at compatative analysis. So far as I know, nobody has tried to use this data to develop any general results, though Abraham has discussed reasons for some inter-country differences.[9]

From an international sample, Houthakker has used linear regression techniques to make comparisons both of total private saving and of personal saving.[10] It proved impossible to analyse corporate savings separately because of non-uniformity of data, but the differences between private and household saving threw some light on this. The general conclusion drawn by Houthakker is that there is no reason to suppose that the intercept of a linear regression of personal savings on personal disposable income is significantly different from zero – in other words there is no evidence that personal savings are not proportionate to personal disposable income. This disputes the views of Kuznets, who suggested that household savings were in fact relatively higher in richer countries than poor ones.[11] Data were not available for many really poor countries, which tend to be those with the least good statistics and with the highest proportion of activity outside the monetised sector, making saving and investment difficult to estimate. It would therefore be dangerous to draw from Houthakker's analysis the conclusion that an inability to save because of poverty was not a general bottleneck to the development of very poor countries. Nevertheless, a few Latin American countries were represented in the Houthakker sample, and they were not by any means all the most wealthy. It is likely that most Latin American countries have reached the stage where a failure to save more cannot primarily be attibuted to low levels of *per capita* income. This is confirmed by the fairly high total savings ratios shown by some of the countries in Table 1.

In spite of defending the thesis that personal savings tend to be proportional to income, Houthakker showed that total private savings did rise at a faster rate than the total income of the private sector. What this implied was that corporate saving became more important in wealthier countries. In Latin America the savings of private corporations are often combined with public ones for statistical purposes. This makes their behaviour very difficult to analyse. The statistical problem is made worse by the frequent absence of good profit data. Corporate saving is apparently often very important. One reason why it might be of greater importance in all developing countries than its share of total output would suggest is the relative weakness of capital markets, and the need for a firm to retain its profits for its own expansion. I know of no studies of what factors determine the proportion of profits that corporations in developing countries distribute to their shareholders, though this is a subject that has received a good deal of attention in developed countries.

(e) Personal Savings

Studies that are not principally concerned with aggregate saving tend to concentrate on personal saving, usually in the context of particular countries. In this regard, there are numerous theories offering plausible hypotheses to be tested. The most straightforward assumption is that people will on the average increase their savings more than proportionally as their income increases. This, of course, is the Keynesian consumption function. The implied savings function is simple to use and to understand and has considerable intuitive appeal. Some cross-section budget studies in developed countries also seem to support it, with a higher proportion of income saved at higher levels of income than at lower ones. It is still a function that is quite commonly used in macro-economic models.

Unfortunately, research on trends in the ratio of national savings to income in developed countries showed that in spite of considerable increases in income per head the proportion of income that was saved had shown little tendency to rise. We have already discussed research that has looked at the relationship between aggregate saving and income. Most of the theories, however, concentrated on the behaviour of individual households and produced reasons why marginal propensities to consume might be lower if calculated from cross-section budget data and also if calculated in the short period rather than over a long period. Among the innovations was Duesenberry's 'relative income' hypothesis, where the proportion of income saved depends on the family's relative position in the national income distribution, rather than on its absolute income.[12] Some people have suggested that countries behave a bit like families in this respect. The so-called 'international demonstration effect' of observing other countries with higher consumption patterns may lead to a reduction of the national propensity to save.

Since then a number of other theoretical hypotheses have been suggested. An important set of theories make saving a function of an individual's expected income over his lifetime. This 'normal income' will include within it returns and capital gains on assets, and a desired relationship between normal income and assets has been introduced by some writers. Some theorists contrast normal income with 'transitory' income, which equals the difference between current income and normal income. One of the best known of these theories is Friedman's 'permanent income' hypothesis.[13] It is assumed that there is a zero marginal propensity to consume out of transitory income except in so far as the existence of such income changes expectations about future normal income. In Friedman's version, savings are proportional to normal income, although, as Farrell has shown,[14] this is not necessary for the main elements of the theory to hold. Friedman's explanation of budget study findings of a positive relationship between the share of savings and the level of income is that at any moment the higher income groups contain a more than proportionate share of those whose current income exceeds their normal income, and the lower income groups a smaller proportion.

Friend has used a version of this theory to examine the Argentinian propensity to consume and save.[15] According to his approach (explained in Friend and Taubman),[16] saving is in part a linear function of the difference between the actual stock of assets held and desired assets, which are themselves a function of normal income, and in part a linear function of transitory income. Two major problems with this formulation and related ones are that one cannot observe normal income and the desired level of assets directly. The first problem has sometimes been tackled by comparing the behaviour of different families in which one would expect on *a priori* grounds that current income would contain differing proportions of normal and transitory incomes (e.g. farmers versus civil servants). In tackling the second problem, information on the behaviour of the same family over a period of years would be extremely helpful in separating differences in asset-holding between families into those that are apparently a question of taste for asset-holdings and those that reflect a difference between desired and actual assets. Presumably in this context assets should include durable consumer goods and income the imputed return on such goods. This is already done in national income statistics for housing and could, in principle, be extended to other durable goods, but the practical difficulties are enormous. In practice assets are usually taken to be financial assets. Even here, however, there are very considerable problems, since generally there are no data on asset-holdings in Latin America and one has to take some proxy, such as savings in the previous year or years. An approximation to normal income has also to be derived from past income. Friend ran a large number of regressions on Argentine time-series data for the period 1950–63; but, frankly, his introducing a distinction between current and normal income, and introducing a proxy to represent asset-holdings did not make any significant differences to the result. The marginal propensity to consume out of transitory income, though slightly lower than that out of normal income, was not significantly different from it. The introduction of lagged savings as a proxy for asset-holdings explained nothing. The result was that however the time-series regressions were formulated, the Argentine marginal propensity to consume differed little from 0·75 (i.e. an additional dollar's worth of personal income would lead to an additional 25 cents of personal saving). Friend also calculated marginal propensities to consume from the data of a 1963 urban household survey. The before tax marginal propensity to consume was 0·65 – which is reasonably consistent with the after tax marginal propensity of 0·75 derived from time-series.

The same problems – the inadequacy of savings data, and difficulties in finding suitable proxies for asset-holding – were among those confronting Lester Taylor, who made a very interesting attempt to test a rather elaborate savings function in Colombia.[17] His underlying model allows saving to include the acquisition of both financial assets and durable goods. It also explicitly recognises the possible effect of interest rates and price changes on saving. The effects of inflation on saving have, of course, been explored by others and form part of a separate chapter to this book. From the time-series analysis of ten countries, Landau found little correlation between aggregate saving and the rate of inflation.[18] For personal saving in Colombia, however, Taylor found that price changes appeared to have a negative effect on saving, although the coefficient (i.e. the relationship) was not very significant. The interpretation placed on this by Taylor was that inflation lowers the rate of interest on savings, so that often the rate paid by the savings institutions accessible to the lower income groups has been substantially negative. Potential saving has been diverted into car purchases (which depreciate very slowly in Colombia) and into expenditure on lotteries.

Apart from Taylor's work, the effect on savings of movements in the real rate of interest does not seem to have been much studied in Latin America, and few have suggested that rises in interest rates might be important in raising personal savings. This no doubt reflects the common view in developed countries that interest rate changes are unimportant. It can be argued that whatever motive one has to save, the difference between getting a 6 per cent rate in money terms (say 3 per cent in real terms) and 4 per cent in money terms (1 per cent in real terms) is likely to be disregarded. This is particularly the case where the rate of inflation moves largely unpredictably within a small but limited range, so that nobody knows what rate of return he is likely to obtain in real terms. Houthakker found interest rate differences unimportant in explaining international differences in savings rates.[19] A difference between an expected negative rate of return and a significantly positive one, however, may be important. An interest rate reform in Korea in 1965 which allowed real interest rates to rise very sharply indeed had a markedly positive effect on personal savings, and provides some evidence that this sort of a change might be of great assistance in curbing inflation. On the other hand, J. G. Williamson found that higher real interest rates in a cross-section of Asian countries (not including Korea) had an insignificant or even a negative effect on saving.[20] One possible explanation of the latter result could be that some Asians are 'target' savers, and save to obtain a particular income objective or with the intention of obtaining some desired level of assets, which are more easily reached with high interest rates than with low ones. An alternative and more plausible explanation is that in many Asian households savings and investment are interdependent, and that interest rates may have more the effect of discouraging investment than of encouraging savings.

The distorting effects of inflation, and of negative real interest rates, may have had some effect on the observed negative saving in Chile (see Table 4), though one can scarcely believe that the main reason is other than statistical. If, for example, either gross domestic capital formation or personal incomes were consistently underestimated, and expenditure estimates were consistently overestimated, then this might give rise to the negative savings observed continuously over a period of years. Mamalakis has analysed the Chilean process of constructing the national accounts and suggests that all of these errors are possible.[21] Depreciation figures, too, have probably been overestimated. Notwithstanding these statistical defects, however, part of the reason for the negative savings was an ability to borrow for consumption purposes at low or negative interest rates without an escalation clause so that the rising money debts of the household sector were offset by inflation.

Table 4. Household Saving as a Percentage of Household Disposable Income in Seven Latin American Countries, 1957–67

	Bolivia	Chile	Colombia	Honduras	Peru	Uruguay	Venezuela
1957	...	...	6·3	4·2	13·0	6·3	...
1958	0·4	...	1·4	4·4	12·3	7·5	...
1959	−1·2	...	2·3	5·5	9·1	2·9	...
1960	1·2	−10·4	2·5	7·5	11·3	5·6	10·7
1961	−2·5	−3·6	3·5	5·7	12·3	10·3	9·7
1962	4·4	−3·3	4·1	7·6	11·3	10·4	3·4
1963	1·1	−7·8	1·8	6·0	7·5	11·2	6·7
1964	6·4	−4·6	0·9	6·7	...	...	7·6
1965	2·3	−2·3	3·4	5·8	...	...	4·3
1966	2·1	−3·3	−0·3	3·5	...	...	5·0
1967	...	−9·0	1·9	2·0	...	...	4·7

Source: U.N., *Yearbook of National Accounts Statistics* (1968).

Table 4 illustrates how difficult it is, in fact, to make any useful deductions from available time-series information. The figures are too unstable to be plausible, and no deductions can be made from the direction of their movement. The only country to have what appears to be a clear trend of a rising share of savings in disposable income is Uruguay – at a time when *per capita* income was falling!

Another important set of savings theories are associated with the name of Modigliani, and in particular with his unpublished paper with Brumberg.[22] An individual plans his savings on the basis of his expected normal lifetime income. He plans to dissave during retirement what he has saved during his working life. This has two consequences. If real *per capita* incomes are rising, succeeding generations have larger lifetime incomes and hence save more, so personal savings should be a function of the rate of growth of output. It is possible to carry out international comparisons to see whether savings rates have been correlated with economic growth rates. Houthakker regressed domestic savings rates on growth rates of national income, and found clear evidence of the Modigliani–Brumberg effect.[23] The problem with this formulation is that it is very difficult to separate cause and effect by ordinary (i.e. using a single equation) regression methods. Often it may be more or less obvious what is cause and what is effect. Here it is not. A high savings rate may imply a high growth rate because of the effects of higher investment on incomes as well as the other way round. This is true, of course, for all regressions involving saving (of the type we have described), but the mutual interaction in the other relationships is much smaller, since the effect that a higher saving rate has on raising the absolute level of income (as a consequence of higher investment) is much smaller proportionately than its effects on the growth rate. A similar problem can arise in trying to use short-run cyclical fluctuations to provide information on savings functions – fluctuations might be due to shifts in investment and hence in a movement along a stable savings formation, or they might result from a structural shift in a savings function. The latter is usually assumed to be less likely, and most writers on this subject have assumed that they were estimating a stable savings function in a changing world. There seems to be a consensus that the immense complications inherent in trying to estimate the parameters of a whole system of simultaneous equations is not worthwhile.

Another interesting conclusion reached by Modigliani and Brumberg is that since a growing population means a smaller ratio of the retired to the labour force (in other words, a larger proportion of savers to retired dissavers) one might expect an increase in savings where the labour force and population were growing. This would make sense were it not that a growing population also means a larger dependent population under the age of 15. Even in countries with low mortality rates and a population that has been growing only slowly for many years (like Britain), the proportion of the population under the age of 14 is of the order of twice that over 65. The proportion is close to twenty times in countries with population growth rates around 3 per cent, as they are for most Latin American countries. Leff has regressed the share of income saved (in logarithmic form) on the log of the dependency ratio, *per capita* income and the rate of growth of income for seventy-one countries. [24] He finds that differences in the dependency ratio are significant in explaining international differences both in the share of income saved and in savings per head. This is also true if the regressions are carried out separately for developed and underdeveloped countries. These findings strengthen the general case for believing that *per capita* income growth in Latin America would be faster with slower rates of population growth.

The net gain to the understanding of private savings in Latin America resulting from the use of these rather sophisticated formulations of the consumption function has not been very great. To some extent this may be because the savings theories used were developed to explain behaviour in wealthier countries where the purchase of financial assets and consumer durables is much more widely practised. But most of the problem stems from the obvious futility of attempting to test precise theories about the behaviour of rational men possessed with clear expectations of the future, using figures derived as a residual on the basis of very shaky national income data, when in fact individuals are operating in a highly uncertain environment under conditions of very rapid economic and social change. A great deal more might be learnt, however, if we could obtain much more detailed case studies that examined household savings behaviour in a sample of families over a number of years.

(f) Personal Savings and the Functional Distribution of Income

All the studies described so far have treated personal income as though the sources of income did not matter. This goes counter to at least one assumption that is very commonly made in growth models, viz. that the propensity to save out of profits is much greater than the propensity to save out of wages. The propensity to save out of rent is also thought to be low.[25] The argument is essentially the intuitive one that the entrepreneur has a great incentive to save and the opportunity to do so. He may also be anxious to expand his firm with his own resources rather than sell shares, in order to maintain personal control. The case for assuming that profit income is more likely to be saved than other income is rather less strong for income paid on dividends to ordinary shareholders. Scattered, individually insignificant shareholders plus modern managers do not collectively add up to the Schumpeterian entrepreneur. Undoubtedly, however, some of the savings recorded as being made by incorporated enterprises and some part of household savings would accord with this intuitive explanation of why profits are more likely to be saved. In addition, profits fluctuate more than other categories of income, and for this reason it is less likely that their recipients will adjust their patterns of consumption in response to a rise in profit income as quickly as they would to a rise in other forms of income.

Unfortunately, for most countries in Latin America it has not proved possible to divide household incomes into their various components, and it is particularly difficult to separate profit income from rent. Diaz Alejandro attempted to compare the marginal propensity to save for wage and non-wage income in Argentina.[26] The marginal propensity to save out of wage income was not significantly different from zero, while that for non-wages was; on the other hand, this interpretation is based on the much larger standard error for savings out of wages, rather than a difference in the marginal propensities to save, which appeared to be larger for wage than for non-wage income. It is difficult to accept that this really was the case, and it seems very likely that the difficulty results from the fact that the method of estimation used by Diaz Alejandro (with gross domestic saving regressed on saving out of both profits and wages) runs into considerable problems of multicollinearity.

Houthakker also found that the marginal propensity to save out of employment income was not significant in explaining international differences, and in fact used a consumption function which made savings simply proportional to other income.[27] For several Asian countries Williamson adopted Houthakker's method of analysis of this problem.[28] He expressed all the variables as deviations from their means over a national time-series, and regressed total personal savings on wage and salary income, on non-labour income and on taxes. This is described as a short-run function. He also tested a long-run function, expressing national averages as a deviation from the averages of the group of Asian nations. He found, as expected, that the short-run marginal propensities to save exceeded the long-run one. He also found surprising evidence that in several of the countries, and for the group as a whole, direct taxes had no significant effect in explaining aggregate personal savings in the short-run functions, but did have a large negative effect in the long-run function for all the Asian nations taken together. The most interesting result of the study was a very large difference between the marginal savings rate out of employment income, which was often not significantly different from zero and did not exceed 10 per cent, and the marginal savings rate out of profits, which ranged from 25 per cent upwards and was generally much higher. As far as I know, nobody has attempted anything similar for Latin America. Williamson's findings support Lewis's view that it is not income inequality *per se* that leads to high savings rates, but that it is the source of income that is important.

The view that the propensity to save out of profits is likely to be greater than the propensity to save out of rent accords with the widely held view of the *latifundista* as an inefficient and idle farmer, making a low return on a very large acreage, which provides more than enough income for him to live comfortably in the capital city, or even abroad. These is certainly some evidence for this view. Sternberg examined the behaviour of landowners in the Central Valley of Chile, where landowners are very highly concentrated.[29] In 1955 1·1 per cent of the landholders were estimated to own 72·7 per cent of total farm land (though a much smaller percentage if one takes arable land – 36·8 per cent – or irrigated land – 21·6 per cent), while 77·1 per cent of landholders owned 1·1 per cent of the farm land (though a higher percentage of the other categories). Sternberg interviewed the owners and managers of twenty large landholdings, owning between them about 900 square miles of land, and with a reported gross income of some £1·25 million in 1960 at the exchange rates then prevailing. Net income was some 35 per cent of this. 27 per cent of this net income was reinvested in the farm, and some 4 per cent went in taxes. The percentage of the disposable income then remaining that was saved was generally low – about 5 per cent – but one exception saved 89 per cent and another only 1 per cent. The implication drawn by Sternberg is that an undesirably high percentage of income is consumed by the large landholder, and spent, as he documents, on relatively luxurious items. Only about 30 per cent of expenditures were for food and utilities and housing (either imputed or actually paid), even though the average family had a house both on the farm and in Santiago. The failure to save, or to invest off the farm, clearly reduced the resources available for other investments below what they might have been, while the consumption patterns of the landholders encouraged the production and import of luxury goods.

The great inequality of landownership and income, and the high levels of consumption by landowners were not in Chile a necessary price paid for agricultural efficiency. Sternberg found that medium-sized farms from 250–1250 acres were more efficient, whether measured in terms of productivity per man or per hectare. It is obviously dangerous to try to draw too general conclusions from the study of only a small sample. A recent study of entrepreneurial characteristics among *latifundistas* in two areas of Colombia makes it very clear that large landholders in Latin America cannot be classed simply as technologically backward, or uninterested in making more than a low but steady return from their land.[30] Some were vigorous entrepreneurs, not all successful, while others were traditionalists with little desire to maximise profits. In contrast with Sternberg's sample, the Colombian traditionalist invested only a small proportion of his capital in agriculture but spent a high proportion of his working time on the farm. The majority of his capital was in stocks or other real estate.

If landowners are often criticised for a failure to save, one should not give the impression that they are the only Latin Americans who have a taste for luxury goods or multiple residences. It would be a mistake to think of all Latin American industrialists as thrusting single-minded entrepreneurs, depriving their families of all but a meagre subsistence, while they plough back all available income into their growing businesses. Casual empiricism suggests that this is not so, and that a great many Latin American industrialists run medium-sized firms, comfortably insulated from foreign competition by protective barriers and enjoying as a consequence a fairly high degree of monopoly. The incentive for such an individual to devote his resources to the expansion of his business or to seek eagerly for new fields of endeavour may be no greater than for a *latifundista*, and his taste for high living is unlikely to be smaller.

(g) *Savings and the Incentive to Invest*

It has sometimes been argued, particularly in those countries in which profits are high and the distribution of income is clearly becoming no more equal and possibly the reverse, that the growth of output might be faster and produced at lower cost if there were a redistribution of income away from profit earners towards less affluent parts of society, which would have different consumption habits. This argument is seldom spelt out in any rigorous way, but is quite often implied by common statements about the need to redistribute income in order to enlarge the market for consumer goods, in order to offset the fact that industrialisation on the basis of import substitution is proving to be harder and harder, as an increasing proportion of imports have been replaced by domestic production. There is no doubt that when the main incentive to invest has been provided by the opportunity to obtain protection against imports a drying up of this opportunity may reduce investment, and hence *ex post* savings, unless and until some other object of investment is found. It is possible that if the market for consumer goods among the poorer income groups were expanded this would provide such a market, and it is also possible that this might enable firms to achieve economies of scale in certain lines of production, become internationally competitive, begin exporting and produce a further widening of the market and an added incentive for investment.

The way the argument is expressed does not usually make it clear whether what is expected to happen is something like the above sequence of events, which would make it open to the objections that each step in it is extremely hypothetical, or whether the argument is based on a confusion about the relation between the distribution of income and the incentive to invest. Using national income statistics produced for a study of the Mexican economy that was sponsored by the World Bank (which covered the decade of the 1940s with a degree of detail that has never been available since), Sturmthal observed that an apparent shift in the distribution of income towards profits during the 1940s did not lead to an increase in capital formation.[31] He then raised the question of whether this might be a sign that a very unequal distribution of income might not weaken the incentive to invest. But if in fact profits were not being used to finance investment, they must have been financing consumption, thereby providing an incentive to invest in the things which capitalists consumed. It might, of course, be argued that these were goods in which there were no economies of scale, or which were normally imported, causing a strain on the balance of payments, but this is not made clear. Unless there is an obvious sign of a deficiency of aggregate demand, it makes little sense to talk about the desirability of 'widening the market' in order to 'increase the incentive to invest'.

Has there been a general deficiency of aggregate demand? This is something that one can scarcely attempt to answer on a continent-wide basis, and even for individual countries the issues are extraordinarily complex. It is clear that in most countries there is a great deal of disguised unemployment in urban service industries, since if one assumed that all those whose occupations are classified as service industries had a productivity even remotely resembling the wage level in the industrial sector, the implied pattern of demand would be quite unlike that ever experienced in countries that are now developed. There is also a good deal of open unemployment and unutilised capacity in many industries, although precise information on this is extremely hard to obtain. Nevertheless most countries hover on the edge of rapid inflation or balance of payments difficulties, or both, and it is difficult to believe that an expansion of aggregate demand would usually do more than increase the rate of inflation or worsen the balance of payments. What policies or practices are to blame for the fact that an economy can simultaneously appear to have reached capacity in a sector or sectors (e.g. those capable of competing in the world market and so earning foreign exchange) while there are large quantities of unemployed resources is a matter of very great importance, but one that I do not want to try to tackle here. The point I want to make is that until one overcomes the particular bottlenecks that lead so readily to inflation and balance of payments crises with the expansion of aggregate demand, it is not sensible to argue that private savings are limited by an ability to invest.

A view that might appear to dispute this is the argument by Albert Hirschman that investment in Latin America is held back by a lack of opportunities rather than of potential savings,[32] but his argument is quite distinct. Hirschman describes savings that are 'frustrated', implying that in the absence of investment opportunities potential savers build houses and buy durable consumer goods, or spend their money on other things. This does not have the same results as a lack of inducement to invest in a Keynesian macroeconomic model, since it is not implying that *ex ante* savings exceed *ex post* investment and that the two are brought into equality by a deficiency of aggregate demand and a fall in income. One might perhaps test Hirschman's idea by comparing, say, different regions and looking at consumption and investment patterns in each to see whether a difference in visible investment opportunities had made a difference to the proportion of income consumed and invested, or had diverted investment from construction to other activities. I know of no attempt to make such a test at all systematically, though Hirschman's ideas were published more than ten years ago and are potentially of great significance.

Hirschman is, in effect, arguing that the supply of private savings is elastic to investment opportunities. This is similiar to the belief that they are responsive to interest rates, a belief which (as already mentioned) has not been tested very widely in Latin America, either as a practical policy to try to increase savings sharply (as in Korea), or as a subject of econometric investigation. Other research might also usefully consider whether savings might be responsive to the growth of suitable financial institutions. It is quite possible that a wider and more efficient banking system might encourage potential small savers to hold savings deposits rather than consumer durables, and it is also possible that more efficient capital markets might encourage large savers to purchase local securities rather than foreign ones. A preference for foreign securities is widely alleged to be a common one, though one cannot tell from the usual balance of payments statistics just how serious it is. These possible effects – they are no more than this – further strengthen the usual case for improving capital markets, which is that by improving the allocation of investible resources greater economic efficiency and hence faster development might be achieved.

(h) Conclusion

This is a subject in which theoretical speculation is still far ahead of empirical findings. There is some small evidence that the share of incomes saved in Latin American countries is greater in richer than in poorer countries and some likelihood that the saving out of profit income is greater than out of wages, and also out of rents. It is certainly possible that attempts to obtain a much more equal distribution of income would reduce total savings. But none of these findings has been established beyond doubt. To some extent this has been because the number of studies has been very small, but mainly because the information that is available in national statistics is quite inadequate to answer the questions to which it would be most interesting to obtain answers.

The gradual inprovement of national income accounts may help to improve our knowledge of the factors determining savings. A more promising approach, however, would be the carrying out of small but carefully designed surveys of saving and expenditure, covering the same groups of people over a period of several years. Properly carried out, this would provide reliable and comparable time-series and cross-section data from which to make deductions and with which to test hypotheses. Such data could not by its nature be collected quickly and it is likely that progress in this field will be slow, but nevertheless this is the most attractive direction in which further research might move. Because of the great importance of this subject, and because our present knowledge is so scanty, we must hope that such research begins soon.

NOTES

1. Those who are interested in the role of financial institutions in the process of development should read two books on Mexico – one by R. W. Goldsmith, *The Financial Development of Mexico* (1966) and the other by Brothers and Solis, *Mexican Financial Development* (1965). Goldsmith has also brought together almost all available shreds of evidence on the sources of saving in Mexico.

2. For example, L. D. Taylor, 'Personal Saving in Colombia' (mimeo., Bogotá, 1968; forthcoming in *Estadística*) argues this for Colombia, and M.

Mamalakis, 'Negative Personal Saving in the Chilean National Accounts: An Artifact or Reality?' (Yale Growth Centre Discussion Paper no. 36) does so for Chile. I should like at this point to record my gratitude to Luis Landau for providing me with some unpublished material, including both these papers.

3. 'Differences in Savings Ratios among Latin American Countries' (Ph.D. thesis, Harvard, 1969), pp. 116–21.

4. By the term 'statistically significant' we mean that the chances of the events which were observed to occur together being quite unrelated to one another in any way are very small – sometimes 1 in 10, more often 1 in 20 or 1 in 100.

5. S. Kuznets, 'Quantitative Aspects of the Economic Growth of Nations, v, Capital Formation Proportions: International Comparisons for Recent Years', in *Economic Development and Cultural Change* (July 1960), pt ii; S. Kuznets, 'Quantitative Aspects of the Economic Growth of Nations, vii, The Share and Structure of Consumption', in *Economic Development and Cultural Change* (Jan 1962), pt ii; H. S. Houthakker, 'On Some Determinants of Saving in Developed and Underdeveloped Countries', in E. A. G. Robinson (ed.), *Problems in Economic Development* (1965).

6. L. Landau, 'Determinants of Savings in Latin America' (Harvard University Project for Quantitative Research in Economic Development, Report no. 13, mimeo., 1966); L. Landau, 'Differences in Savings Ratios among Latin American Countries' (Ph.D. thesis, Harvard University, 1969).

7. N. Leff, 'Marginal Savings Rates in the Development Process: the Brazilian Experience', in *Economic Journal* (Sept 1968).

8. L. Landau, 'Brazilian Saving: A Note' (Harvard University Project for Quantitative Research in Economic Development, Report no. 137, 1969).

9. W. I. Abraham, 'Savings Patterns in Latin America', in *Economic Development and Cultural Change* (July 1964).

10. Houthakker, in *Problems in Economic Development*, ed. Robinson.

11. Kuznets, in *Economic Development and Cultural Change* (July 1960), pt ii.

12. J. S. Duesenberry, *Income, Saving and the Theory of Consumer Behaviour* (1949).

13. M. Friedman, *A Theory of the Consumption Function* (1957).

14. M. J. Farrell, 'The New Theories of the Consumption Function', in *Economic Journal* (Dec 1959).

15. I. Friend, *The Propensity to Consume and Save in Argentina* (Documento de Trabajo, Instituo Torcuato di Tella, Buenos Aires, 1966).

16. I. Friend and P. Taubman, 'The Aggregate Propensity to Save: Some Concepts and their Application to International Data', in *Review of Economics and Statistics* (May 1966).

17. Taylor, op. cit.

18. Landau, 'Differences in Savings Ratios Among Latin American Countries'.

19. H. S. Houthakker, 'An International Comparison of Personal Savings', in *Proceedings of the 32nd Session of the International Statistical Institute* (1961).

20. J. G. Williamson, 'Personal Saving in Developing Nations: An Intertemporal Cross Section from Asia', in *Economic Record* (June 1968).

21. Mamalakis, op. cit.

22. F. Modigliani and R. E. Brumberg, 'Utility Analysis and Aggregate Consumption Functions, An Attempt at Integration' (mimeo., 1953).

23. Houthakker, in *Problems in Economic Development*, ed. Robinson.

24. N. Leff, 'Dependency Rates and Savings Rates', in *American Economic Review* (Dec 1969).

25. W. A. Lewis, 'Economic Development with Unlimited Supplies of Labour', in *Manchester School of Economic and Social Studies* (May 1954).

26. C. F. Diaz Alejandro, *Exchange-Rate Devaluation in a Semi-Industrialized Country* (1965).

27. Houthakker, in *Proceedings of the 32nd Session of the International Statistical Institute* (1961).

28. Williamson, op. cit.

29. M. J. Sternberg, 'Chilean Land Tenure and Land Reform' (Ph.D. thesis, University of California, Berkeley, 1962).

30. J. E. Grunig, 'Economic Decision-Making and Entrepreneurship Among Colombian Latifundistas', in *Inter-American Economic Affairs* (summer 1969).

31. A. Sturmthal, 'Economic Development, Income Distribution and Capital Formation in Mexico', in *Journal of Political Economy* (June 1955).

32. A. Hirschman, *The Strategy of Economic Development* (1958).

6. Inflation and the Financing of Economic Development

ROSEMARY THORP[1]

(a) Introduction

THE central topic of this book being the financial aspects of the development problem in Latin America, it might appear that in the chapter on inflation we should turn immediately to the analysis of the direct effects of inflation on the sources and uses of development funds, public and private, domestic and foreign. However, to narrow the question in this way would be to run the risk of severely distorting the problem. A central argument of one school of thought on inflation in Latin America is not so much that inflation provides a desirable means of financing development – quite the contrary – but rather that an ongoing inflation has to be tolerated in the short run in the pursuit of development. Given this line of argument, it would be misleading to discuss the direct effects of inflation on savings and investment without exploring the broader direct and indirect relationships between inflation and growth. Further, it will be clear that underlying such a discussion are highly controversial issues. A person's view of the relation between inflation and growth, and his interpretation of the empirical evidence differ greatly according to his view not just of the origins of the typical inflationary process, but even of the whole framework of development in Latin America. Thus to approach the question of the relation between inflation and growth we must first begin with some understanding of the major schools of thought on the origin of inflation in Latin America. These will be described in section (c) below; section (b) sets the scene with a brief review of the significance of the topic first in quantitative terms and secondly in policy terms. In section (d) we analyse the relations between inflation and growth and the relevant empirical evidence. Section (e) proceeds to such conclusions as are possible at this time given the unsatisfactory state of the empirical evidence.

(b) The Dimensions of the Question of Inflation

Table 1 presents the basic data on the post war experience of inflation and growth in Latin America. It will be seen at once that we are dealing with a problem of no mean order: every country of South America with the single exception of Venezuela appears in the strong or moderate inflation categories at one time or another, and the annual rate has run as high as 470 per cent for Bolivia (1956) and 102 per cent for Argentina (1959). The rather slow growth rates shown in Table 1 for many of the larger Latin American countries reveal the other side of the problem: whatever the relation between inflation and development, the recent depressing performance in terms of growth of most of the larger Latin American countries makes it imperative its nature should be clarified.

A further dimension adding even more to the importance of the problem comes from the serious policy issues at stake. Much of the interest in the subject of Latin American inflation in the last ten or fifteen years has been engendered by the impact of anti-inflation programmes implemented at various times in every country suffering from severe inflation. As will be explained below, these programmes have been based on a specific analysis of the nature of inflation, namely an analysis centring on the need to curb excess demand and restore an orderly and 'undistorted' market. In almost every case the consequences of such a programme appear to have been severe depression, social unrest and a sharpening of inflationary pressures. This fact has been a major stimulus to the development of alternative analyses, and points up the importance of considering and clarifying the issues. What has given the issue even more significance has been the insistence of the International Monetary Fund on the implementation of such programmes as a precondition of borrowing from the Fund. This leverage has been made the more effective by the fact that U.S. Treasury loans and other such sources of funds have typically been linked with the acceptance of I.M.F. recommendations.

(c) The Background: The Various Approaches to the Analysis of Inflation

(i) *The Structuralist Approach.* The standard analytical categories of demand pull and cost push inflation were discarded in the second half of the 1950s by a number of Latin American economists looking for a framework of analysis more suited to the chronic and clearly deep-rooted problem of inflation in Latin America. The resulting 'structural-

G

Table 1. Latin America: Average Annual Percentage Changes in the Cost of Living and in Real Income *Per Capita*, by Country, 1950–1969

| | Cost of living[a] | | | | Real income per capita |
	1950–55	*1955–60*	*1960–65*	*1966–69*[c]	*1950–67*[d]
Relatively stable countries[b]					
Cuba	0	0[e]	…	…	…
Venezuela	1	2	0	0	2·6
Nicaragua	( )	−2	2	2[f]	2·6
Panama	0	0	1	1	2·9
El Salvador	4[g]	0	0	1	2·4
Guatemala	3	−1	0	3	1·3
Dominican Rep.	0	0	3	3	1·6
Costa Rica	2	2	1	2	1·5
Paraguay	( )	( )	…	2	1·0
Honduras	5	1	4	2	1·4
Mexico	( )	( )	2	3	3·1
Ecuador	2	0	4	4	1·9
Bolivia	( )	( )	5	5	3·0
Moderate inflation countries[b]					
Bolivia	( )	6[h]	( )	( )	−2·4
Mexico	10	6	( )	( )	3·4
Peru	6	8	10	10	3·1
Colombia	4	10	14	10	1·4
Nicaragua	15	( )	( )	( )	5·2
Rapid inflation countries[b]					
Argentina	17	38	27	18	0·7
Uruguay	13	25	35	36[i]	−0·3
Chile	47	24	29	24	1·2
Paraguay	47	11	…	( )	0·1
Brazil	18	28	62	29	2·4
Bolivia	108[h]	( )	( )	( )	−1·1

[a] Unless otherwise stated, the price change is between December of one year and December of the year following.

[b] For each five-year time period, countries are grouped according to the average annual rate of increase of prices in that period. A blank indicates that that country has been placed in a different group for the years in question. 'Relative stability' indicates a price rise of less than 5 per cent, 'moderate inflation' between 5 and 15 per cent a year, and 'rapid inflation' rates in excess of 15 per cent a year.

[c] The figures for 1969 are in most cases the change between October 1968 and October 1969.

[d] The growth rate given is the annual average for the period during which the country appears in that group.

[e] 1956–7 only.

[f] 1966–7 only.

ist' school of thought has become strongly associated with Chile and with ECLA,[2] although perhaps its first representative was a Mexican, Juan F. Noyola (see 44). The emergence of the school has been well chronicled and there is no need to record again the major contributions in the area.[3]

To identify a single structuralist theory is hardly possible. There is rather a structuralist approach, with many variations on the theme. This approach consists in viewing inflation as generated in the course of the attempt to develop in the face of structural rigidities, that is, certain fundamental facets of the economic, institutional and socio-political structure of the country which in one way or another inhibit expansion. These can perhaps best be defined by description. In the long period of export and foreign capital oriented growth preceding the Great Depression of the 1930s, there emerged in the individual economies of Latin America certain fairly well-defined characteristics, chief among which are the following. First, all countries relied heavily on primary products for their export revenue, and typically only on a very small number of products. Second, an internal financial structure was lacking. During the phase of export-led growth, capital had come from abroad, government revenue had come from foreign trade taxes or from foreign bonds, and thus there had been no need to develop internal financial institutions or habits of saving. Third, fairly large urban populations had grown up centred on commerce and service activities associated with the export sector. Fourth, the infrastructure, such as it was, was principally geared to primary exporting activities rather than to the development of domestic industry. Fifth, the land tenure system was the traditional form characterised on the one hand by landlords who were not interested in land for its direct production potential, and on the other by tenants and

---

Notes to Table I—*continued*.

g 1953–5 only.

h The periods taken were 1951–6 and 1957–60, since, given the extremely drastic stabilisation in 1957, in this instance this was the division which appeared to make most sense.

i Excluding 1967. The figure for 1968 is the change between January 1968 and January 1969.

Sources: I.M.F., *International Financial Statistics*; O.E.C.D. Development Centre, *National Accounts of Less Developed Countries, 1950–1966* (Paris, July 1968); ECLA, *Economic Survey of Latin America* (1965–7); O. Sunkel, 'El Trasfondo Estructural de los Problemas del Desarrollo Latinoamericano', in *Trimestre Económico*, xxiv, 133 (Jan–Mar 1967) (reprinted in English in *Weltwirtschaftliches Archiv*, xcvii, 1).

workers who were not in a position to exploit its potential. Sixth, the income distribution was very unequal, as a result of the tenure system and the enclave nature of the export economy. And last, the industrial sector was fairly small and vegetative in nature, stifled by the availability of imports and by the narrow market generated by the unequal income distribution and the preference for foreign goods among those with money.

Given economies which fitted more or less closely to this general pattern, the impact of the Great Depression and the effective end of the era of export-led growth was profound. The structuralist characterises the subsequent widespread inflationary pressures as the inevitable concomitant of being forced by the collapse of export markets and internal growth aspirations to attempt a very different growth strategy, namely internally oriented development based on the substitution of domestic production for previously imported manufactured goods.[4] The essence of the problem was that this change in strategy was attempted within the context of an unplanned, essentially *laissez-faire* economy, while at the same time it required radical non-marginal changes in structure beyond the power of the price mechanism to achieve. Further, the successful operation of the price mechanism was inhibited not just by the non-marginality of the changes required. Of the numerous assumptions underlying the 'optimising' ability of the market system, perhaps the most conspicuously invalid was that of the mobility of resources. For the market mechanism to work well, factors must both wish to respond to profit opportunities and be free in a meaningful sense to do so. If we consider for instance the agricultural sector, the invalidity of both assumptions will be immediately apparent. The peon tied by debt and ignorance to his *patrón* could not respond to a profit opportunity. Far from capital moving freely in response to profit, there was no market in which such movement could take place. Given the imperfections of the system, the result of attempting major structural change had to be shortages and disequilibria on many fronts.

The structuralists do not disregard the great diversity of inflationary experience in Latin America. The ability of their model to accommodate this variety of experience is discussed below (pp. 203–4). It is true, however, that the details of the model are usually left vague. In particular the timing of the emergence of inflation and its implications for their theory are not carefully examined. The impression sometimes given is that inflationary pressures followed immediately on the collapse of export markets early in the 1930s. Yet inflation was not great during the 1930s, except in Chile where it had anyway been in existence since the nineteenth century. The disequilibria became gradually more acute, in part as a consequence of the kinds of policies pursued in these years, such as the neglect of infrastructure and poorly designed import substitution policies.

The central part of the structuralist writing consists in the elaboration of the nature of such bottlenecks and their relation to inflation. The major bottlenecks considered are food output, foreign exchange and finance. Let us consider each briefly in turn.[5] First, it will be obvious from what has been said that the agricultural sector has been a major bottleneck. Rising urban populations plus rising income generated by import-substituting activities lead to a growing demand for food. But supply responds little, for lack of either appropriate motivation or means. The inelasticity of supply constitutes a 'structural' inflationary factor which the market system is powerless to eliminate, since it is rooted in institutions and value systems.

In so far as this structural factor results in greater import demand, this merely reinforces the second major structural bottleneck at work: foreign exchange. As primary exporters, the rate of growth of the export revenues of the Latin American economies is typically limited by the growth of demand for such products in developed countries. For reasons which need not be repeated here[6] this demand has grown sluggishly since the 1930s (with the exception of oil). On the other hand the attempt at industrialisation implies an import demand which rises at least as rapidly as income and characteristically more rapidly (Seers, 55). The resulting balance of payments problem results sooner or later in exchange rate adjustment. However, this does little good: export prices are typically determined by the world market, supply is inelastic in the short run, and devaluation therefore has little effect on foreign exchange revenue. The monopolistic structure of the industrial sector and the lack of domestic substitutes mean that the demand for imports is inelastic; rising import costs are passed on by monopolistic producers and rising consumer prices generate wage demands which in turn are granted. Export sector costs rise with rising import prices, wages and final goods prices. The inflationary repercussions of the devaluation eliminate the stimulus to the supply of the export good before it has time to take effect. At the same time, the disequilibrium itself generates continued pressures to high cost import substitution,[7] which forms a further link in the inflationary process. Again it is the inflexibility of the economy which is responsible for the aggravation of the pressures. Specifically, the infrastructure, particularly in power and transport, is inadequate and cannot be quickly adapted. The rapid growth in urban populations further accentuates inadequacies of infrastructure.

The export sector also acts as a 'bottleneck' in a sense by virtue of the tendency to instability in export proceeds. A temporary fall in export revenue, given a low level of reserves, may necessitate devaluation, with subsequent inflationary repercussions. By the time exports recover it would therefore be unrealistic to return to the old rate; further, there will probably now also be demand pull inflationary pressures operating owing to the renewed expansion of exports.

It is also argued that this instability aggravates inflation through the downward fluctuation in public revenue it induces.[8] Since public expenditure cannot easily be cut (consisting as it does largely of wages and salaries), deficit financing is the inevitable result. The structuralist logic is not usually very clear on this point, however: given the fall in demand, deficit financing is not inflationary in itself, although the additional credit expansion induced by the method of financing the deficit might be, and the more so since the market is imperfect and the rise in demand may not affect the sector where there is slack. However, the more significant inflationary consequences probably derive from the measures necessitated by the downward fluctuation in exports.[9]

The lack of internal sources of finance forms the third structural bottleneck – though one which is rejected by some who claim to belong to the structuralist school (see the discussion on pp. 189–90 below). As explained above, this financial bottleneck is itself a heritage of export-led growth. For a government faced on the one hand by inadequate public revenues, very limited internal private capital for investment, and a highly unequal income distribution leading to a concentration of power which makes radical tax reform unthinkable, and on the other by the imperative of growth, the resulting recourse to inflationary means of finance is itself to be considered a structural phenomenon. A low rate of private investment is also considered partly responsible (together with inappropriate choice of techniques) for the failure of industry to absorb the rapidly growing urban populations, thus creating a further structural pressure on public spending, since employment in services has to be expanded to absorb the excess labour force (Sunkel, 65).

Many structuralists have refined on the above analysis by adopting the distinctions initially developed by Sunkel (65): inflationary pressures are classified as 'basic', 'exogenous' and 'cumulative', and acting and reacting upon them are 'propagation mechanisms'. 'Basic' pressures are the structural features described above (the food supply bottleneck, the foreign exchange bottleneck, factors such as population pressure and inadequate infrastructure, the rigid tax structure and the low rate of capital formation). 'Exogenous' factors are those which come from outside, such as rising import prices in time of war. 'Cumulative' pressures are effects of the inflation itself which in turn worsen basic inflationary pressures. Most notable among these are the effect of price controls (including exchange rate controls), which are frequently imposed during inflation and which discourage investment, usually precisely in the bottleneck sectors (agriculture, exports, infrastructure). They also include the adverse effect of inflation on investment and savings, both on volume and on allocation. 'Propagation' mechanisms are those which pass on the inflationary impulse while not being directly inflationary: they consist in the various ways each group defends itself against inflation – by wage readjustment, by monopolistic passing on of cost increases, or in the case of the public sector by raising nominal public expenditure (Sunkel, 65, p. 111).

Some structuralists would reject the third category of structural bottleneck described above, deficit financing resulting from a taxation bottleneck. Olivera, for instance, defines 'structural inflation' as that which is inevitable given, first, the need for structural transformation, and therefore for relative price adjustments, and, second, the fact of downward price rigidity (Olivera, 45–7). Assuming a passive money supply,[10] he shows that these factors lead to an upward movement of the price level on average, which could be amplified by propagation mechanisms to give an inflation as high as 25 or 30 per cent a year, for an initial structural gap between, say, supply and demand for food of only 3 per cent a year.[11] He considers it totally unhelpful to begin describing as 'structural' inflations which result from *ex ante* investment exceeding *ex ante* savings, 'however deeprooted in the economic structure such propensity might be' (46, p. 331). This he would label 'structural proneness to inflation', as distinct from 'structural inflation'. The former leads to a type of inflation which he claims is adequately described as excess demand inflation.

There would indeed seem to be a case for dividing off this kind of bottleneck from the others: it does appear to be clearly demand inflation, and the rigidity in question is clearly political rather than economic. But those who disallow this category of structural inflation do set themselves rather clearly apart from the structuralist school *per se*, since by making the distinction they de-emphasise several important characteristics of the structuralist school.

First, for the structuralist it is imperative to make clear the nature of this kind of inflationary financing, since he wishes to reject as facile the analysis which would argue that such inflation can be prevented by eliminating the budget deficit. He therefore needs such a category. He may then be guilty of placing cases indiscriminately within that category, but that is another matter. Second, structuralists quite specifically do not find the demand pull/cost push categorisation useful. A food price inflation originating in an agricultural bottleneck could also be described as sectoral demand inflation. Any inflation which is commonly described as structural usually has elements of both demand and cost. Third, Olivera wants to exclude one symptom of 'structural proneness to inflation' (deficit financing) while retaining for his model of true structural inflation factors which are just as much part of structural proneness – that is, the wage–price spiral and other propagation mechanisms and the assumption of a passive money supply. And lastly, and closely related to the previous point, any attempt to divide off inflation for lack of tax reform from the others on the ground of political versus economic rigidity cannot be sustained. The inelastic response of the agricultural sector can just as much be traced back to the political impossibility of land reform. It is one of the chief assets of the structuralist school that it wants to avoid the attempt to define a clear borderline between political and economic factors.

(ii) *The Income Shares Approach*. This approach will be described only briefly, since it often appears to be more a variant of the structuralist approach than a separate category – and indeed, it will be argued here, is only comprehensible when it does merge into the structuralist school. It is based on the propagation mechanisms as described by Sunkel; for some analysts these become the key inflationary mechanisms, to the point where the writers in question have earned at least in name a separate label. Inflation is seen as an instrument for reconciling conflicting social groups: total product is expanding more slowly than is compatible with the aspirations of different sections of the community, and the solution of weak governments is to respond to all aspirations. The conflict is worked out through a continuous rise in prices, which erodes the gain first of one group, then of another. As Hirschman shows, this school of thought preceded the emergence of the structuralist school *per se* in Chile, and is still a common framework of analysis of the Chilean problem.[12] Simonsen puts forward a similar analysis of Brazil (63); Galbraith[13] and others have used similar explanations of Latin American inflationary tendencies in general.

However the argument, if proposed in its 'pure' form, raises several problems. First, it can surely not be intended as an explanation of the initiation of inflation. Secondly, it appears to postulate a continuing and implausible degree of money illusion – that is, if inflation is really to continue to play primarily a conflict-resolving role, people have to be assumed never to learn that achieving gains in money terms brings them nothing in real terms. When wage claims and the other propagation mechanisms are seen, as in the structuralist approach, principally as defence mechanisms, then there is no need to assume that people are so vulnerable to money illusion. Different groups are seen as being forced into a battle to maintain shares in the pie, rather than as pursuing an eternally self-defeating quest for a larger share. Presumably also the structuralist response to the conflict argument consists in pointing out that the only practicable way around it lies in increasing the rate of growth of total product; thus it becomes necessary to analyse structural restraints on growth. Certainly, both schools come together in holding that short-run demand restraint can only lead to intolerable economic depression, social tension and even political instability.

(iii) *The Monetarist Approach.* This approach, since it stems directly from the orthodox excess demand approach of much writing on inflation in developed countries, requires only a relatively brief description. The monetarist observing a Latin American country sees inflation as stemming from and primarily sustained by expansionary monetary and fiscal policy. As analysed for example by Costanzo,[14] the 'principal causes' of inflation in Latin America are government deficit spending, expansionary credit policy and the exchange operations of central banks. Of these, the first is predominant and results chiefly from the financial policy of state-owned enterprises, which are unwilling to charge the public what the service costs; the resulting deficit is the larger because of their considerable inefficiency. Credit expansion has frequently been governed by the notion that to lend for directly productive activities is not inflationary, a notion which ignores time lags and the possibility that supply may not be able to expand at all. Multiple exchange rates have invariably led to a need for subsidisation by the Central Bank (a spread develops between export and import rates which results in the Bank paying more to exporters for their exchange than it receives from importers) and therefore to further expansion of the money supply.

The bottlenecks which dominate the structuralist analysis are in no way denied by the monetarist; however, the causal chain is reversed. It is held that undistorted and freely operating market incentives would in general lead to the elimination of such bottlenecks, that these have arisen simply through the distortions which inevitably accompany inflation.[15] Thus for example a monetarist looking at deficient agricultural production argues that this is to be blamed not on any inherent structural condition such as land tenure, but on government policy which largely through price controls but also by unfavourable input-pricing has consistently undermined profit opportunities in agriculture and thus led to the low level of investment for which the structuralists have more sociological if not Machiavellian explanations. The price controls themselves appear to be in practice an inevitable concomitant of inflation, imposed by a government concerned to mitigate its unpopular effects. Similarly, the policy of price control so frequently applied to transport and power (whether public or private) must bear primary responsibility for the existence of inflationary pressures derived from infrastructure. If privately owned, a low level of investment must result, with consequent bottlenecks and high costs. If the enterprises are in public hands, then either the same is true, or the necessary subsidies generate further pressure on the public purse. The foreign exchange bottleneck is likewise to be explained largely in policy terms. Again a frequent concomitant of inflation has been a misguided control of the exchange rate, which in turn has prevented the normal adjustment of the market. Given unfavourable terms of trade for traditional exports, without policy discrimination against the export sector resources would have shifted and non-traditional exports would have appeared. Instead, high import tariffs, themselves a reaction to the balance of payments problem resulting from inflation, have added to the bias already contained in unfavourable export exchange rates against the emergence of new lines. Further, in certain cases where the world market has been good (copper, for example) policy has inhibited investment and reduced the country's ability to make the most of the market opportunity. The generally low level of capital formation which features in the structural analysis is associated for the monetarist at least in part with the inflationary environment.[16]

The failure of the tax structure to provide the revenue for developmental activities forced on the government is commented on, but the conclusion drawn is not that therefore inflation was inevitable, but first that the tax structure should have been reformed (for the structuralist, true but irrelevant), and second that without inflation and if necessary with correspondingly less government activity, the private sector would have come forward to play a larger role and so relieve this 'structuralist' pressure on the government's purse.

An analysis which attributes so-called structural problems to inflation itself and attributes that inflation to excess demand arising primarily from government spending leads to a rather simple policy prescription, such as forms the base for the I.M.F.-sponsored stabilisation programmes mentioned above. First and foremost, the budget deficit must be ended, by raising public utility rates, ending subsidy payments, cutting public expenditure, reorganising and increasing efficiency in the nationalised enterprises, and by increasing taxes and reducing tax evasion. Secondly, credit to the private sector must be restricted. The combination of these two policies should restrain the increase in the money supply to a non-inflationary figure, namely to that justified by the expected increase in real output, with an adjustment where relevant for any expected change in velocity of circulation (usually none). Thirdly, all distortions in the market mechanism must be abolished; externally, the exchange rate should be left to find its own level. The response to the new situation on the part of supply will be such that the immediately depressing effect of the cuts in credit and government spending will be short-lived. Felix summarises it well: 'the assumption is that output in all the major productive sectors is quite elastic to changing relative prices so that resources will shift quickly from activities depressed to activities stimulated by the curtailment of inflation – quickly enough so that unemployment will be mercifully brief and social tensions will not be raised to boiling point' (23, p. 584). Since expansion of credit directly leads to expansion of imports, external equilibrium will be restored by credit restriction and by the stimulus given to exports and to import substitution by the renewed health of the investment climate.

The points at issue between monetarist and structuralist may now be identified. First it must be stressed that the structuralist should not deny that monetary variables in some sense determine inflation. Structuralists may write at times as if inflation is a totally non-monetary phenomenon – but implicit in their analysis must be the assumption that the monetary system is having to respond to pressure, in order that a given rate of growth and level of employment be achieved. There is always a sense in which the rate of inflation can be 'explained' in terms of the quantity of money, the desire for liquidity, the level of output and so forth. But for the structuralist this is not the point. The real issues are the direction of causation, with the whole debate about the price system underlying this, the values of the parameters relating monetary variables to the real variables of output and employment, and the relevance of introducing political and social variables into the analysis.

It can now be seen what was meant by saying that one's whole analysis of inflation, and even of development strategies in general, is crucial to the more specific problem at hand. Firstly, one's interpretation of the inflationary process is vital in colouring one's interpretation of cause and effect and thus of the empirical evidence relevant to inflation and the financing of development. For example, the monetarist points to the relatively poor export performance associated with higher inflation and attributes the blame to inflation; thus less inflation would improve developmental possibilities. The structuralist reverses the argument and stresses the role of foreign demand in depressing exports, and the relevance of relatively poor export performance in causing inflation.

Secondly, the possible evil effects of inflation are never denied by either school. But the weight given to bad effects versus good is strongly determined by one's view of the power of a market mechanism undistorted by inflation or the resulting controls to lead to development. That is, the view of the alternative to inflation being radically different, the assessment of its consequences tends to be too. The structuralist, sceptical of the potential of free enterprise and seeing structural bottlenecks as preceding inflation, sees stabilisation by restrictive financial policy as not merely irrelevant but positively harmful to the goals of development. He thus will tend to play down the quantitatively indeterminate evils of inflation and to stress the possibility of counteracting them. The monetarist, believing in the potential for development given by free enterprise in a healthy economy, i.e. in a viable alternative, is therefore inclined to stress the many negative effects of inflation, though he may have just as little evidence of their quantitative significance.

(d) The Relationships between Inflation and Development

Now that the fundamentally different positions on the origins of inflation in Latin America have been clarified, we can turn to our more specific concern in this chapter: the relationships between inflation and development. We shall divide this somewhat arbitrarily into the case for and the case against inflation promoting growth, reviewing the empirical evidence for each in turn.

(i) *The Case for Inflation Promoting Growth.* Arguments under this head divide into those which claim some direct growth-promoting function for inflation, and those which see a given rate of growth as necessitating some measure of inflation, since the steps required to eliminate inflation would only do so at a cost in terms of growth. The reasoning behind the latter claim usually turns on a mixture of economic, social and political factors.

Let us consider first the directly growth-promoting mechanisms. First, inflation is supposed to promote growth by redistributing income towards profits. The propensity to save out of profits being higher than out of wages, this redistribution 'forces' an increase in the aggregate marginal propensity to save,[17] which is assumed to generate greater investment.

In fact no school advocates this line of argument as a reason for encouraging inflation in Latin America. It has commonly been supposed to be part of the structuralist case; however, it sits very uneasily with other elements in the structuralist position. First, it necessitates worsening income distribution: structuralists typically take a moderate or left-wing position and such a consequence would be extremely embarrassing to them. Second, as an argument for growth it rests on certain assumptions which are directly contradicted by other structuralist contentions. Specifically, it assumes that a redistribution to profits implies redistribution to a group that can be relied on to use these resources productively, and that not only the propensity to invest but also the feasibility of private investment is high. These assumptions run counter to the structuralists' contentions about the high propensity to consume or to invest non-productively among upper income groups, and the structural constraints which inhibit investment.[18] Thus it is not surprising that structuralists join with monetarists in arguing that the forced saving aspect of inflation is not only inequitable but also extremely inefficient as a growth mechanism (see for example, Prebisch, 51, p. 2; Griffin, 26, pp. 195–203).

The second version of this kind of argument is equally one which is not actually applied in the Latin American case, although again some appear to consider it to be part of the structuralist position. It consists simply in the claim that the existence of inflation aids the process of drawing more resources into the growth process. At times the argument appears to rest on money illusion: rising money returns to factors draw a response in excess of that to be predicted on the basis of real returns. Or it is again derived from the redistributive effect of inflation, but this time the emphasis is on the rising expectations created by rising profits (Kaldor's 'animal spirits' of entrepreneurs). We need not pursue the argument, however, since it will already be clear that it implies a system responsive to price incentives, the denial of which is the basis of the true case for structural inflation.

Turning then to the arguments for inflation promoting growth in some indirect sense, the first of these states that only inflation permits necessary relative price changes. The form of this argument has already been outlined above. That there is a certain necessary degree of inflation, given the downward rigidity of prices and the need for major structural adjustments in the course of development, and that in this sense inflation can be growth-promoting, is not only true but has been cogently argued by an outstanding representative of the monetarist school of thought (Dorrance, 16). The problem lies not in the validity of the argument but in determining how much inflation should be allowed for on this score.

Relative price adjustments are in themselves an argument for a very moderate rate of inflation, though how moderate depends in part on one's assumptions about the speed with which the system adjusts to price signals. It is clear that Dorrance is talking about annual rates that are well below 10 per cent. He suggests that the highest growth rates will be associated with relatively stable prices (annual increases of less than 5 per cent), although there is only a definite falling off of performance once the rate of price increase exceeds 10 per cent. As explained above, however (see p. 189), the structuralist goes on to argue that inflation on this count can be well over an annual rate of 10 per cent, once it is realised first that the inelasticities of supply may be such that a large change in relative prices has little or no effect on the original disequilibrium, and second that there exist powerful propagation mechanisms.

Implicit in the above argument is the assumption that such propagation mechanisms cannot in any simple fashion be controlled in the short run – at least not without sacrificing the goals of development and policies which in the longer run should prove fundamentally anti-inflationary. This leads us directly to the next argument, which forms the core of the structuralists' case for inflation being a necessary concomitant of development, once that inflation already exists. It runs as follows:[19] (i) The root causes of inflation are structural; excess monetary demand, if it exists, is a symptom of a deeper disequilibrium, not a cause. (ii) At the same time the techniques of short-run stabilisation inevitably consist in attacking symptoms not causes: the budget deficit, the supply of credit, the wage-price spiral. (iii) The depression which will result from such measures will be extremely severe in the typical Latin American country. First, business is highly dependent on bank credit. Second, the sensitivity of labour to wage restraint and unemployment will result in strikes which further depress output. Third, the decline in public revenue, as a result of the fall-off in internal and external trade (the latter normally being what has precipitated stabilisation), combined with increased non-payment of taxes in a time of credit stringency, leads, if not to the abandonment of the programme, then to even greater cuts in public spending in an attempt to balance the budget. (iv) Such a depression will not achieve the reallocation of resources and subsequent resumption of growth in a new pattern which is postulated in monetarist logic, since the economic system is insufficiently flexible. (v) The programme as a whole will in fact have cost push inflationary effects, which in turn accentuate the problem of eliminating the budget deficit and lead to further cuts in real public spending as it rises in current prices. These cost push effects come through the increases in public utility tariffs and the removal of price controls in the attempt to restore the market mechanism and eliminate subsidies, and through the increases in import duties which are essential given the urgency of the balance of payments problem. (vi) There is every likelihood that the social tension created by the above combination of rising prices, restraints on wages and acute unemployment will lead to the abandonment of the programme. But even if the creation of depression is carried to the point where the rate of price increase slows down, when the restrictions on demand are relaxed inflationary pressures will return, since the structural pressures on the price level remain unaltered. In fact they may even have been aggravated, since the alleviation of bottlenecks such as those in infrastructure and agriculture will only come through government investment. It is this category of public spending which will have borne the brunt of the heavy expenditure cuts in the course of the attempt at stabilisation, since around 80 per cent of government current expenditure typically consists of wages and salaries. The one apparently positive sign which may have appeared is an improvement in the balance of payments. But this will be entirely the result of the effect of depressed internal activity on imports. There will probably in fact be some increase in external short-term debt, to the I.M.F. and others, and thus possibly even a worsening in the basic situation.

Thus since short-term stabilisation is not only irrelevant but actually positively harmful to growth and to the longer-term structural changes which are the only way inflationary pressures can be genuinely reduced, given an ongoing inflation, this has to be tolerated in the short run. Anything that can be done to mitigate either the speed of the inflation or its undoubtedly adverse side effects should be done, provided this is at a sufficiently low cost to the structuralist's development strategy.

The final argument for inflation promoting growth is derived directly from the structuralist analysis already described, and from the contention that government investment is crucial for the elimination of bottlenecks preventing growth. In this it overlaps with the preceding argument, since the case against short-run stabilisation is in part that government investment must proceed, inflation or no. But it is also more positive: given the financial bottleneck described above, the argument goes, the only way to carry out this government investment is by government deficit spending which necessarily leads to inflation. That is, inflation is the only politically acceptable form of tax. Ideally the development strategy financed by inflation should be aimed at institutional changes which will eventually permit growth without inflation – as it is claimed happened in Mexico but not in Brazil, the two case studies which we discuss below.

(ii) *The Empirical Evidence on the Case for Inflation Promoting Growth.* Perhaps the first point to be made here concerns the inadequacy of the empirical evidence. Structuralist literature abounds in elaborations of the structuralist position, but attempts to formulate and test hypotheses are rare in the extreme. Given the enormous importance of the issues which we have tried to illustrate in section (*b*), this imbalance is extremely serious.

The evidence, such as it is, comes from a wide area of empirical work; this is implicit in the contention that what is at issue here is really the whole problem of strategies of development. We can divide the relevant material into five areas: first, there are statistical investigations of the postulated positive relation between inflation and private investment described above. Second, we can examine evidence on the causes of inflation, and in particular of each of the so-called structural bottlenecks. Third, we should look at evidence on the ability of the structuralist thesis to explain why various countries have experienced such varied rates of inflation. Fourth, the analysis of the effect of stabilisation attempts itself constitutes evidence relevant to the structuralist claim about the inevitability of inflation, and further evidence on causes of inflation. And fifth, we should examine case studies of successful growth with inflation, which form the basis for the argument that inflation can be the justifiable cost of public investment essential for growth.

Statistical evidence on inflation and growth. The evidence on this count is thin. There is more evidence on the specific adverse effects inflation is postulated to have on investment, but this is taken up below when the positive case against using inflation to promote growth is considered. What is in question here is whether inflation *per se* appears directly to stimulate private investment, primarily by redistribution towards profits.

Some writers derive evidence against such a stimulus from the falling off of growth rates which appears to be associated with rather high rates of inflation (e.g. Dorrance, 16). But it is clear from the case against short-run stabilisation outlined above that this evidence cannot be taken at face value. If inflation has typically precipitated inappropriate stabilisation policies which accelerate inflation and severely hamper growth, then this will confuse any underlying statistical relation between inflation *per se* and growth. Thus it is hardly surprising that a plot of the cost of living data from Table 1 against the growth rates for the same time periods shows no marked straightforward correlation between inflation and growth, but does suggest a falling off of growth rates at high rates of price increase (Brazil being the single notable exception).

Turning to other kinds of evidence, we must relate it to two questions: first, does redistribution occur, and second, when it does, is investment positively associated with inflation? The evidence on the first point suggests that in a prolonged inflation in Latin America the redistributive effects are negligible, as far as this can be determined from the data available on labour's share in G.N.P. Chile appears to be the most notable example of this (Felix, 23, p. 280).

Turning to the second question, there is some sign, for what it is worth, of a positive correlation. For example, Ternent (66), comparing Brazil, which he describes as at least until 1960 a case of demand inflation unhampered by severely restrictive policies, and Colombia, predominantly cost push, finds over the period 1948 to 1964 a positive correlation between inflation and private investment for Brazil and a zero correlation for Colombia. If the years 1954–64 are taken, the correlation is significantly negative for Colombia. But in Brazil both inflation and investment were rising with time, and in any case, as Ternent points out, the causality underlying the relationship could perfectly well run either way (particularly as in the data partly government-owned companies are included in the private sector). And as will emerge below, there were other characteristics of this period in Brazil which were probably more important in explaining the correlation between inflation and investment. We can conclude then that there is no strong evidence in favour of inflation stimulating private investment – which is hardly surprising since the theoretical case for it doing so is so plainly inapplicable to Latin America.

The origin of inflation in structural bottlenecks. Evidence on this does not lend itself to easy review. This is partly because what statistical evidence there is in the form of correlations raises the constant problem of interpretation. This problem is particularly evident when correlation analysis is used to explore the relation between inflation and the money supply (Harberger, 28, Delfim Netto *et al.*, 13). The money supply in each case comes out as highly significant as an explanatory variable – but as Baer points out in his review of such work (3), if changes in the money supply are simply symptoms of institutional difficulties, what have we really explained and what policy conclusion can we draw?[20] Since the structuralist specifically asks us to go beyond the figures at their face value, we need to examine a wide area of literature, not directly bearing on inflation, which can shed light on the structuralists' claim that in Latin America we are confronted with poorly integrated economies where inappropriate factor prices, supply rigidities rooted in institutional factors, unequal income distribution and low propensities to invest all imply a system which both requires structural changes and is unresponsive to the price mechanism as a means for accomplishing them. The task of review therefore becomes somewhat unwieldy.

The case for poor responsiveness to the price system in the context of Latin America has perhaps been most completely argued by Balogh in a paper published by ECLA (4). Many of the empirical facts underlying such an analysis are widely accepted and evidently true: unequal income distribution, the unresponsiveness of the tax system, the poor performance of primary exports, the rising demand for imports with industrialisation and urbanisation. The paper by Seers we have already quoted so frequently (56) documents such characteristics, and evidence may be found in a large number of country studies produced by ECLA. For the agricultural sector in particular the work of CIDA[21] documents the case for the effect of tenure institutions on performance.[22] The high propensity to consume of upper income groups, as well as many other structural features, is documented in a study of Chile by Kaldor (32), where he finds that Chilean property owners consume over 60 per cent of property income while for British property owners the figure is only 30 per cent.

Further support for the structuralist case comes from the undoubted fact that such structural defects in Latin American economies preceded inflation. Unequal income distribution, an unproductive agriculture with tenure systems undermining both the incentive and means to higher productivity, defective tax and financial structures – all these preceded the emergence of inflation and so can hardly be attributed to that inflation alone (Seers, 56). Monetarists occasionally play into the structuralists' hands by pointing out that such structural conditions also existed in, say Cuba, yet Cuba has had price stability (Eder, 18). Since Cuba also was conspicuous for its stagnation during the thirty-five years prior to the revolution, this makes the structuralists' point very neatly.

Turning to more detailed work which attempts to clarify the origin of particular bottlenecks, we find a lack of systematic efforts to test specific structural hypotheses, drawing together the kind of evidence described above and relating it in a convincing fashion to the theory. One notable exception to this is a recent study by Edel on the food supply bottleneck (17), a study which is sufficiently unusual and important to justify a detailed summary here. Edel explores two hypotheses: first that agriculture has lagged behind its required rate of growth, and second that where the lag has occurred, it has been associated with inflation. Taking eight Latin American countries, he finds that food output was adequate in Mexico, Brazil and Venezuela, but inadequate in Argentina, Chile, Colombia, Peru and Uruguay. This is consistent so far with the structuralist position, since the latter countries have all experienced inflation, while of the former, special circumstances in each case show how the exception can prove the rule. In Venezuela export revenue has until recently been available to fill any structural gap. Mexico accomplished structural reform in agriculture following the revolution and its very moderate inflation can in part be attributed to that.[23] Brazil's inflation has been caused by other factors, the adequacy of food supplies being usually explained in terms of the 'open' frontier which at least until the 1960s permitted an easy supply response.[24]

The search for a strict association between food prices and inflation meets the problem of what constitutes evidence. 'A proponent of the lagging agriculture argument may see food shortages as delivering exogenous shocks to the inflationary mechanism, accelerating it, or restarting it at any time that it slows down, without claiming that once the mechanism is started, food prices need grow faster at all times' (17, p. 69). Thus qualitative studies are more helpful evidence. Edel examines the role of food supplies in various stabilisation attempts and finds clear evidence of their significance with regard to inflation.

Granted a bottleneck, though, we still have to establish the relative roles of policy versus structural conditions. Schultz (54), Bray (7, 8) and Mamalakis (39) among others have for instance blamed the poor performance of Chilean agriculture on poor rates of return, in turn attributable to government manipulation of prices, itself a reaction to inflation. Rates of return in Chilean agriculture are certainly low, but to quote Edel again, 'these may result from inadequate technological progressivity in adopting cost-cutting innovations, rather than simply from price distortions' (17, p. 100). The chief argument of the price distortion school seems to rest on the low price of meat relative to wheat; this in itself, as Edel shows, is no explanation of the inadequate performance of the sector as a whole. The degree of price control on foodstuffs does not appear to be systematically associated with the performance of agriculture country by country, and testing for response to price reveals some response in Colombia and Chile but none in Argentina, Uruguay or Peru (17, p. 41). On the other hand there is considerable evidence accumulating, through the work of CIDA mentioned above as well as others, to the effect that tenure is related to low productivity (17, ch. 5).

The second kind of empirical work we can examine is constituted by country studies of inflation which by the presentation of a coherent picture based on quantitative and qualitative material provide evidence of the origin of inflation in the economic and institutional structure. Such studies have mostly been primarily concerned with the analysis of stabilisation programmes and as such will be discussed again later. The best-documented cases are those of Chile and Argentina: in works by Sunkel (65), Kaldor (32), Pinto (48), Sierra (60, 61) and Felix (21) among others,[25] a case is made for Chile fitting very closely to the standard structuralist situation, with special emphasis on the rigidity of the agricultural sector and the low propensity to invest of upper income groups. In works by Eshag and Thorp (19), Ferrer (24, 25) and Diaz Alejandro (14), Argentina's inflation problem is shown to have an unusual character, since the country is exceptional in being a food exporter with a predominantly commercialised agriculture. The problem here originated in Peron's discrimination against agriculture and belated realisation of the interactions between agriculture, the balance of payments and industry. Subsequent attempts at stimulating agriculture with better internal terms of trade or with devaluation or both had no short-run effect on supply but raised internal food prices, and in the case of devaluation import prices too. The resulting inflation eliminated the price advantage to agriculture before it could have any effect on longer-run supply. The farmer's lack of confidence in government price incentives was self-reinforcing.

The explanatory power of the thesis. The third form of evidence for the basic structuralist case derives from the coherence and general applicability of that case. It is sometimes said that the structuralist analysis was evolved in the context of Chile and is a plausible explanation of that economy, but not of general applicability. On the contrary, the structuralists claim that their approach provides a framework for analysing inflationary potential on a very general basis. This was first shown in the historical analysis of the experience of different Latin American countries presented by Seers (56). Pinto (50) presents a very similar analysis, and empirical work such as that of Edel (17) and Mueller (43) shows how apparent exceptions such as Mexico actually strengthen the structuralist case.

The 'potential' for structural inflation is given by on the one hand the strength of a country's aspirations to grow in the face of the structural transformation required of it, and on the other hand by the country's circumstances in a number of crucial respects. Seers and Pinto summarise these as the speed and depth of the readjustment required, the evolution of the external sector, the flexibility of the productive system, the aptitude of social and institutional organs for change and the role played by economic policy.

With the onset of the Depression, the size of urban populations and the need for urban employment were such that the larger countries of Latin America were forced into financial unorthodoxy in an attempt to continue developing by expanding their already existing industrial base. They form the first of the group U countries as classified by Seers.[26] The two smaller countries which attempted to follow the same route, Bolivia and Paraguay, faced a greater depth of readjustment and consequently experienced the most violent inflation. Chile too experienced very serious inflation, given the extremely unfavourable evolution of her external sector and her acute lack of aptitude for change in regard to social and institutional characteristics. Mexico experienced a much less violent inflation, for a number of reasons. First, the revolution of 1910 introduced an exceptional degree of aptitude for change, including in particular a land reform which, as was mentioned above, was responsible for the lack of an agricultural bottleneck.[27] Second, the flexibility of the productive system was fairly great owing to an unusual diversity of exports. Further, the slowing down of inflation in Mexico was associated with a reduced importance of the agricultural and public sector bottlenecks, as Mueller shows (43). This increased responsiveness was itself associated with government policy.[28] The moderate inflation in Peru (until 1966–8) was associated also with diversified exports, and a social institutional situation which is less rigid than that, say, of Chile or Argentina, in the sense that wage earners had less power to defend themselves: worsening income distribution was permitted rather than a tight wage–price spiral, a consequence which also relieved some of the pressure on the agricultural bottleneck by reducing the rate of growth of aggregated demand for food (Thorp, 67).

Turning to Seers's second group,[29] these followed a more orthodox financial policy after the Depression, which, as Seers shows, was permitted to them for reasons entirely in line with the structural analysis. In the small countries of Central America and the Caribbean and in Ecuador, 'both the need and the opportunity . . . were lacking' (56, p. 32), given smaller urban populations, banking systems largely in foreign hands, and a dearth of any industry to form a base for expansion. In the case of Venezuela, as mentioned above, the evolution of the external sector was until recently so favourable that growth was possible essentially without structural transformation.

The failure of monetarist stabilisation remedies. The fourth kind of evidence comes from the consequences of trying to apply the monetarist remedy to an inflationary situation which is argued to be structuralist at root. The measures which form part of such a remedy were outlined above; they have at one time or another been applied in a very similar fashion in every country of Latin America which has experienced rapid inflation. The accumulating evidence of costly failure has been responsible for several countries breaking with the I.M.F. (Argentina 1964–5) or at least holding out against pressure (Colombia 1966, Chile under Frei), and also for some growth in the flexibility of I.M.F. policy. The I.M.F. has been willing recently to go along with somewhat unorthodox programmes (e.g. Colombia 1966–7) and has come further towards accepting the overwhelming importance of not sacrificing public investment. On the other hand, several Latin American governments now appear to be following orthodox policy on a voluntary basis and independent of pressure from the Fund.

The bones of the structuralist analysis of the operation of the so-called 'orthodox economic policy' were set out above. Detailed empirical substantiation of the various points can be found in several case studies, especially those on Argentina and Chile mentioned above,[30] and can hardly be adequately summarised here. The empirical studies bring out in each case the severely depressing effects of the programmes on output, while at the same time inflationary pressures are aggravated. Thus for example in Argentina in 1959, the first year of a drastic stabilisation programme, output fell while prices rose 102 per cent. The apparent improvement in the following two years is shown to originate in an inflow of foreign exchange (Eshag and Thorp, 19). This inflow was temporary in nature, being partly due to the stabilisation credits themselves and partly to an inflow of foreign capital associated primarily with Frondizi's reversal of policy towards the petroleum industry. This inflow more than counterbalanced the internal credit restraints and made possible some resumption of growth; when the inflow came to an end during 1961 the underlying structural conditions were left unchanged (except for an increase in the external debt burden) and the history of 1962–3 repeats that of 1959, with the same vicious circles operating in the manner outlined above. The extreme effects on production that such restrictive policies are bound to have are further illustrated by Maynard and Rijckeghem (40) in an econometric study of the Argentine economy. They show that given the high dependence of industry on credit, such a policy affects output and costs very heavily; the depression originates on the *supply* side. Felix also provides evidence to support his contention that both in Argentina and Chile credit restraints not only are severe but also discriminate against precisely the sectors which should be encouraged – that is, those with export potential (23, p. 394).

Thus structuralists contend that such studies show first that inflation has deeper roots than monetarist policy implies, and second that inflation cannot be ended rapidly without active harm to more fundamentally anti-inflationary policies. The monetarist response is first to argue that the policies did not work because they were not wholeheartedly applied. The structuralist reply to this is that the reasons for their abandonment were inherent in the internal contradictions of the programmes (which raised prices yet demanded reduced government expenditure, depressed output and employment yet expected wage restraint to be feasible) and in the socio-political context in which they were applied. Secondly, the monetarist points to instances where the policy appears to have worked – for example Peru in 1959, where stabilisation was followed by an immediate recovery in output, a rather moderate rate of inflation and balance of payments equilibrium. Here the structuralist response is that the exceptions merely go to prove the rule. The success of the Peruvian programme can be shown to be explicable in terms of an export boom which began at the crucial moment for reasons quite independent of the programme. The inflow of foreign exchange nullified the effect of credit controls, permitting compliance with the letter but not the spirit of the I.M.F.'s requirements, and allowed a rising supply of imports; thus internal activity was not depressed, tax revenues rose rather than fell, and the task of balancing the budget could be accomplished with little reduction in expenditure. Control of inflation was made the easier by a weak labour movement which was held well in control (Thorp, 67).

The recent experience of Argentina, where the rate of price increase has been greatly reduced in 1967–9, also appears to be a case of fulfilling the letter rather than the spirit of orthodox policy. Again an inflow of foreign exchange via rising exports has made it possible to comply with I.M.F. regulations as to the money supply without creating a situation of shortage of credit. The military government was also able to control wages very firmly, then to proceed to expand demand via government spending, so stimulating internal activity and employment at the same time that price rises were restrained. The increases in production assisted the slackening of inflationary pressures and the increase in employment was presumably designed to ease labour discontent.[31] The labour troubles in May and June 1969 threatened to disrupt the programme, but appear to have been suppressed with the arrest of the main union opponent of the government and the maintenance of a state of siege (still in force at the time of writing). This highlights again two crucial variables: the ability of the government to squeeze labour's share and the evolution of the external sector.

One further case should be mentioned here: Bolivia underwent a drastic stabilisation programme in 1956 which brought an absolute fall in the price level (Eder, 18). Prior to stabilisation inflation had broken all Latin American records (470 per cent in one year) and the corruption, speculation and distortion pervading the economy as a result of the inflation and the controls accompanying it had reached an extreme point (80 per cent of all Bolivia's foreign trade was said to be smuggled, for example). An abrupt stabilisation effort led to increased supplies of goods on the market and lower prices. But no structuralist would fail to agree that there *can* come a point where the disutility of inflation is so great that certain short-run gains come simply from ending it. As Eder himself shows, the increase in supplies generated by the restoration of a healthy price system is actually primarily a matter of reallocation: food formerly withheld from the market began to be brought in, people who had spent their time holding places in queues now went back to the fields to work. The longer-term stimulus to overall growth is another matter: Eder's own evidence on agricultural production appears to suggest that the entire source of the expansion was sugar, which he himself says was promoted far beyond the point of rationality. G.D.P. *per capita* fell during 1956–64; prices still rose over 70 per cent in the same period, and it is clear that the burden of what stabilisation was achieved fell heavily on labour (Walther, 70).

Table 2. Mexico and Brazil: Average Annual Rates of Growth in *Per Capita* G.D.P. at Constant Prices and in the Cost of Living, 1940–65

| | Mexico: | | Brazil: | |
	G.D.P. per capita	Cost of living	G.D.P. per capita	Cost of living (*São Paolo*)
1940–5	4·4	16	...	...
1945–50	3·5	11	3·4	11
1950–5	3·6	10	2·7	18
1955–60	3·0	6	2·9	28
1960–5	2·9	2	1·8	62

Sources: As Table 1, also M. W. Mueller, 'Structural Inflation and the Mexican Experience', in *Yale Economic Essays*, v, 1 (spring 1965), 156.

Inflationary financing of government investment. The fifth point to be examined is evidence for the contention that inflation can successfully be used to finance development, not through the forced saving mechanism as it is usually understood, but by its financing of government developmental expenditures. The extra saving is accomplished by the increased share of government in total income. The key examples of this role of inflation in Latin America are claimed to be Mexico and Brazil. Rates of growth in income and in prices are given in Table 2; it will be seen that each has experienced a period where high growth rates were accompanied by inflation (Mexico 1940–55, Brazil 1945–60), although in the Brazilian case the inflationary pressures were considerably greater.

In fact Mexico's experience is by no means unique; several other countries have experienced similar rates of inflation and growth. But what is unusual is the way in which the Mexican case can be interpreted as an instance where inflation was used to promote growth.[32]

The typical picture we have sketched in for the 1930s and 1940s for the larger Latin American countries where the size of urban populations forced action on the government, is one of increasing government deficits stimulating inflation while other structural bottlenecks gradually emerged. That is, food supplies failed to respond, while the inefficiencies of import-substituting industrialisation, plus its own mechanics in terms of generating greater import requirements, resulted in a gradually tightening external bottleneck, which was worsened to a greater or lesser extent by export trends. At the same time, infrastructure was typically neglected (in Argentina for instance net investment in railways was negative over the period 1935–55). In a sense, then, many governments were using inflation to grow by deficit financing which stimulated internal demand; however, what makes Mexico particularly interesting is that she did so not just in the short-term sense of stimulating the level of activity. Where in other countries the expansion of the money supply went largely to current expenditures or transfers, in Mexico in an important degree it went to infrastructure. The huge public works of the end of the 1930s and the 1940s in agriculture encouraged an increasingly prosperous commercial agriculture.[33] This permitted an expansion both of agricultural exports and of domestic food supplies, which grew more rapidly than G.N.P. 1946–56 (Solis, 64; Mueller, 43). Infrastructure services were often provided below cost, with a view to stimulating private investment both in agriculture and in industry. Industrial growth was aided by a growth rate of exports which was adequate to permit the imports necessary for industrialisation; export growth was favoured by Mexico's unusual diversity of exports as well as by the investment in agriculture. Further, by the 1950s tourism, again deliberately favoured by government policy, began to emerge as a major exchange earner. Meanwhile important institutional changes, such as the growth of financial intermediaries, the emergence of Nacional Financiera, and changes in banking regulations (for example banks were required to hold government bonds and to lend to non-traditional activities), led to increased bank financing of industry. Solis argues that these changes permitted so large a part of the burden of financing public investment to be taken up by the banking system, that by the mid 1950s the inflationary effects of government investment could be substantially ameliorated. Meanwhile private savings played an increasing role (Solis, 64), at the expense of some worsening of the distribution of income.[34]

Thus the reduced inflation after 1956 can be explained in terms of reduced bottlenecks. This occurred partly as a direct result of the use of inflation (which contributed to the agricultural and industrial expansion, and thereby via both exports and industrial import substitution had repercussions on the foreign exchange bottleneck), and partly as a result of prudent institutional changes aimed at increasing the sources of non-inflationary finance.

In Brazil the notable period of inflationary promotion of growth occurred in the 1950s, especially under President Kubitschek (1956–61). Industry expanded at 10 per cent a year and tripled in size over the 1950s, expanding from 26 per cent of G.N.P. in 1949 to 35 per cent by the early 1960s. This came about while prices rose 20 per cent per annum 1949 to 1959, and subsequently accelerated. Meanwhile Argentina, for example, with a larger share of industry at the end of the 1940s, experienced virtual stagnation in income *per capita* over the same period, accompanied by a similar rate of inflation.

Part of the explanation of Brazil's growth lies in factors such as the size of the market and the performance of exports, which was sufficiently favourable not to hamstring industrialisation but not so favourable as to relax the incentive to industrial promotion. But the key element lay in government policy, firstly in a foreign exchange policy which particularly after 1953 was very effective in promoting import-substituting industry and in encouraging the entry of foreign capital, and secondly in extensive government investment, especially in energy and transport. This was greatly expanded under Kubitschek under the *Programa de Metas* (1956), which set five-year targets for basic industries (Baer, 1, ch. 3). The tax increases which would have made possible such a programme without inflation were less acceptable to the business community than was inflation,[35] *given* the government's known commitment to growth, if necessary at the expense of stability. The stimulus to growth came partly through the rising level of activity and partly through the supply effects of improved infrastructure. (It seems probable that within the private sector the more usual form of the forced saving mechanism also operated to increase private investment. See Baer, 1, ch. 6.)

Thus in both Mexico and Brazil the expansion of the government's share was also probably accompanied by redistribution towards profits and against wages – the traditional forced saving mechanism – and it is suggested that in both cases there must come a 'day of reckoning'. But for Brazil there also appears to have been a day of reckoning in a further sense: the enormous industrialisation push, and the channelling of public investment so strongly in this direction, was achieved at the expense of other areas, especially agriculture, education and non-traditional exports. These have emerged in the 1960s as bottleneck areas, which directly or indirectly may have tended to worsen inflation and reduce growth. It appears to be factors of this nature, rather than the acceleration of inflation *per se*, which were responsible for halting at least temporarily the period of rapid growth with inflation.[36] However, the current resumption of growth, with inflation of some 20 per cent a year, suggests that the continued potency of the mechanism for Brazil is very much an open question.

What these case studies suggest, then, is that it is possible to use inflation to further long-term growth – and that this may be done more or less successfully. In particular, given the evils of inflation to which we turn in the next section, success would seem to include eliminating eventually the 'need' for inflation: the key difference between Mexico and Brazil appears to be Mexico's success in carrying out institutional change and financial innovation to achieve this goal. But it is an odd kind of argument that is being used. Firstly, every analyst would prefer the alternative: the raising of finance by non-inflationary means. It is 'merely' that this may be politically impossible. Secondly, it is a case for inflation which can only really be made *ex post*. A government which announced too boldly its intentions of pursuing and expanding inflationary development policies would not only bring down on itself the wrath of international lending agencies, but would also produce a loss of confidence on the part of private capital and would probably accelerate the inflationary spiral quite unnecessarily as prices and wages rose in anticipation of such inflationary action.

Summary and review. Attempting to sum up the evidence on the case for inflation promoting development, we find that the evidence for any direct growth-promoting function is extremely weak. However, there is considerable evidence accumulating which shows that inflation may have to be tolerated in the pursuit of development. This body of evidence takes two main forms: evidence for the basic structuralist arguments on the origin of inflation, and evidence on the impossibility of short-run stabilisation without a sacrifice both of growth and of the longer-run reforms which might genuinely lead eventually to growth with stability.

However, there is one serious gap in the evidence, a gap which constitutes the weakest aspect of the structuralist case. There is as yet no clear indication either in theory or in practice as to how a structuralist can handle a short-term crisis situation of dwindling exchange reserves and accelerating inflation without sacrificing his goals. Suggestions about import restrictions and a greater degree of planning must confront the fact that today's problems are in part the result of inefficient policy; capacity for manipulating the economy cannot be acquired overnight. Meanwhile, structuralist measures such as land reform tend if anything to be inflationary in the short run. The 'structuralist stabilisation programme' which Frei has recently attempted to put into effect in Chile has been shown to be a misnomer (Sierra, 61); in the event, it was both orthodox and unsuccessful. This is an area of ongoing research among structuralists, especially at ECLA;[37] if this chapter does nothing more than illustrate the need for such work, given the damaging effects of other solutions, then it will have achieved an important goal.

(ii) *The Case against Inflation Promoting Growth.* Part of the case against inflation is obviously contained in the monetarists' response to the specific arguments for inflation. These counter-arguments were discussed in the preceding section as they became relevant and will not be reviewed again here. The specific areas where it is claimed that inflation hinders growth can be summarised as follows.

The effect on the supply of capital funds, domestic and foreign. The effect on domestic supply of funds can be further divided into the effect of inflation first on the savings decision directly, and second on the investment decision, and thereby indirectly on the volume of funds made available for domestic investment.

The impact on the savings decision comes primarily through one of the inevitable concomitants of inflation rather than through inflation itself: the control of interest rates. In Chile during a period when inflation averaged more than 60 per cent per annum the commercial bank rate never exceeded 16 per cent. The real negative rates engendered by such interest rate control cannot, it is argued, do otherwise than discourage savings even given extensive evasion. Savings will be further discouraged by the decrease in the liquidity of money and financial claims expressed in money terms in a time of inflation, in conjunction with an increased desire for liquidity with increased uncertainty – also a consequence of inflation. The impact of these liquidity considerations will be felt primarily on the decision how to allocate a given volume of savings, which is discussed below, but may also result in increased consumption, especially in a poor country where money represents the form of savings most widely available. 'A communal shift away from holdings of financial assets is almost certain to be associated with a decline in total savings' (Dorrance, 15, p. 44). The pressure for liquidity will also, it is suggested, show up as an increased pressure for distribution of profits, i.e. reduced corporate saving.

The first of the effects on the investment decision, an increased preference for holding foreign assets, will result in similar pressure and in reduced availability of funds for local investment. A second effect on the investment decision will be felt through the rise in the price of investment goods relative to consumer goods which is empirically associated with inflation and decreases the rate of return on investment. This effect is noted by Dorrance (15, p. 52) and explained in terms of the high import content of investment, the excessive exchange depreciation caused by inflation and the nature of protective import policies.

The effect on the volume of funds from abroad is also felt primarily through the exchange depreciation associated with inflation. If this is greater than the amount of the internal inflation, the real net return to the foreign investor is reduced and foreign investment is discouraged. Further, the prospect of exchange controls which may go with the worsening balance of payments situation resulting from inflation may also deter the foreign investor.

The effect on the productivity of capital. Inflation will tend to misallocate funds and so reduce their productivity, either directly, primarily through the uncertainty as to the movement of prices in general and particularly relative prices, or indirectly, via the price controls inevitably accompanying the inflation.

Examples of the first are biases in favour of inventory investment, at the expense of longer-term fixed investment, and in favour of investment in luxury housing and real estate more generally. As explained above, inflation both increases the desire for liquidity and makes money undesirable as a form of liquidity; inventories form a relatively liquid investment with opportunities for speculative profit if relative price movements can be correctly anticipated, and particularly when inflation accelerates inventory investment will rise sharply (see Shaalan, 58, for a full analysis). Savers looking for assets other than money to hold in an inflationary situation also turn readily to real estate, which is known to provide an excellent inflation hedge (and therefore continues to do so).

An example of the second is the neglect of investment in infrastructure, which is liable to occur anyway in a time of uncertainty given its long-term nature, but which is much accentuated by lags in the adjustment of public utility rates. This may be partly bureaucratic slowness and partly a short-term, and short-sighted, anti-inflationary policy. A desire to avoid the undesirable consequences of inflation also lies behind another example: price controls on food not balanced by adequate producer subsidies discourage investment in agriculture. A further occasion can be the temporary pegging of exchange rates, another common phenomenon in time of inflation, which squeezes exporting profits to the point of discouraging investment.

Inflation, it is argued, will also tend to lead to inefficiency in given uses. This occurs principally through the increased difficulty of rational decision-taking in a time of rising prices, since these confuse accounting practices. Specifically, illusory profits tend to be generated by the understatement of depreciation implied by the use of historical cost. This is claimed to lead to firms bankrupting themselves by excessive distribution of profits.

Inflation, finally, is said to discourage the adoption of innovations and therefore to slow down the rate of increase of the productivity of resources. The greater the uncertainty as to future price movements, the larger the return businessmen require to induce them to adopt a cost-cutting innovation. This is seen by Harberger as perhaps the strongest argument against inflation as a growth promoter (Harberger, 29, p. 320).

The effect on the balance of payments. The chief repercussions on the balance of payments have been mentioned already among the various aspects of the distorted allocation of resources under inflation. Through income and substitution effects operating on exports and imports, the initial effect of inflation is to worsen the current account of the balance of payments, to a greater or lesser extent depending on supply and demand conditions at home and abroad. The result will sooner or later be exchange rate adjustment in some form; to the extent that the rate is in fact pegged over periods of time, export supply may be severely depressed. To the extent that over a longer time period, and partly as a consequence of the depression of exports, the exchange rate adjusts by more than the internal inflation, capital inflow is discouraged.

(iv) *The Empirical Evidence against Inflation Promoting Growth.* Assessing the arguments and empirical evidence for the harmful effects of inflation meets with three constantly recurring problems. First, since the structuralists accept such harmful effects in principle, the interesting question becomes the quantitative importance of such effects. Given the scanty empirical evidence, it is hardly surprising that this can rarely be determined. Second, we are constantly confronted with the problem of attempting to assess what might actually have been the situation in the absence of inflation: that is, to assess the effect of inflation we have to envisage the relevant alternative. And third, we meet repeatedly the problem of establishing causation.

The effect on the supply of capital funds, domestic and foreign. The reduction of financial asset holding in a strong inflation is *a priori* very reasonable and is borne out empirically (Dorrance, 15, p. 43), as is the prevalence of (official) negative real rates of return on savings. However, the association of these with a reduction of total savings is less clear, and is open in any case to problems of interpretation. First, the predicted association of pressures for liquidity with increased profit distribution is not supported empirically. Ternent (66) finds that the percentage of retained profits in the total rises with inflation in Colombia and Brazil. Data from the Instituto de Economía (33) show an increase for Chile in the 1950s. There was some decline in household savings rates in Argentina and in Chile in the 1950s – both strong inflation countries. However, Felix argues (23) that import-substituting industrialisation itself tends to redistribute income against the higher income households who consume the good formerly imported but now produced at higher cost domestically. The depression of savings 'may, therefore, be due at least in part to the redistributive effect of import substituting industrialisation, rather than to the supposed depressive effect of inflation as such on the propensity of households to save' (Felix, 23, p. 380). Davis, looking for an explanation of Chile's remarkably low level of investment, shows that the rate of return on corporate investment in Chile is extremely low and suggests high labour costs as the chief explanation (12). Mamalakis, however, finds (39) the foreign exchange constraint to be the most important influence hampering investment and in turn attributes this to inflation (but see below).

Evidence on the negative effects on saving and investment is thus not as yet clear-cut; on the opposite side we have the evidence of Brazil, where inflation does not appear to have inhibited investment, despite legal ceilings on interest rates. The answer lies largely in evasion of controls, but also in good part in the possibility of institutional adaptation: already existing financial institutions develop methods of increasing the real return they can offer and new institutional forms spring up (the new credit and finance companies of Brazil, for example, where a depositor becomes a shareholder and receives interest in the form of a dividend which is not subject to a legal ceiling).[38]

The higher ratio of the price of investment goods to that of consumer goods which Dorrance finds empirically associated with inflation is an interesting phenomenon which again must have discouraged investment. Dorrance provides evidence of a correlation from data for nine Latin American countries (15, p. 81). But if Dorrance is right in associating the rise with industrialisation policies, then once more the argument is open to reversal: the significant fact *may* be that structural balance of payments problems led to import-substituting industrialisation, inflation and to the relative price shift in question.

Turning to the effect on the inflow of foreign capital, *a priori* there must be a disincentive effect if the exchange rate depreciates by an amount in excess of the internal price rise. For six strong inflation countries, Dorrance finds that exchange rates on average moved down by 75 per cent more than internal price levels rose over the years 1953 to 1959 (15). But Dorrance's data are for only six years; taking a longer period, 1950 to 1968, for the three Latin American countries included in his sample, Argentina, Brazil and Chile, gives the reverse result for both Brazil and Chile.[39] Further, if the investment is in the export sector, then the major components of an investor's costs and returns are given in foreign currency in any case, which very considerably reduces the significance of the argument. More impressive evidence comes from the negative association between the amount of inflation and the inflow of U.S. investment into Latin American countries which Dorrance observes over the years 1950 to 1961. But the correlation is no longer so clear when more recent years are included: taking 1950 to 1968, the moderate inflation countries received considerably more investment.[40] And the price stability and high U.S. investment in Central America and Venezuela may both reflect a particular export-oriented growth pattern, rather than being causally related to each other. Further, the fact that foreign investment flowed strongly into Brazil under Kubitschek reveals how easily government policy (in this case subsidy) and a strong growth trend can outweigh the effect of inflation. Only when foreign capital begins to anticipate stabilising action and so a fall in growth rates as a consequence of inflation is it really deterred. And finally, the significance of the deterrent effect of inflation on foreign capital is called into question at a more fundamental level by the growing school of thought among structuralists which sees foreign investment as having on balance negative developmental effects.[41]

The effect on the productivity of capital. The evidence on the effect of

H

inflation on productivity via distortions in resource allocation which derive from that inflation, does not suggest as yet that such effects are very serious. On the build-up of inventories, it is clear first of all that inflation *per se* does not lead to excessive investment in stocks. Neither Shaalan (58, p. 255) nor Dorrance (15, p. 54) find a correlation, and this is confirmed by Baer's discussion of inventory investment in Brazil (1, p. 128). The actual distortion is more temporary: there appears to be a tendency for inventory investment to accelerate with an acceleration of inflation, then to level off. This is found to hold for Brazil, Chile, Colombia and Mexico by Shaalan (58, p. 254). Roughly, according to Dorrance (15, p. 54), when the variability of the rate of inflation doubles so do inventories as a percentage of total investment.

On excessive investment in luxury housing, the evidence is not compelling. Felix points out (23, pp. 372–3) that non-inflationary countries such as Venezuela are also notorious for luxury housing. Baer finds no sign of excessive investment in real estate in Brazil, and attributes this to one of the ways in which inflationary situations tend to contain built-in mechanisms to control the evil effects of inflation – in this instance rent control (Baer, 1, pp. 129, 134).

The impact of controlled rates and prices in deterring investment is perhaps the most serious of the distortions of inflation, if an indirect one. No structuralist would wish to deny the contributory role of price controls in the poor performance of agriculture, for example. The importance of controlled rates in leading in particular to infrastructure bottlenecks is widely acknowledged: in the public sector, once a deficit exists then enormously strong pressures are immediately generated against investment in that sector, since this is seen as directly inflationary.

The effect of inflation on rational decision-making, on the other hand, remains a hypothesis, while an intuitively reasonable one. Baer and Simonsen (2) find for a small sample of Brazilian firms that profits were overstated by 20 per cent in 1958, when prices rose 16 per cent, and by 44 per cent in 1963, when prices rose nearly 50 per cent. But they only suggest, rather than show, that the result of the illusory profits may be undue decapitalisation. And some counter-evidence comes from an exploration of Brazilian businessmen's attitudes to inflation: the majority of those surveyed considered the inflationary environment had been favourable to development.[42]

Finally, the effect on the adoption of innovations is an untested, if plausible, hypothesis, and moreover raises the following problem: if there is more investment with inflation than with the relevant alternative, and if most technical progress is correctly argued to be 'embodied', may there not be more rapid innovation with inflation than without?

There is one further kind of evidence which could shed some light on the impact of inflation on the productivity of capital in general, via any of the above mechanisms. If there is clear evidence that marginal capital output ratios rise with inflation, then despite the numerous problems of data involved and the many other influences at work, would this not suggest that inflation has an adverse effect on the productivity of investment? However, Baer finds a negative correlation for Brazil 1947–60, at an average annual rate of inflation of about 20 per cent (1, p. 130), and Shaalan finds the same for Colombia, at an average annual rate of inflation just under 10 per cent (58, pp. 254–5). In any case the problem with the test is that since the marginal capital output ratio is itself dependent on the rate of growth, what we may in fact be observing is the relationship between inflation and growth itself. Thus it is not surprising that Shaalan finds a positive correlation for Argentina and Chile, where we have already argued that stabilisation programmes produced both depression and increased inflationary pressures. It is particularly clear in the case of Argentina that in years of increased inflation the higher marginal capital output ratios reflect short-run spare capacity, not less efficient investment. It is significant that during the periods covered by the data neither Brazil nor Colombia undertook serious stabilisation programmes.

The effect on the balance of payments. The impact on capital flows has already been discussed. The impact on the current account is clearly adverse in principle; however, as usual, the evidence on the extent of the damage is less clear. De Vries (69) finds no association between domestic inflation and the performance of major exports, though inflation did tend to deter the expansion of minor exports. Dorrance (15), using data from Lovasy (37), calculates that comparing 1958–9 with 1953–4, the weighted average [43] of the volume of exports for eight high inflation countries rose only 5 per cent, compared with 19 per cent for eight with moderate inflation and 24 per cent for sixteen stable countries. Dorrance notes that export price indices moved 'by approximately the same amount' for each group (15, p. 61). In fact according to his data export prices fell on average 16 per cent for the high inflation group as compared with 5 per cent for the stable countries and 10 per cent for the moderate inflation group – and if the volume had not risen so little the price fall would presumably have been greater. This suggests that it is very relevant to ask how far Lovasy's results in fact indicate an unfavourable export position leading to inflation, which may then subsequently lead to a further worsening of the balance of payments position. The unfavourable export position itself often of course results in part also from domestic pricing and exchange rate policy.

Summary and review. Summing up the evidence on the case against inflation as a developmental tool, it is clear that inflation has some detrimental effects on growth. This is not disputed: the widespread agreement on the evil effects of inflation is evidenced in structuralist writers such as Sunkel (65), Felix (23), Prebisch (51) and Sierra (61), to name but a few. At the same time, there is nothing conclusive in the empirical evidence to show that its bad effects cannot be successfully counterbalanced – by the dynamism of a growing economy, by government policy, or by chance effects such as the concomitance of rent control and inflation. But this is to talk of annual rates of 20 or perhaps 30 per cent. There appears to be further widespread agreement even among structuralists that once inflation exceeds this, the distortions become excessive and inflation has to be restrained.[44] However, it is worth noting that this consensus appears to be rooted in little more than a 'feeling for the situation'. It was only at much higher rates in Bolivia that the distortions became so clearly apparent.[45]

(e) Conclusion

What is the effect of inflation on the financing of development in Latin America? It should have become clear that we are not faced here with a simple situation where we can perceive inflation's effects on savings and investment, sum them up as good or bad on balance and proceed to policy conclusions. Instead we have a complex web of interactions, made the more confusing at every turn not only by the conspicuous lack of good empirical evidence, but also by the repeated introduction of political and social variables considered crucial by some and irrelevant by others.

To the writer at least, the most important point is that we cannot expect to look in any simple sense for the effect of inflation on the financing of development. This is essentially the wrong question: where we have inflation, for better or worse, continuing inflation in the short run is inevitable in the pursuit of acceptable development goals and structural reforms which may ultimately end inflation. It is conceivable that the bad effects of inflation on growth could be shown to be sufficiently great as to make this position self-contradictory. At the moment that does not appear to be the case.

It will be clear then that for the writer the structuralist framework emerges as the more convincing: the analysis which points up inevitability of inflation is intrinsically structuralist and rests on the structuralist's view of the development process. This is not to say that the structuralist analysis is without problems. The problems of short-run policy formation and the tendency to conceive of inflation as a totally non-monetary phenomenon, and hence perhaps to underplay the dangers of deficit financing, have already been commented on. Most important of all, perhaps both schools could be said to share a common weakness in the failure to face up to political realities. The monetarists fail to admit the relevance of the social and political consequences of their anti-inflationary policies. It may be that the structuralists, also, having very valid long-term policy prescriptions, will ultimately have to face, more fully than they have done, the extent to which the political and technical implications of structuralist measures are incompatible with present political, social and administrative systems in Latin America.

REFERENCES

1. W. Baer, *Industrialization and Economic Development in Brazil* (Irwin, Homewood, Ill., 1965).

2. W. Baer and M. Simonsen, 'Profit Illusion and Policy Making in an Inflationary Economy', in *Oxford Economic Papers* (July 1965).

3. W. Baer, 'The Inflation Controversy in Latin America: A Survey', in *Latin American Research Review*, ii, 2 (1967).

4. T. Balogh, 'Economic Policy and the Price System', in ECLA, *Economic Bulletin for Latin America*, vi, 1 (1961). Reprinted in Balogh, *The Economics of Poverty* (Weidenfeld & Nicolson, 1966).

5. S. L. Barraclough and A. L. Domike, 'Agrarian Structure in Seven Latin American Countries', in *Land Economics*, xlii, 4 (Nov 1966).

6. J. Bergsman and S. Morley, 'Import Constraints and Development: Causes of the Recent Decline of Brazilian Economic Growth: A Comment', in *Review of Economics and Statistics*, xi, 1 (Feb 1969).

7. J. O. Bray, 'Elements of the Agricultural Situation in Chile' (mimeo., Stanford University, Calif., 1961).

8. J. O. Bray, 'Acerca del Problema Agrario en Chile', in *Cuadernos de Economía* (University of Chile), ii, 4 (1964).

9. R. de Oliveira Campos, 'Two Views on Inflation in Latin America', in A. O. Hirschman (ed.), *Latin American Issues* (Twentieth Century Fund, New York, 1961).

10. G. A. Costanzo, *Programas de Estabilización Económica en América Latina* (Mexico, 1961).

11. T. E. Davis, 'Eight Decades of Inflation in Chile, 1879–1959: A Political Interpretation', in *Journal of Political Economy* (August 1963).

12. T. E. Davis, 'Changing Conceptions of the Development Problem: The Chilean Example', in *Economic Development and Cultural Change*, xiv, 1 (Oct 1965).

13. A. Delfim Netto, A. C. Pastore, P. Cipollari and E. P. de Carvalho 'Algunos Aspectos de Inflaçao Brasileira', in *Estudos ANPES*, i (São Paulo, 1965).

14. C. F. Diaz Alejandro, *Exchange Rate Devaluation in a Semi-Industrialised Country: The Experience of Argentina 1955–1961* (Cambridge, Mass., 1965).

15. G. S. Dorrance, 'The Effects of Inflation on Economic Development', in W. Baer and I. Kerstenetsky (eds), *Inflation and Growth in Latin America* (Irwin, Homewood, Ill., 1964).

16. G. S. Dorrance, 'Inflation and Growth: The Statistical Evidence', in *I.M.F. Staff Papers*, xiii, 1 (March 1966).

17. M. Edel, *Food Supply and Inflation in Latin America* (New York, 1969).

18. G. J. Eder, *Inflation and Development in Latin America: A Case Study of Inflation and Stabilization in Bolivia* (Michigan International Business Studies no. 8, University of Michigan, 1968).

19. E. Eshag and R. Thorp, 'The Economic and Social Consequences of Orthodox Economic Policies in Argentina in the Postwar Years', in *Bulletin of the Oxford University Institute of Economics and Statistics*, xxvii (Feb 1965). (Reprinted in 25.)

20. D. Felix, 'Industrialisation and Stabilisation Dilemmas in Latin America' in *Journal of Economic History*, xix, 4 (Dec 1959).

21. D. Felix, 'Structural Imbalances, Social Conflict and Inflation: An Appraisal of Chile's Recent Anti-Inflationary Effort', in *Economic Development and Cultural Change*, viii, 2 (Jan 1960).

22. D. Felix, 'An Alternative View of the "Monetarist–Structuralist" Controversy', in A. O. Hirschman (ed.), *Latin American Issues* (Twentieth Century Fund, New York, 1961).

23. D. Felix, 'Monetarists, Structuralists, and Import Substituting Industrialization: A Critical Appraisal', in W. Baer and I. Kerstenetsky, *Inflation and Growth in Latin America* (Irwin, Homewood, Ill., 1964).

24. A. Ferrer, *The Argentine Economy* (University of California Press, 1967).

25. A. Ferrer, M. Brodersohn, E. Eshag and R. Thorp, *Los Planes de Estabilización en la Argentina* (Editorial Paidos S.A.I.C.F., Buenos Aires, 1968).

26. K. B. Griffin, *Underdevelopment in Spanish America* (Allen & Unwin, London, 1969).

27. J. Grunwald, 'The "Structuralist" School on Price Stability and Development: The Chilean Case', in A. O. Hirschman (ed.), *Latin American Issues* (Twentieth Century Fund, New York, 1961).

28. A. Harberger, 'The Dynamics of Inflation in Chile', in C. Christ *et al.*, *Measurement in Economics: Studies in Mathematical Economics and Econometrics* (Stanford, 1963).

29. A. Harberger, 'Some Notes on Inflation in Latin America', in W. Baer and I. Kerstenetsky (eds), *Inflation and Growth in Latin America* (Irwin, Homewood, Ill., 1964).

30. A. O. Hirschman, *Journeys Toward Progress* (Twentieth Century Fund, New York, 1963).

31. A. O. Hirschman, 'The Political Economy of Import Substituting Industrialisation', in *Journal of Political Economy*, lxxvi (Dec 1968).

32. N. Kaldor, 'Economic Problems of Chile', in *Essays on Economic Policy*, ii (Duckworth, London, 1965).

33. Instituto de Economía, Universidad de Chile, *Formación de Capital en las Empresas Industriales* (Santiago, 1961).

34. I.M.F., *International Financial Statistics* (Washington).

35. N. Leff, 'Export Stagnation and Autarkic Development in Brazil, 1947–1962', in *Quarterly Journal of Economics*, lxxxi (May, 1967).

36. N. Leff, 'Import Constraints and Development: Causes of the Recent Decline in Brazilian Economic Growth', in *Review of Economics and Statistics*, xlix, 4 (Nov 1967).

37. G. Lovasy, 'Inflation and Exports in Primary Producing Countries', in *I.M.F. Staff Papers*, ix (1962).

38. M. J. Mamalakis, 'Forced Saving in an Underdeveloped Country', in *Economía Internazionale*, xvii (Aug 1964).

39. M. J. Mamalakis, 'Public Policy and Sectoral Development. A Case Study of Chile 1940–1958', in C. W. Reynolds and M. J. Mamalakis, *Essays on the Chilean Economy* (Irwin, Homewood, Ill., 1965).

40. G. Maynard and W. van Rijckeghem, 'Stabilisation Policy in an Inflationary Economy: Argentina', in G. F. Papanek (ed.), *Development Policy: Theory and Practice* (Harvard University Press, Cambridge, 1968).

41. A. McBean, *Export Instability and Economic Growth* (Harvard University Press, Cambridge, 1966).

42. A. Monti, 'Una Política de Desarrollo sin Inflación' (mimeo., ILPES, Santiago, Feb 1968).

43. M. W. Mueller, 'Structural Inflation and the Mexican Experience', in *Yale Economic Essays*, v, 1 (spring 1965).

44. Juan Noyola Vazquez, 'El Desarrollo Económico y la Inflación en Méjico y Otros Paises Latinoamericanos', in *Investigación Económica* (Mexico, 4th quarter 1956).

45. J. H. G. Olivera, 'La Teoría no Monetaria de la Inflación', in *Trimestre Económico*, xxvii (Feb–Mar 1960).

46. J. H. G. Olivera, 'On Structural Inflation and Latin American Structuralism', in *Oxford Economic Papers*, xvi, 3 (Nov 1964).

47. J. H. G. Olivera, 'Aspectos Dinámicos de la Inflación Estructural', in *Desarrollo Económico*, vii, 27 (Oct–Dec 1967).

48. A. Pinto, *Ni Estabilidad ni Desarrollo – la Política del Fondo Monetario Internacional* (Santiago, 1960).

49. A. Pinto, 'El Analisis de la Inflación "estructuralista" y "monetarista"', in *Revista de Economía Latinoamericana*, no. 4 (1961).

50. A. Pinto, 'Raíces Estructurales de la Inflación en América Latina', in *Trimestre Económico*, xxxv, 1 (Jan–March 1968).

51. R. Prebisch, 'Economic Development or Monetary Stability: The False Dilemma', in ECLA, *Economic Bulletin for Latin America*, vi, 1 (1961), 1 ff.

52. R. Prebisch, 'Commercial Policy in Underdeveloped Countries', in *American Economic Review, Papers and Proceedings*, xlix, (May 1959).

53. C. W. Reynolds, *The Mexican Economy: Twentieth Century Structure and Growth*: to be published.

54. T. W. Schultz, 'The Economics of Chilean Agriculture', in Schultz, *Agriculture and Economic Growth* (McGraw-Hill, 1968).

55. D. Seers, 'A Theory of Inflation and Growth in Underdeveloped Countries Based on the Experience of Latin America', in *Oxford Economic Papers*, N.S. xiv (June 1962).

56. D. Seers, 'Inflation and Growth: A Summary of Experience in Latin

America', in ECLA, *Economic Bulletin for Latin America*, xii, 1 (Feb 1962).

57. D. Seers, 'Inflation and Growth: The Heart of the Controversy', in W. Baer and I. Kerstenetsky, *Inflation and Growth in Latin America* (Irwin, Homewood, Ill., 1964).

58. A. S. Shaalan, 'The Impact of Inflation on the Composition of Private Domestic Investment', in *I.M.F. Staff Papers*, ix, 2 (July 1962).

59. B. N. Siegel, *Inflación y Desarrollo: Las Experiencias de Méjico* (Centro de Estudios Monetarios Latinoamericanos, Mexico, 1960).

60. E. Sierra, 'La Investigación de la Inflación y las Políticas de Estabilización', in *Revista de Economía y Administración*, 4th year (Universidad de la Concepción, 1967).

61. E. Sierra, *Políticas de Estabilización: la Experiencia Chilena en el decenio 1956–1966* (mimeo., ILPES, Santiago, June 1969).

62. M. Simonsen, 'Inflation and Money Markets', in H. Ellis (ed.), *The Economy of Brazil* (University of California Press, Berkeley, 1969).

63. M. Simonsen, *A Experiencia Inflacionaria no Brasil* (Instituto de Pesquisas e Estudos Sociais, 1964).

64. L. Solis, 'Inflación, Estabilidad y Desarrollo: el caso de Méjico', in *Trimestre Económico*, xxxv, 3 (July–Sept 1968).

65. O. Sunkel, 'La Inflación Chilena: un Enfoque Heterodoxo', in *Trimestre Económico*, xxv (Mexico, Oct–Dec 1958). English version: 'Inflation in Chile: An Unorthodox Approach', in *International Economic Papers*, no. 10 (London and New York, 1960).

66. J. Ternent, 'Inflation and Private Investment in Latin America' (unpublished doctoral dissertation, University of Oregon, March 1967).

67. R. Thorp, 'Inflation and Orthodox Economic Policy in Peru', in *Bulletin of the Oxford University Institute of Economics and Statistics*, xxix (Aug 1967).

68. United States Department of Commerce, *Survey of Current Business*.

69. B. A. de Vries, *Export Experiences of Developing Countries* (Johns Hopkins Press, Baltimore, Md, 1967).

70. T. Walther, 'Stabilization Policies in Latin America 1956–1960' (unpublished doctoral dissertation, New School, 1964).

NOTES

1. I would like to thank the Centre for Latin American Studies, University of California, Berkeley, for financial support. I would also like to thank Albert Fishlow and Ernest Nadel for very helpful comments on an earlier version.

2. United Nations Economic Commission for Latin America.

3. See especially Seers, 55, pp. 192–5, for a good bibliographical comment. Pp. 185-8 of this section draw heavily on the works listed there, and perhaps most heavily of all on the really excellent article by Seers published by ECLA in 1962 (Seers, 56, pp. 23–51).

4. This strategy will be referred to by ECLA's term: import-substituting industrialisation. For an excellent analysis of it, see Hirschman, 31.

5. The bottlenecks have been amply and clearly described by numerous writers. The following summary omits many details of the argument. For more detail, see Felix, 22. Seers, 55, gives a very full presentation of the foreign exchange bottleneck.

6. The reasons form the core of the Prebisch–Singer thesis concerning the unfavourable trend in the terms of trade of primary products. See for example Prebisch, 52. Felix, 22, pp. 88–9, gives a good brief summary.

7. See Seers, 55, pp. 179–80, for a good discussion of why it is high cost.

8. This argument is peculiar to Chile, where the dependence of public revenue on copper taxes is unusually high.

9. *Given* a low level of reserves which impel action. This seems to be the significant point which McBean does not explore in his analysis of the impact of export revenue fluctuations, in which he shows that there is no obvious statistical evidence of any significant impact of such fluctuations on domestic activity or price levels (McBean, 41).

10. That is, 'the flow of money exchanged for goods and services accommodates itself to price level variations rather than the other way round' (Olivera, 46, p. 326).

11. 47, p. 266. To get this result he assumes that a 1 per cent rise in the price of food leads to a 0·9 per cent rise in money wages the following year, and that a 1 per cent rise in wages leads to a 0·9 per cent rise in manufactured goods prices within the same year. The latter assumption in particular appears somewhat strong, as wages are not the only component of costs.

12. Hirschman, 30. See also Davis, 11.

13. In a speech to a conference on 'Technology and the Third World' at Stanford University, October 1969.

14. Costanzo, 10. See also Campos, 9, for a well-known monetarist's exposition.

15. See the discussion of the relations between inflation and growth, section (*d*) below, for a fuller explanation of this.

16. See below, section (*d*) for a full discussion.

17. As Haberler points out (quoted in Mamalakis, 38) the additional saving *is* voluntary. The term is something of a misnomer.

18. See Mamalakis, 38, for an excellent analysis of the term 'forced saving', its use in the literature and its weaknesses as a growth-promoting mechanism in less-developed countries.

19. Eshag and Thorp, 19.

20. This is not to deny the very great importance of such work. The interactions of the different variables and the kind of lags involved have to be understood, even if 'causes' lie deeper.

21. Comité Interamericano de Desarrollo Agricola. Country studies have so far been published on Argentina, Brazil, Columbia, Chile, Ecuador, Guatemala and Peru, and others are under way.

22. See also Barraclough and Domike, 5.

23. See Mueller, 43, and the discussion of Mexico below.

24. Baer, 1.

25. See Grunwald, 27, pp. 97–8, for further references.

26. U for unorthodox. Classified in descending order of size, the group U countries are Brazil, Argentina, Mexico, Colombia, Chile, Peru, Uruguay, Bolivia and Paraguay.

27. In an indirect fashion. See the discussion of Mexico below, pp. 208-9.

28. See Solis, 64, and the further discussion of Mexico below.

29. Group O (orthodox) – Venezuela, Ecuador, Central America and the independent Caribbean States.

30. Sunkel, 65; Pinto, 48; Sierra, 60, 61; Felix, 21; Eshag and Thorp, 19; Ferrer, 24, 25; Diaz Alejandro, 14.

31. M. Brodersohn, paper read to Stanford–Berkeley Colloquium of Latin Americanists, April 1969.

32. The following analysis of Mexico draws very heavily on a paper by Solis (64).

33. The public works benefited the larger holdings rather than the *ejidos* set up by the agrarian reform, which until recently have performed very poorly. Nevertheless this expansion of commercial agriculture is linked by several analysts directly to the revolution and the land reform, through the change in attitudes in regard to holding land, and through the 'revolutionary heritage' necessitating public investment in rural areas. This commitment could apparently be fulfilled by investment which notoriously neglected the true children of the revolution, the *ejidatarios*. See Reynolds, 53, and Edel, 17, pp. 119–27, and the references given there.

34. The increasing role of private savings is denied in an earlier study by Siegel (59), but his data are poor and his conclusion cannot be relied on. See Reynolds 53.

35. There were in fact substantial increases in indirect taxes in 1957 and 1958, which were also years of much slower inflation than the average for 1955–60.

36. The various analysts disagree on the most relevant causes. See for example, Leff, 35, 36; Baer, 1; Bergsman and Morley, 6.

37. See the work of Sierra (60, 61) and Monti (42) available in mimeographed form from ECLA.

38. See Simonsen, 62, for a description both of the detrimental effects of inflation on money and capital markets in Brazil, and of the extent to which the system was able to adapt.

39. The data are from 34, and Dorrance's methodology was used.

40. The calculations were based on data given in 68, October 1969.

41. See for example Griffin, 26, ch. 3.

42. Raimer Richers, 'O Empresario e a Inflacao Brasileira', in *Revista de Administracao de Empresa* (May–Aug 1962), quoted by Baer, 1, pp. 131–2.

43. Country totals are weighted by 1959 export values.

44. Monetarists of course put the ceiling much lower – between 5 and 10 per cent a year, depending on the author.

45. The problem is that given that this consensus exists, it may be to some extent its own justification. As suggested above, as inflation accelerates the investment climate may be affected just by the belief that restrictive measures must be in the offing. As soon as growth decelerates but built-in inflationary mechanisms continue to operate, all eyes are turned to inflation as the culprit and stabilisation measures indeed follow.

7. The Role of Foreign Capital

KEITH GRIFFIN

THE apparent role of foreign capital in financing investment in Latin America varies enormously from one country to another. This can be seen by comparing the deficit on the current account of the balance of payments (which measures the net inflow of foreign capital) with total gross domestic savings. In the period 1960–7 foreign savings accounted for —7·2 per cent of total gross savings in Venezuela, i.e. there was a net capital outflow. On the other hand in Nicaragua in 1965–7 over a third of total savings originated abroad. The average for Latin America as a whole probably is about 12 per cent.[1]

Foreign savings may be transferred to an underdeveloped country in several ways. A large proportion of the capital inflow in Latin America consists of grants and loans from the U.S. government. Some of this foreign aid is in the form of cash grants, some takes the form of gifts of surplus agricultural commodities, but most consists of loans tied to purchases of goods produced in the United States. Another major source of foreign aid is the international lending agencies, notably the World Bank group and the Inter-American Development Bank. Finally, there are private foreign savings. In principle these savings could be transferred through grants, purchases of financial assets (e.g. equities or government bonds) or through direct investment. In practice only the latter is important, and most of this is done by large U.S. corporations.

The consequences of a given capital inflow for the recipient country depend, at least in part, upon the precise manner in which the savings are transferred. Gifts and grants, for example, are a one-way transfer; they do not give rise to a return flow of resources. Loans, in contrast, give rise to fixed repayment obligations which occur over a specified number of years. This inevitably introduces a certain amount of inflexibility into a country's balance of payments accounts. Direct private investments also lead to a reverse flow of resources – in the form of repatriated profits – but the amount and duration of this reverse flow usually is indeterminate. Some indication of the composition of the capital inflow in Latin America – and the extent of profit repatriation, amortisation and interest payments – is provided in the table below.

In the period 1961–8 there was an average yearly inflow of public grants and loans, after deducting amortisation and interest charges, of approximately $572 million. This was more than offset, however, by a net outflow of resources associated with private foreign capital of about $703 million. The net contribution of all foreign capital movements was to aggravate Latin America's balance of payments difficulties

Table 1. Capital Movements in Latin America: Annual Average 1961–68
(millions of dollars)

1. AID grants[a]	131·4
2. Foreign loans[b]	938·0
3. Amortisation of foreign loans	310·9
4. Interest on foreign loans	186·8
5. Net movement of foreign grants and loans	571·7
6. U.S. direct private investment[c]	360·5
7. Profit and interest repayments on (6)[c]	1,063·1
8. Net movement of private capital[c]	−702·6
9. Net movement of all capital	−130·9

[a] Figures for grants refer to authorisations, not disbursements.

[b] Loans of the World Bank group, AID, Export–Import Bank and the Inter-American Development Bank.

[c] Average of the period 1960–7.

Source: Organisation of American States.

by $131 million a year. In other words, the reverse flows associated with (earlier) foreign capital substantially exceed the current inflow of capital. If all the capital inflow in this period had been in the form of grants, the region would have been better off by $1,561 million a year! Clearly the composition of capital imports makes a difference. Alternatively, if all foreign capital were confiscated and governments were to default on the foreign debt, the balance of payments of the region would improve by $131 million – assuming efficiency in the confiscated enterprises were maintained.

(a) The Macro-economics of Foreign Capital

Economists tend to view the role of foreign capital in rather abstract terms, ignoring the precise way in which the savings are transferred. Many models have been constructed which attempt to show how capital imports affect the aggregate behaviour of an economy.[2] The usual point of departure is the Harrod growth equation: $g = sk$, where g is the proportional rate of growth of national income, s the proportion of national income saved and invested, and k the incremental output–capital ratio. If a country receives an inflow of foreign capital, a, expressed as a fraction of its national income, the growth rate rises to $g = (s + a)k$.

Some economists argue that the marginal propensity to save is higher than the average, so that a given inflow of foreign capital has two effects: first, it supplements domestic savings and leads to a higher rate of accumulation of capital and, second, it raises *per capita* income and hence the proportion of income saved. As a result capital imports increase a country's capacity for growth. Eventually, it is argued, growth will become 'self-sustaining' and the need for further foreign aid or private foreign investment will cease.

Other economists argue that the difficulties experienced by many underdeveloped countries, particularly those in Latin America, arise not from their inability or unwillingness to save but from their inability to acquire foreign exchange by exporting. Accordingly, these economists view the role of foreign capital not as supplementing savings but as supplementing foreign exchange earnings. It is the 'foreign exchange gap', not the 'savings gap', which restrains growth. The implication of models which emphasise the 'foreign exchange gap' is that potential domestic savings are being frustrated because at least some of the capital goods necessary to undertake desired investment are not produced domestically and cannot be obtained from abroad. If additional foreign exchange were available the level of investment and the rate of growth would increase.

In an *ex post* or accounting sense the foreign exchange and savings gaps must be equal, but it is argued that they need not be identical *ex ante*. The weakness of this argument is that it assumes domestic and foreign resources cannot be substituted. Suppose, for example, that foreign exchange is the binding constraint on growth. In this case the theory implies that although domestic production can be increased – and the community is willing to refrain from consuming too much of it – it is impossible either to increase exports or substitute domestic production for imports. Output which is not consumed can neither be sold abroad nor used to replace goods purchased abroad.

In other words, it is assumed that the economy is extremely rigid: it can produce neither capital goods, nor export goods nor import substitutes. It is possible, of course, that a country is unwilling rather than unable to introduce policies which would earn or save foreign exchange. In such cases it might appear that foreign exchange is the binding constraint, but it is the unwillingness to reduce domestic consumption in order to expand exports or reduce imports which is the source of the difficulty. Thus, ultimately, there can be only one constraint on investment, viz. savings, and it is the contribution of capital imports to total savings that is important for economic growth.

(b) Capital Imports and Domestic Consumption

Most models of economic growth are based on the assumption that any increase in foreign capital is devoted entirely to raising the rate of capital accumulation. In other words, capital imports supplement domestic savings rather than consumption. I have argued at some length elsewhere that on theoretical grounds one should expect the opposite.[3] That is, capital imports act essentially as a substitute for savings and a large proportion of foreign capital ultimately is used to increase consumption rather than investment.

If one takes planned growth rates seriously, this is what one would expect to happen. That is, governments have, and are encouraged by foreign lenders to have, growth targets. From these targets and an assumption about the incremental output–capital ratio the amount of investment needed to achieve the target can be estimated. This investment can be financed either from domestic savings or from capital imports. Assuming the government wants to achieve its growth objective at the lowest possible cost in terms of reduced current consumption, it will substitute foreign capital for domestic savings to the fullest extent possible.

Is there any evidence that this in fact happens? Yes, there is.

A group from the Organisation of American States recently calculated a savings function for eighteen Latin American countries using data from about 1960. The group used multiple regression analysis, regressing current domestic savings (S_t) on current national product (Y_t) and the net capital inflow (A_t). Their results were as follows:[4]

$$S_t = 0 \cdot 1716\,Y_t - 0 \cdot 6702\,A_t : R^2 = 0 \cdot 75$$
$$(0 \cdot 005) \qquad (0 \cdot 204)$$

The equation indicates that savings are positively associated with current income and inversely associated with capital imports. About two-thirds of all capital imports, in fact, were used to supplement consumption and only about a third was used to increase investment.

These results are supported by a time-series analysis of a single country. In a study of Colombia in the period 1950–63, I smoothed out the biannual coffee cycle by using a two-year moving average and then regressed domestic savings on foreign capital. The estimated equation is as follows:[5]

$$\frac{S}{Y} = 21 \cdot 5 - 0 \cdot 84 \frac{A}{Y}; \ R^2 = 0 \cdot 43$$
$$(0 \cdot 29)$$

That is, in Colombia it appears that about four-fifths of the capital inflow was used to supplement consumption and only about one-fifth to supplement capital accumulation.

Lastly, Luis Landau ran a series of regressions on time-series data for twenty Latin American countries. These were multiple regression equations. The dependent variable was *per capita* savings and the explanatory variables were *per capita* income plus either the export surplus (i.e. net capital outflow), export proceeds or a price index of exports. Landau found that of the last three independent variables, only the export surplus gave consistently good results.[6] His findings are summarised below.

Partial regression coefficient	Export surplus	Export proceeds	Price index of exports
Positive (+)	18	11	8
Negative (−)	0	2	7
Not significant statistically	2	7	5

In all the countries studied except Brazil and the Dominican Republic, Landau found a statistically significant positive association between savings and the export surplus. In other words, everything else being equal, the larger the inflow of foreign capital the lower domestic savings.[7]

Thus there is some basis in theory and fact for supposing that capital imports contribute relatively little towards financing development; most capital imports are used to finance consumption. This in itself may not be undesirable. Increased consumption of certain items may actually raise the productivity of labour or contribute indirectly to faster growth. Even if this did not occur, one might defend an increase in consumption provided that it helped to raise the material well-being of the poorest members of the community. On the other hand, if most of the capital imports are used to subsidize the consumption of the rich, neither the productive capacity of the economy nor the welfare of those most in need is increased. It would be very hard to justify borrowing abroad and incurring repayment obligations if the capital imports were used largely to subsidise the consumption of relatively prosperous groups.

Obviously, one cannot reach a final judgement on the role of foreign capital without knowing to what extent it supplements consumption rather than investment, to what extent the increased consumption and investment so financed raise national income, and to what extent the increased consumption goes to the poorest classes. A great deal depends upon the precise mechanism by which capital imports reduce domestic savings.

First, public savings may decline. This may happen if either tax receipts fall or there is a change in the composition of government expenditure. Tax revenues will decline if (1) the government reduces taxation, or (2) less effort is made to collect taxes, or (3) given inflation and an inelastic tax system, tax rates are not raised periodically. Equally important, the government may respond to increased foreign capital by changing the composition of its expenditure in favour of public consumption. State capital formation may remain virtually unchanged, and be financed in effect by foreign savings, while the expansion of government expenditure is directed towards providing more public consumption, e.g. higher salaries for civil servants and teachers, increased employment on the railways, greater social security benefits, etc.

Second, foreign capital may lower private domestic savings. The foreign capital may be channelled to private indigenous entrepreneurs via easy credit loans from industrial development banks or similar institutions. The availability of debt finance on soft terms may reduce the incentive of local investors to save. Alternatively, private foreign capital may enter the economy through participation in mixed enterprises. In this case it is probable that foreigners will supply at least some capital that indigenous entrepreneurs would have saved themselves – out of retained profits, for instance. Yet another alternative is for private foreign capital to establish wholly owned enterprises. In this case they are likely to compete directly with local investors – and, indeed, may be granted special tax and import privileges which enable them to do so. Foreign capitalists may pre-empt the most profitable investment opportunities and the strong, direct competition faced by local investors may tend to reduce the supply of indigenous entrepreneurship and savings.

Finally, capital imports may reduce domestic savings by stimulating the consumption of importables and exportables. The increased availability of imported goods which foreign capital facilitates may lead to an increase in their consumption. Perhaps even more likely, the increased availability of foreign exchange which accompanies capital imports may induce the government to adopt or maintain inappropriate exchange rates or other trade policies. The consequence of these policies may be to reduce the effort devoted to exporting and to increase domestic consumption of potential export goods.

It is difficult to generalise further without specifying more accurately the type of capital import one is considering. Accordingly, we shall next discuss the role of foreign aid in Latin America and then examine the importance of private foreign capital.

(c) The Contribution of Aid

The amount of aid authorised for Latin America was no higher in 1968 than it was in 1961. In real terms it was considerably lower, since world prices rose substantially in the last decade. Moreover, in *per capita* terms it was lower still, since the population of Latin America grew nearly 3 per cent a year in this period. Finally, the absolute amount of dollar aid to Latin America is likely to decline in the current decade. Thus there is a very pronounced trend for real aid per head to fall.

Table 2. Latin America: Aid Authorisations, 1961–68
(millions of dollars)

	1961	*1967*	*1968*
Grants and loans	1172	1711	1947
U.S. Government	605	1052	942
World Bank	277	167	579
Inter-American Development Bank	290	493	427
Compensatory finance	1255	391	429
Total	2426	2103	2376

Source: Organisation of American States.

The distribution of foreign aid among the various countries of the region appears to be totally arbitrary. There is no evidence that donors systematically reward those countries which are making rapid progress, nor is there evidence that those countries which are encountering difficulties receive special attention. Uruguay and Peru have received approximately the same amount of aid, yet *per capita* income was rising rapidly in the latter and falling in the former. There certainly is no

I

correlation between poverty and aid authorisations, as a glance at Table 3 will indicate. Colombia and Brazil have virtually the same *per capita* income, yet Colombia received more than twice as much aid per head as Brazil. Chile is over twice as rich as Honduras, yet received about three times as much aid. Obviously, the allocations are largely based on political criteria, as is most evident, perhaps, in the case of Haiti.

Table 3. Aid Authorisations *Per Capita*, 1961–67
(U.S. dollars)

Argentina	33·77	Haiti	2·45
Bolivia	64·48	Honduras	48·42
Brazil	22·74	Mexico	28·24
Chile	142·18	Nicaragua	70·98
Colombia	53·93	Panama	104·30
Costa Rica	92·86	Paraguay	51·06
Dominican Republic	53·09	Peru	38·83
Ecuador	35·15	Trinidad and Tobago	64·69
El Salvador	37·94	Uruguay	39·72
Guatemala	20·87	Venezuela	69·81

Source: Organisation of American States.

So far we have made no distinction between one type of aid and another. Clearly, however, there are enormous differences between an AID grant of $1 million; a loan from IDA of $1 million at a rate of interest of 0·75 per cent, with a ten-year grace period and forty years to amortise the debt; and a loan of $1 million from the 'ordinary resources' of the Inter-American Development Bank, bearing an interest rate of 6·81 per cent, with a grace period of four years and only twelve years to amortise the debt.

These different types of foreign assistance can be made more comparable by calculating the 'grant element' of each type of loan. A loan on purely commercial terms would contain no grant element at all, and should not be considered foreign aid. At the other extreme, a gift contains a 100 per cent grant element. In between are various kinds of loans which contain concessional elements of one sort or another. Assuming that the alternative to a concessional loan was a commercial loan at 9 per cent, a research team at the O.A.S. has estimated the grant element of the foreign assistance received by Latin America in the period 1961–7. They discovered that the average grant element of loans was only 37·8 per cent, and the grant element for all foreign assistance was only 46·8 per cent. Moreover, if the effects of tied aid are taken into account, the grant element falls further, to somewhere in the range 38·3–42·2 per cent. In other words, about 60 per cent of the nominal aid given to Latin America should not be considered aid at all; these are resources provided on commercial terms. The remaining 40 per cent, however, represents a donation by the donor countries to the region.

The conclusion so far is that aid to Latin America is increasing very slowly if at all, it is arbitrarily distributed and much of it is provided on essentially commercial terms. Moreover, as we argued in the previous section, most aid leads to higher consumption rather than investment. We now wish to argue that the impact of foreign aid on the total investment programme may result in a lower output–capital ratio. As a consequence, the slight increase in aggregate investment which capital inflows finance tends to be offset in whole of in part by the reduced effectiveness of investment, so that the rate of growth of national income fails to rise perceptively.

Obviously, an important step in the analysis is the hypothesis that the output–capital ratio will tend to fall as aid increases. Why does this occur?

One reason is the motives of the aid donors.[8] Donor countries use aid as an instrument to achieve many objectives, among which economic development is only one. Political objectives are paramount, and in most instances these can best be achieved and goodwill in the recipient country established by concentrating on large, dramatic, highly visible projects which can stand as monuments to the generosity of the donors. The demand for monumental projects is likely to create its own supply, but in the process the effectiveness of investment will almost certainly diminish.

In other cases the involvement of donors in the politics of the host country goes far beyond the financing of monumental projects. In Brazil, for example, U.S. assistance in the early 1960s was reduced and lending by the World Bank suspended until a military regime came to power in 1964. The Pearson report noted that the

United States suspended disbursement of a $100 million loan in August, 1961, when one President resigned (after less than a year in office), released part of the loan again later in the year, and then suspended it again during the protracted debate between the partisans of the parliamentary, as against the presidential, form of government. . . . The World Bank also suspended new project loans between 1961 and 1964, though it made disbursem ents on existing loans. Only after the change of government in April, 1964, and the establishment of more coherent internal policies did aid to Brazil take on a sustained and developmental character.[9]

A second reason why foreign aid tends to reduce the effectiveness of investment is that aid agencies have certain ideological biases against government ownership of directly productive activities. Since aid usually is channelled directly to the government of the recipient country, this ideological bias tends to alter the pattern of investment in favour of social overhead capital and economic infrastructure – transport facilities, electric energy, housing and schools. Road construction is encouraged; factory construction is discouraged. It is possible, of course, that in some countries infrastructure deserves priority, but a general bias against directly productive activities should tend to lower the aggregate output–capital ratio. In the table below one can see that only about a third of the sector loans to Latin America were allocated to directly productive activities (agriculture, mining and industry); the remaining two-thirds were spent on social and economic infrastructure.

Table 4. The Percentage Composition of Sector Loans, 1961–67

Agriculture	14·8
Mining	4·9
Industry	13·2
Transport	19·4
Communications	1·3
Electric power	21·5
Multisectoral loans	7·8
Water and sewage	6·8
Housing	6·1
Education	2·0
Public health	0·3
Government	0·1
Not classified	1·7
Total	100·0

Source: Organisation of American States.

Furthermore, quite apart from motives and ideology, the administration of aid programmes tends to lower the effectiveness of investment. If an agency is going to lend $60 million to a country it would normally prefer to finance one project costing $60 million than 60 projects costing $1 million each. By concentrating on a few large projects the agency can reduce the difficulties of supervising its projects and keep down its administrative costs. For this reason, aid programmes tend to sponsor large dams rather than small irrigation schemes, major highways (such as the Pan-American highway) rather than secondary roads, university buildings rather than small rural schools, etc. Again, there is no presumption that large projects have a higher rate of return than small projects. If anything, the opposite may be true, and any systematic tendency to alter the pattern of investment in favour of large schemes is likely to alter the output–capital ratio.

One of the great difficulties with project aid is that assistance normally can be used only to finance the foreign exchange costs of a project. This practice induces countries, first, to select projects which are intensive in foreign exchange and, second, to design any given project so as to maximise the foreign exchange component of total costs. This additional bias in project selection and design reduces still further the impact on growth of any given volume of investment.

Finally, there is tied aid. From the recipient's point of view tied aid tends to lead, first, to a higher cost of imported goods – since the prices of goods imported under tied aid agreements will almost certainly be higher than world prices – and, second, to a continuing flow of high cost imports in the form of spare parts and ancillary equipment complementary to the aid-financed imports. Thus a country may become 'locked in' to a high cost source of supply via tied aid, and this might permanently lower the competitiveness of its investments. It certainly is not obvious that a larger volume of aid that is tied is preferable to less aid that is untied. Indeed the practice of tying aid greatly increases the costs of investment to Latin America, lowers the aggregate output–capital ratio and reduces the international competitiveness of aid-financed activities. There are few precise estimates of the costs of tied aid, but it is becoming accepted that the direct 'excess costs' of aid-financed imports are about 12–24 per cent. The indirect costs are indeterminate, but they clearly are not negligible.

Thus, for all the reasons enumerated in this section, the contribution of foreign aid to financing development in Latin America has not been very great. In the past there has been virtually no correlation between the amounts of aid received and a country's growth performance. An important reason for this, as the Pearson report noted, is that 'much aid was given in ways which did not make it as efficient a contribution to development as it could have been'.[10]

(d) The Importance of Private Foreign Investment

The role of private direct investment in promoting economic development is a subject surrounded by controversy. On the one hand there are those who emphasise the positive aspects of foreign investment. These include a transfer of capital, foreign exchange, technology and managerial techniques; the creation of employment opportunities and the training of labour; plus the payment of taxes to the host government. Others go further, claiming that 'in many developing countries, the external economies radiating from foreign investments involve notable improvements in infrastructure and social overhead facilities. Foreign investors can also stimulate local enterprise. . . .'[11] At the other extreme are those who believe the large international corporation is simply an instrument of neocolonialism.

Some of the alleged benefits of private foreign investment (e.g. increased tax payments and increased employment) would arise from any investment, however financed. Other benefits (e.g. the transfer of technology and managerial techniques) could be obtained not only through direct investment but also through management contracts or joint ventures. Still other benefits (e.g. increased foreign exchange) could be obtained as easily by borrowing abroad as by encouraging private direct investment. Thus one must beware of statements which seem to imply that private foreign investment has a special or unique contribution to make in accelerating development.

Perhaps the most likely contribution of private overseas investment is the provision of capital and foreign exchange. In practice, however, it seldom provides much of either, and when it does so, severe social and political tensions are likely to be created. If the rate of profit on foreign investment exceeds the rate of growth of the host economy, an increasing share of the nation's total assets will tend to be in foreign hands, and a growing proportion of the capitalist class will be composed of aliens. This is certain to be unacceptable in most underdeveloped countries, Latin America not excluded. As Felipe Pazos has said, 'A workable capitalist system is one which is made up of local capitalists, not foreign capitalists and local workers. The latter obviously has adverse social implications.'[12]

The problem of alienation of the stock of capital is avoided if foreigners repatriate their profits rather than reinvest them in the host economy. If the rate of repatriation of profits exceeds the rate of growth of exports, however, balance of payments problems for the host economy will be created. Foreign investment, far from contributing to foreign exchange receipts, detracts from them. In fact, foreign investment will make a net addition to foreign exchange only if the rate of investment is greater than the net profit rate.[13]

U.S. private foreign investment in Latin America has declined sharply since the late 1950s and the stock of foreign-owned capital is growing less rapidly than the region's G.N.P. Moreover, there has been a radical change in the composition of foreign investment. Until recently, most private overseas investment was in the extractive industries, particularly petroleum. Venezuela, in fact, was by far the largest recipient of private foreign capital. Today, however, most foreign investment is going into import-substituting industries in the manufacturing sector. Between 1957 and 1967 the share of manufacturing in total U.S. direct private investment rose from roughly 10 per cent to 60 per cent. The absolute amount invested, however, rose much less dramatically. The change in composition was due in large part to the decline in investment in petroleum from $965 million in 1957 to only $6 million in 1967.

Table 5. Net Inflow of U.S. Direct Private Investment

	1957		*1965*		*1967*	
	$ million	*%*	*$ million*	*%*	*$ million*	*%*
Petroleum	965	62·3	−37	−6·2	6	1·5
Mining	150	9·7	67	11·2	93	21·8
Manufacturing	166	10·7	411	69·0	259	60·5
Other	268	17·3	155	26·0	69	16·2
Total	1550	100·0	596	100·0	427	100·0

Note: Figures are net of amortisation.

Source: U.S. Department of Commerce, *Survey of Current Business*.

It is clear from the above table that private foreign capital is making a small and declining contribution to total investment in the region. We have already seen, in Table 1, that its contribution to foreign exchange receipts is negative, profit and interest repayments exceeding direct investment by over $700 million a year.

Now let us consider more carefully how private overseas investment is financed. Much of the literature is misleading in that it implies that for each million dollars invested by foreigners there is a transfer from abroad of foreign savings of an equivalent amount. In general, only about a quarter of the investment by U.S. manufacturing subsidiaries in Latin America is financed by what the U.S. Department of Commerce calls 'U.S. funds', i.e. fresh capital exported by the United States. Another quarter is provided from 'internal funds', i.e. from retained profits of the subsidiary. The remaining half consists of 'foreign funds', i.e. funds raised locally on the capital market or borrowed from local banks.   In other words, half the U.S. investment in manufacturing in Latin America is financed by Latin American savings. If all direct foreign investment ceased, on this reckoning 'foreign' investment would decline by only 50 per cent. If all foreign assets were confiscated, and the existing enterprises were run no less efficiently, total 'foreign' investment would decline by only 25 per cent. Most of the resources used to finance foreign investment in Latin America are generated within the region; they are not contributed from abroad.

Table 6. Financing of U.S. Manufacturing Subsidiaries, 1958–65

	$ million	%
U.S. funds	1100	26·5
Foreign funds	2044	49·5
Internal funds	993	24·0
Total	4137	100·0

Source: U.S. Department of Commerce, *Survey of Current Business*.

Thus the quantitative effects of private overseas investment on transferring savings and foreign exchange are negligible. If foreign investment is important in Latin America, it must be for its qualitative effects. These qualitative effects, however, may be adverse, e.g. if the competition from foreign investors reduces the supply of local entrepreneurship. This has been recognised in a recent paper by Professor Hirschman. He speaks of 'the displacement of local factors and stunting of local abilities which can occur in the wake of international investment . . . as when local banks or businesses are bought out by foreign capital; this has in fact been happening recently with increasing frequency in Latin America'.[14] Hirschman's analysis leads him to 'a simple conclusion: strictly from the point of view of development, private foreign investment is a mixed blessing, and the mixture is likely to become more noxious at the intermediate stage of development which characterizes much of present-day Latin America'.[15] I concur with this opinion.

(e) International Capital Movements in a Dynamic World

Most explanations of international trade and capital movements are based on static models, but the world in which we live is radically different from the world implicit in the most widely accepted theories. We live in a world characterised by continuous and rapid change, and this change is largely a consequence of changes in resource endowments and the availability of factors of production. A growing country's factors of production are not 'given', they are themselves produced – as a result of the accumulation of capital, the provision of widespread technological education and the acquisition of practical skills through experience.

The industrial countries grow rapidly, and hence are able to adjust quickly to changed circumstances, because they produce their own means of production. It is the rapid accumulation of capital per man, changes in technique and the expansion of knowledge – in short, rapid technical progress – which distinguishes the economically strong countries from the weak. Technological progress is a product of the wealthy countries; it is endogenous to their economies and it is this which makes them so dynamic. As a result of rapid technical progress new consumer goods are designed and manufactured, methods of production are improved and new inputs are created. This activity causes relative prices to change and induces a continuous reallocation of resources towards the most productive sectors. In consequence the innovating country enjoys rapid and substantial shifts in its comparative advantage.

Change, of course, also is occurring in the underdeveloped countries, but the rich countries are the centre of change, the creators of change, while the poor simply adapt passively as best they can. Moreover, endogenous change in the rich countries is a product of growth, and the fact that income per head is rising quickly enables the rich to respond and adjust swiftly and with minimum disturbance to any exogenous shocks that may occur. The rapid growth of man-made fibres and synthetic rubber, for example, have made a small but positive contribution to the prosperity of the industrial nations, but these same innovations have been a threat to the growth and stability of several underdeveloped nations. They have forced primary producers to accept lower prices and allocate resources to previously unattractive activities; failure to do so would have resulted in even lower levels of income and consumption.

Sir Dennis Robertson suggested over fifteen years ago that there were severe disadvantages to free international trade if technological progress is concentrated systematically on a few countries, and if the rest of the world is constantly being displaced and loses markets as a result of innovations elsewhere. He draws an analogy between the poor and the rich, technologically dynamic countries on the one hand, and the relationship between a servant and an inventive scientist on the other:

> The simple fellow who, to the advantage of both, has been earning a living by cooking the dinner for a busy and prosperous scientist wakes up one day to find that his master has invented a completely automatic cooker, and that if he wants to remain a member of the household he must turn shoeblack. He acquires a kit and learns the technique, only to find that his master has invented a dust-repelling shoe, but would nevertheless be graciously willing for him to remain on and empty the trash-bins. Would he not do better to remove himself from the orbit of the great man, and cultivate his own back-garden? And if he can find some other simple fellows in the same case with whom to gang up and practise the division of labour on a less bewildering basis, so much the better for him.[16]

The technical dynamism of the rich countries affects not only international commodity flows but also factor flows. The conventional theory suggests that, broadly speaking, capital would tend to move from the rich countries to the poor (where its scarcity would ensure a high return) and labour would tend to move from the poor countries to the rich. The equilibrating movements would continue so long as factor rewards differed from one country to another. In practice, however, there is a tendency for factor movements to be disequilibrating and for differences in factor rewards to become wider rather than narrower over time. This too is a consequence of rapid technical progress.

As a result of continuous bursts of innovation, investment opportunities are created and profit rates are maintained at a high level. The innovating and expanding sectors and countries tend to attract capital from areas which are growing less rapidly. In other words, technical progress leads to high profit rates in the rich countries and this in turn causes capital to move out of the poor countries. This tendency for capital to be attracted to the capital-abundant countries and regions rather than to the capital-scarce regions has been noted by many economists, but since the facts conflict with what the conventional theory predicts economists have had to rely on non-economic explanations. 'Capital flight' – the very term suggests that in some sense it is unnatural – has been explained in terms of adverse expectations generated by wars, revolutions and general political instability. I do not wish to deny that such political events can and do influence international capital movements, but the basic explanation lies in the nature of the international economic system. This is a disequilibrium system which creates cumulative movements in economic activity and widening disparities in income, and the fundamental cause of the disequilibrium is the concentration of technological progress in the wealthy economies.

Table 7. Rate of Return on Book Value of U.S. Direct Private Investment in Latin America

	Manufacturing	Petroleum	Total
1951–59	11·0	24·3	14·8
1960–67	10·2	15·5	12·5
1951–67	10·5	18·9	13·4

Note: Earnings are net of local taxes.
Source: U.S. Department of Commerce, *Survey of Current Business*.

Some capital, of course, is attracted to Latin America and the other underdeveloped countries by investment opportunities in particular extractive or manufacturing industries, but the net movement favours the rich countries, or would do so if financial resources could move freely across international boundaries. We have shown above that the net movement of resources is adverse to Latin America (Table 1), that private foreign investment is declining (Table 5), and that most foreign investment is financed from resources generated within Latin America (Table 6). Contrary to what many people believe, the profit rate on foreign investment in Latin America is not high. Moreover, it has been falling. Investment in petroleum and some mining activities has yielded high profits in the past, but profits on investment in manufacturing are modest – even when these are expressed as a percentage of book value rather than the more realistic replacement value.

Conventional international trade theory would predict that savings would flow from developed countries, where they are abundant and hence the return on investment is low, to underdeveloped countries, where savings are scarce and the return on investment is high. The conventional analysis is depicted in the top half of the accompanying diagram, in which the savings curve shifts inwards in the developed country and outwards in the underdeveloped, in response to international capital movements. This process continues until the rate of return is the same in both countries.

In the bottom half of the diagram we present an alternative theory. Technical progress in the developed country shifts the marginal efficiency of investment schedules (I_1) to the right. In the underdeveloped country, however, I_1 may shift to the left. This would occur, for example, if technical progress in sugar-beet production reduced the profitability of extracting sugar from cane. These shifts of the investment schedules raise the profit rate in rich countries and lower it in the poor ones. As a

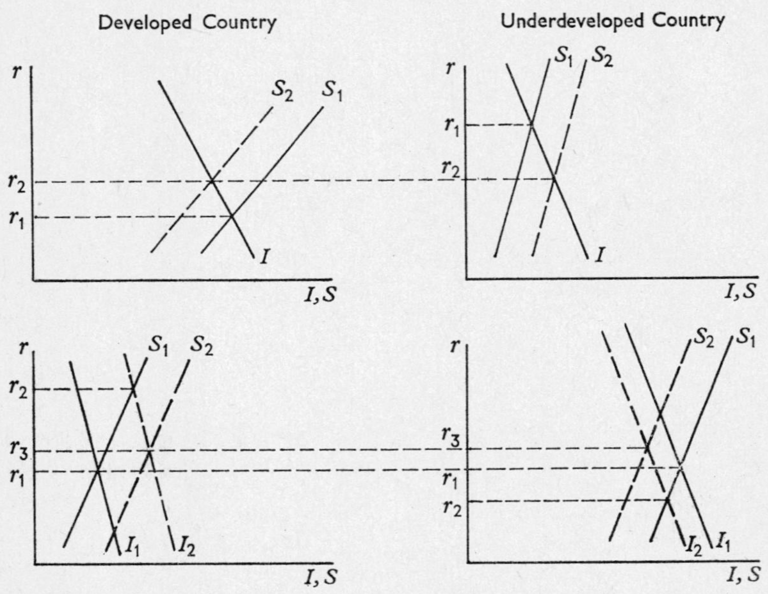

result, savings will tend to flow from the latter to the former, and this will continue until the return on capital is the same in both countries. The international migration of savings in this model is disequilibrating, lowering the level of investment, the capital–labour ratio and the productivity of labour in the poor country and raising them in the rich one.

Thus, in principle, private foreign investment is unlikely to contribute very much to financing development in Latin America, and in practice it has not done so. Indeed, the problem is not to attract foreign savings to the region, but to prevent the region's savings from leaking abroad. Despite capital controls there is evidence that a substantial volume of private Latin American savings is transferred each year to foreign financial centres. For example, the 'errors and omissions' term in Latin America's balance of payments statement has been negative for many years, and appears to be rising. In the period 1946–50 the outflow under errors and omissions was $430 million. In the following five years it rose to $450 million, and in 1956–60 it was $2,100 million. By 1961–5 it had declined somewhat – to $1,500 million – but it was still very substantial. The Economic Commission for Latin America has examined these figures and believes that the errors arise from under-recording of capital movements rather than movements of commodities or services. Their estimate of the total net outflow of private domestic capital from Latin America is $5,000 million over the period 1946–62.[17]

In conclusion, almost all the evidence we have suggests that international movements of capital, whether private or public, are a poor instrument for accelerating development.

NOTES

1. See Chapter 5, Table 3.

2. Several of the models are summarised in R. F. Mikesell, *The Economics of Foreign Aid* (1968), ch. 3.

3. 'Foreign Capital, Domestic Savings and Economic Developments', in *Bulletin of the Oxford University Institute of Economics and Statistics* (May 1970). Much of the material used in the first two sections of this chapter was taken from the above article.

4. Inter-American Committee for the Alliance for Progress, Organisation of American States, *La Brecha Externa de la America Latina 1968–1973* (Washington, Dec 1968), p. 30.

5. 'Coffee and the Economic Development of Colombia', in *Bulletin of the Oxford University Institute of Economics and Statistics* (May 1968), 109–10.

6. Luis Landau, 'Determinants of Savings in Latin America' (Harvard University Project for Quantitative Research in Economic Development, Report no. 13, mimeo., June 1966).

7. Landau rejects this conclusion, claiming that the indirect effects of capital imports on raising incomes may be stronger than the direct effect of capital imports on reducing savings. He provides no evidence to support this hypothesis, however. (Ibid. p. 19.)

8. See Keith Griffin and John Enos, 'Foreign Assistance: Objectives and Consequences', in *Economic Development and Cultural Change* (April 1970).

9. Lester B. Pearson, *Partners in Development* (1969), p. 248. As regards Brazil's experience, the Pearson report might better have been entitled 'Partners in Dictatorship'.

10. Ibid. p. 50.

11. Ibid. p. 101.

12. J. H. Adler (ed.), *Capital Movements and Economic Development* (1967), p. 205.

13. See P. P. Streeten, 'The Contribution of Private Overseas Investment to Development' (Paper presented to the Columbia University Conference on International Economic Development, Feb 1970).

14. A. O. Hirschman, *How to Divest in Latin America, and Why* (Essays in International Finance no. 76, Princeton, Nov 1969), p. 6.

15. Ibid. p. 8.

16. Sir Dennis Robertson, *Britain in the World Economy* (1954), pp. 58–9.

17. ECLA, *External Financing in Latin America* (1965), p. 82.

Notes on Contributors

JORGE ARRATE, Lecturer in Economics at Escolatina, Institute of Economics and Planning, University of Chile; graduate of Escolatina and Harvard; currently doing research on public policy and income redistribution in Chile.

ARTHUR L. DOMIKE, Assistant Co-ordinator, Food and Agricultural Organisation/Inter-American Development Bank Co-operative Programme; formerly F.A.O. Land Tenure Officer in Latin America; graduate of the University of Minnesota; principal author of the CIDA report on *Land Tenure and Agricultural Development in Argentina* (1966).

LUCIO GELLER, Lecturer in Economics and Director of Escolatina, Institute of Economics and Planning, University of Chile; graduate of the University of the Litoral (Argentina) and Escolatina; currently doing research on exchange rate policy and industrialisation in Argentina in the period 1900–30.

KEITH GRIFFIN, Fellow and Tutor in Economics, Magdalen College, Oxford; formerly Visiting Professor, Institute of Economics and Planning, University of Chile; author of *Underdevelopment in Spanish America* (1969) and co-author of *Planning Development* (1970).

TIMOTHY KING, Fellow of Queens' College, Cambridge, and University Lecturer in Economics: at present on leave to the World Bank; graduate of Cambridge and the University of California, Berkeley; author of *Mexico: Industrialization and Trade Policies since 1940* (1970) and co-author of *Regional Economic Development: The River Basin Approach in Mexico*.

ROSEMARY THORP, Lecturer in Economics and member of the Centre for Latin American Studies, University of California, Berkeley; formerly a member of the Institute of Economics and Statistics, Oxford; graduate of Oxford; author of articles on inflation in Argentina and Peru; currently working on a study of agrarian reform in Peru.

LESTER C. THUROW, Associate Professor of Economics, Massachusetts Institute of Technology; formerly Assistant Professor at Harvard; Rhodes Scholar; author of *Poverty and Discrimination* (1969) and editor of *American Fiscal Policy* (1967).

VICTOR TOKMAN, Head of the Chile, Peru and Uruguay Unit, Economic Department of the Pan-American Union; graduate of the University of Rosario, Escolatina and Oxford; author of articles and reports on economic planning, foreign aid and economic development in Latin America; author of a D.Phil. thesis on 'Land Tenure and Socio-Economic Development of the Agricultural Sector in Argentina in the Post-War Period' (1969).

LAURENCE WHITEHEAD, Fellow in Politics, Nuffield College, Oxford; formerly Faculty Fellow at the Latin American Centre of St Antony's College, Oxford; graduate of Oxford; author of *The United States and Bolivia: A Case of Neo-Colonialism* (1969). Currently working on economic policy in Bolivia since 1952.

Select Bibliography

A CONSIDERABLE amount of research on problems of economic development in Latin America has been completed in the last ten years, but so far only a few works of synthesis have appeared. F. Benham and H. A. Holley, *A Short Introduction to the Economy of Latin America* (Oxford University Press for the Royal Institute of International Affairs, reprinted with corrections, 1961) is superficial and out of date. Several major issues, both political and economic, are discussed in A. O. Hirschman (ed.), *Latin American Issues: Essays and Comments* (Twentieth Century Fund, New York, 1961). Keith Griffin, *Underdevelopment in Spanish America* (Allen & Unwin, London, 1969), is up to date and contains a great deal of factual information; the analysis is broadly 'structural' and is concerned primarily with the Spanish-speaking countries of South America. 'Reform-mongering' and the Latin American style of policy-making are the subjects of A. O. Hirschman, *Journeys Toward Progress: Studies of Economic Policy-Making in Latin America* (Twentieth Century Fund, New York, 1963). The studies referred to in the sub-title are of regional planning in north-east Brazil, land reform in Colombia and inflation in Chile. André Gunder Frank, *Capitalism and Underdevelopment in Latin America: Historical Studies of Chile and Brazil*, rev. ed. (Monthly Review Press, New York, 1969) adopts a more radical approach and reaches less optimistic conclusions. C. T. Nisbet (ed.), *Latin America: Problems in Economic Development* (Free Press, Glencoe, Ill., 1969) contains a useful collection of articles reprinted from various journals. The annual United Nations *Economic Survey of Latin America* is a good source of current information and interpretation.

There are several good textbooks on public finance. Perhaps the most widely read is Richard A. Musgrave, *The Theory of Public Finance* (McGraw-Hill, New York, 1959). A new book by Carl Shoup, *Public Finance* (Weidenfeld & Nicolson, London, 1969) is of interest because of the distinction made between consensus criteria and conflict-of-interest criteria and because of the attention given to the tax problems of countries highly dependent on international trade. Another good textbook is A. R. Prest, *Public Finance in Theory and Practice* (Weidenfeld & Nicolson, London, 1967). Few volumes deal with specific problems confronted by underdeveloped countries. The following, however, are worth consulting: Ursula K. Hicks, *Development Finance: Planning and Control* (Oxford University Press, 1965); A. R. Prest, *Public Finance in Underdeveloped Countries* (Weidenfeld & Nicolson, London, 1962); Harley H. Hinrichs, *A General Theory of Tax Structure Change during Economic Development* (Harvard Law School, Cambridge, Mass., 1966). R. J. Chelliah, *Fiscal Policy in Underdeveloped Countries*, 2nd ed. (Allen & Unwin, London, 1970) is primarily concerned with India, but the discussion will be of interest to students of Latin America as well. Contrasts and similarities in rich and poor countries, and in centrally planned and market economies, are the subject of Richard A. Musgrave, *Fiscal Systems* (Yale University Press, New Haven, 1969). This is an excellent book and is certain to become a classic in the literature of comparative economic systems. Specifically concerned with tax reform in Latin America, *Fiscal Policy for Economic Growth in Latin America* (Johns Hopkins Press, Baltimore, 1965) contains the papers and proceedings of a conference held in

Santiago, Chile, in late 1962. This volume is essential reading for those concerned with public policy in Latin America. A useful collection of essays is R. M. Bird and O. Oldman (eds), *Readings on Taxation in Developing Countries* (Johns Hopkins Press, Baltimore, 1966). Additional references to the literature can be found in R. M. Bird and J. M. Teran, (eds), *Bibliography on Taxation in Developing Countries* (International Taxation Programme, Harvard Law School, Cambridge, Mass., 1968).

Many attempts have been made to discover what determines the composition and level of government revenue in the course of economic development. The initial stimulus to this research was provided by W. Arthur Lewis and A. M. Martin, 'Patterns of Public Revenue and Expenditure', in *Manchester School of Economic and Social Studies* (Sept 1956). Several authors have suggested that the relative size of the foreign trade sector plays a crucial role. See in particular J. G. Williamson, 'Public Expenditure and Revenue: An International Comparison', in *Manchester School of Economic and Social Studies* (Jan 1961) and S. R. Lewis, Jr, 'Government Revenue from Foreign Trade: An International Comparison', in *Manchester School of Economic and Social Studies* (Jan 1963). An ambitious but unsuccessful attempt to construct a comprehensive theory has been presented by H. H. Hinrichs. See his *A General Theory of Tax Structure Change During Economic Development* (Harvard Law School, Cambridge, Mass., 1966) and 'Determinants of Government Revenue Shares among Less Developed Countries', in *Economic Journal* (Sept 1965). Hinrichs's views have been criticised by V. Tanzi and C. McCuistion, 'Determinants of Government Revenue Shares among Less-Developed Countries: A Comment', in *Economic Journal* (June 1967), as well as by A. R. Roe, 'The Government Revenue Shares in Poorer African Countries – A Comment', in *Economic Journal* (June 1968). An earlier but still useful article is H. T. Oshima, 'Share of Government in Gross National Product for Various Countries', in *American Economic Review* (June 1957). More recent attempts to explain taxation in underdeveloped countries, which take a variety of factors into account, can be found in R. Thorn, 'The Development of Public Finances During Economic Development', in *Manchester School of Economic and Social Studies* (Jan 1967), and J. R. Lotz and E. R. Morss, 'Measuring Tax Effort in Developing Countries', in *I. M.F. Staff Papers* (1967). For an interesting survey of most of this literature, see R. A. Musgrave, *Fiscal Systems* (Yale University Press, New Haven, 1969), ch. 4.

The Alliance for Progress stressed the need for tax reform. Since the commencement of the programme a great deal of research has been done on the fiscal problems of individual countries. See for example O.A.S., I.D.B. and E.C.L.A. Joint Tax Programme, *Problems of Tax Administration in Latin America* (Johns Hopkins Press, Baltimore, 1965); O.A.S. and I.D.B. Joint Tax Programme, 'Reforma Tributaria en Paraguay' (mimeo., Washington, D.C., June 1966); O.A.S. and I.D.B. Joint Tax Programme, *Estudio Fiscal de Colombia* (Washington, D.C., 1967). Earlier studies include C. S. Shoup *et al.*, *The Fiscal System of Venezuela: A Report* (Johns Hopkins Press, Baltimore, 1959) and J. H. Adler, E. R. Schlesinger and E. C. Olsov, *Public Finance and Economic Development in Guatemala* (Stanford, 1952). The progress achieved is assessed in R. M. Sommerfeld, *Tax Reform and the Alliance for Progress* (University of Texas Press, Austin, 1966) and R. M. Bird and O. Oldman, 'Tax Research and Tax Reform in Latin America, A Survey and Commentary', in *Latin American Research Review* (summer 1968).

It is surprising that so little has been written on the role of the public sector in economic development. One of the best books deals with India: A. H. Hanson, *Public Enterprise and Economic Development*, 2nd ed. (Routledge &

Kegan Paul, London, 1965). Relations between the private and public sectors are discussed in S. A. Mosk, *Industrial Revolution in Mexico* (University of California Press, Berkeley, 1950). Data on the profit and loss position of public enterprises can be found in Andrew Gantt II and Giuseppe Dutto, 'Financial Performance of Government Owned Corporations in Less Developed Countries', in *I.M.F. Staff Papers* (March 1968). Roberto Anguiano Equihua, *Las Finanzas del Sector Público en Mexico* (UNAM, Mexico, 1968) is a rather tedious study of the Mexican case.

Two books sponsored by the World Bank provide an introduction to development banks: W. Diamond, *Development Banks* (Johns Hopkins Press, Baltimore, 1957) and S. Boskey, *Problems and Practices of Development Banks* (Johns Hopkins Press, Baltimore, 1959). The experience of Chile's CORFO is examined in M. Mamalakis, 'An Analysis of the Financial and Investment Activities of the Chilean Development Corporation, 1939–1964', in *Journal of Development Studies* (January 1969), and a more extended analysis by the same author is available in Spanish in Keith Griffin and Eduardo Garcia (eds), *Ensayos Sobre Planificación* (Instituto de Economía y Planificación, Santiago, 1967). Brazil's experience has not been properly studied but some information is available in N. Leff, *Economic Policy-Making and Development in Brazil, 1947–64* (New York, 1968). Mexico's financial system has been studied in considerable detail. A general essay by Javier Marquez draws on this experience: 'Financial Institutions and Economic Development', in H. S. Ellis (ed.), *Economic Development for Latin America* (Macmillan, London, 1961). A more detailed study is D. S. Brothers and M. L. Solis, *Mexican Financial Development* (University of Texas Press, Austin, 1966). Perhaps the most useful discussion, however, is found in C. Blair, 'Nacional Financiera: Entrepreneurship in a Mixed Economy', in R. Vernon (ed.), *Public Policy and Private Enterprise in Mexico* (Harvard University Press, Cambridge, Mass., 1964).

Most of the work on social security systems in underdeveloped countries has been done by the international agencies. Particularly helpful are two articles by F. Reviglio published in the 1967 *I.M.F. Staff Papers*: 'The Social Security System and its Financing in Developing Countries', and 'Social Security: A Means of Savings Mobilization for Economic Development'. The I.B.R.D. report *Financial Aspects of Social Security in Latin America* (Washington, 1962) is a basic document. ILO, *The Cost of Social Security, Sixth International Enquiry 1961–3* (Geneva, 1967) contains data which are analysed in Felix Paukert, 'Social Security and Income Redistribution', in *International Labour Review* (Nov 1968). Some information on Chile can be found in Juan Braun, 'Algunas Sugerencias para Reformar el Sistema Previsional en Chile', in Keith Griffin and Eduardo Garcia (eds), *Ensayos Sobre Planificación* (Instituto de Economía y Planificación, Santiago, 1967). In general it seems clear that a great deal more research is needed on the role of social security systems in underdeveloped countries.

Agriculture, although the largest sector in most underdeveloped countries, usually is taxed relatively lightly. In countries where the *latifundia* system prevails the reason for this is political – the ability of large landlords to block tax legislation and frustrate revenue collection. In countries and regions where large numbers of small holdings prevail it is difficult to tax agriculture for administrative reasons, unless farm output is exported and can be taxed at the ports. Despite the obstacles, most writers agree that agricultural taxation can make an important contribution to development. The best book on the subject is H. P. Wald, *Taxation of Agricultural Land in Underdeveloped Economies* (Harvard University Press, Cambridge, Mass., 1959). Several useful essays are printed in H. P. Wald and J. N. Froomkin (eds), *Agricultural Taxation and Economic Development* (Harvard Law School, Cambridge, Mass., 1954). See in particular W. W. Heller, 'A Survey of Agricultural Taxation and Economic Development', and Philip Raup, 'Agricultural Taxation and Land Tenure Reform in Underdeveloped Countries'. Part v of R. M. Bird and O. Oldman (eds), *Readings on Taxation in Developing Countries* (Johns Hopkins Press, Baltimore, 1965) also should be consulted. Somewhat more recent is the well-written survey by S. R. Lewis, Jr, 'Taxation of Agriculture and Economic Development', in H. M. Southworth and B. F. Johnston (eds), *Agricultural Development and Economic Growth* (Cornell University Press, Ithaca, 1967). A remarkable study of the way taxation in Mexico is used to squeeze the poor peasants to finance industry is Salomon Eckstein, *El Marco Macro-Económico del Problema Agrario Mexicano* (Centro de Investigaciones Agrarias, Mexico, 1968).

Professor Kaldor has suggested that the land tax be based on potential rather than actual yields and also that the land tax be progressive. See his 'The Role of Taxation in Economic Development' and 'Will Underdeveloped Countries Learn to Tax?', in *Essays on Economic Policy*, i (Duckworth, London, 1965). Professor Harberger advocates a system of self-assessment for land taxes combined with a requirement that the owner must sell at his declared value. See A. Harberger, 'Issues of Tax Reform for Latin America', in *Fiscal Policy for Economic Growth in Latin America* (Johns Hopkins Press, Baltimore, 1965). Criticisms of this scheme are discussed and a slightly modified version is presented by John Strasma, *Market-Enforced Self-Assessment for Property Taxes* (Land Tenure Centre, University of Wisconsin, Madison, 1965). An interesting case study of the effects of land taxation is L. Harland-Davis, *Economics of the Property Tax in Rural Areas of Colombia* (Research Report no. 25, Land Tenure Centre, University of Wisconsin, Madison, 1967).

Very little is known about the determinants of savings in underdeveloped countries. It is commonly believed that the proportion of national income saved rises along with the level of *per capita* income. Empirical research, however, suggests that if this tendency exists at all, it is very weak. There is not much evidence that rich countries save markedly more than poor or that the aggregate or private savings ratio rises over time as income per head increases. See S. Kuznets, 'Quantitative Aspects of the Economic Growth of Nations, V, Capital Formation Proportions: International Comparisons for Recent Years', in *Economic Development and Cultural Change* (July 1960), pt ii; S. Kuznets, 'Quantitative Aspects of the Economic Growth of Nations, VII, The Share and Structure of Consumption', in *Economic Development and Cultural Change* (January 1962), pt ii. H. S. Houthakker, using regression analysis, obtains results similar to those of Kuznets: H. S. Houthakker, 'On Some Determinants of Saving in Developed and Underdeveloped Countries', in E. A. G. Robinson (ed.), *Problems in Economic Development* (Macmillan, London, 1965); H. S. Houthakker, 'An International Comparison of Personal Savings', in *Proceedings of the 32nd Session of the International Statistical Institute* (1961). The best econometric work on savings in Latin America has been done by L. Landau. See his 'Determinants of Savings in Latin America' (Harvard University Project for Quantitative Research in Economic Development, Report no. 13, mimeo., 1966) and 'Differences in Savings Ratios among Latin American Countries' (Ph.D. thesis, Harvard, 1969).

There is some evidence from cross-section data that urbanisation and industrialisation are associated with higher savings. A study of Brazil, however, casts some doubt on this proposition: N. H. Leff, 'Marginal Savings Rates in the

Development Process: The Brazilian Experience', in *Economic Journal* (Sept 1968). The distribution of income often is assumed to affect the savings ratio, i.e. the greater the inequality the higher the savings rate. Kuznets, on the other hand, implies that in some underdeveloped countries the upper income groups may have a higher marginal propensity to consume and, hence, changes in the distribution of income would have negligible effects on the rate of savings: 'Economic Growth and Income Inequality', in *American Economic Review* (March 1955). A study of Mexico, in fact, showed that savings rose when inequality declined: A. Sturmthal, 'Economic Development, Income Distribution and Capital Formation in Mexico', in *Journal of Political Economy* (June 1955). Another study of Chile showed that the savings propensity of twenty *latifundistas* in the Central Valley was remarkably low: M. J. Sternberg, 'Chilean Land Tenure and Land Reform' (Ph.D. thesis, University of California, Berkeley, 1962). Sternberg's thesis can be used as partial confirmation of Kaldor's hypothesis that the propensity to consume of the capitalist class in Chile is remarkably high. See N. Kaldor, 'Economic Problems of Chile', in *Essays on Economic Policy*, (Duckworth, London, 1965). Other investigations in Asia, in contrast, have demonstrated that small peasants may save a surprisingly large fraction of their income. See, for example, P. K. G. Panikar, 'Rural Savings in India', in *Economic Development and Cultural Change* (1961–2) and A. Bergan, 'Personal Income Distribution and Personal Savings in Pakistan, 1963–64', in *Pakistan Development Review* (summer 1967). One can conclude tentatively, I believe, that landless agricultural workers and the industrial proletariat are unlikely to save, but that property owners – even small peasants and shopkeepers – are likely to save a significant proportion of their income. In other words, in capitalist countries personal savings are influenced more by the class composition of society than by the level of *per capita* income or its distribution.

The literature on inflation in Latin America is vast, and most of it has centred around the controversy between the 'structuralists' and the 'monetarists'. An early and important statement of the structuralist position is O. Sunkel, 'Inflation in Chile: An Unorthodox Approach', in *International Economic Papers*, no. 10 (1960). R. Prebisch's views are presented in 'Economic Development or Monetary Stability: The False Dilemma', in *Economic Bulletin for Latin America* (Mar 1961). Dudley Seers has constructed a structuralist-type model which emphasises the role of a slowly growing export sector: 'A Theory of Inflation and Growth in Underdeveloped Economies Based on the Experience of Latin America', in *Oxford Economic Papers* (June 1962). The importance of inadequate domestic savings is stressed in Keith Griffin, *Underdevelopment in Spanish America* (Allen & Unwin, London, 1969), ch. v. The views of the Economic Commission for Latin America are well presented in a paper by Dudley Seers entitled 'Inflation and Growth: A Summary of Experience in Latin America', in *Economic Bulletin for Latin America* (February 1962). Also see J. H. G. Olivera, 'On Structural Inflation and Latin American Structuralism', in *Oxford Economic Papers* (Nov 1964).

Two surveys of the controversy are contained in A. O. Hirschman (ed.), *Latin American Issues* (Twentieth Century Fund, New York, 1961): Roberto de Oliveira Campos, 'Two Views of Inflation in Latin America', and David Felix, 'An Alternative View of the "Monetarist" – "Structuralist" Controversy'. The 1963 conference in Rio on inflation in Latin America included representatives of both schools of thought, but the outcome was disappointing nevertheless. The best paper was the 'Closing Remarks' by Arthur Lewis and this has been published, along with the other conference documents, in W. Baer and I.

Kerstenetsky (eds), *Inflation and Growth in Latin America* (Irwin, Homewood, Ill., 1964).

The 'monetarist' views are usually found in the corridors of the International Monetary Fund. The following essays by two outsiders should be consulted, however: Roberto de Oliveira Campos, 'Inflation and Balanced Growth', in H. S. Ellis (ed.), *Economic Development for Latin America* (Macmillan, London, 1961), and Eugenio Gudin, 'Inflation in Latin America', in D. C. Hague (ed.), *Inflation* (Macmillan, London, 1962). An impression of the attitudes of the Fund can be obtained by reading the *I.M.F. Staff Papers*. Three articles in that journal merit special attention: J. Keith Horsefield, 'Inflation in Latin America', in *I.M.F. Staff Papers* (Sept 1950); Graeme Dorrance, 'The Effects of Inflation on Economic Development', in *I.M.F. Staff Papers* (1963); Gertrude Lovasy, 'Inflation and Exports in Primary Producing Countries', in *I.M.F. Staff Papers* (Mar 1962). These articles are criticised by H. Aaron, 'Structuralism versus Monetarism: A Note on Evidence', in *Journal of Development Studies* (Jan 1967).

It is difficult to assess the merits of the various competing approaches without some knowledge of conditions in particular countries. The structural approach was born in Chile. In addition to the previously mentioned article by Osvaldo Sunkel, an essay by Joseph Grunwald deserves close study: 'The "Structuralist" School on Price Stability and Development: The Chilean Case', in A. O. Hirschman (ed.), *Latin American Issues* (Twentieth Century Fund, New York, 1961). Those who read Spanish should also see Anibal Pinto, *Chile – Un Caso de Desarrollo Frustrado* (Editorial Universitaria, Santiago, 1962). Useful historical perspective can be obtained in A. O. Hirschman, *Journeys Toward Progress* (Twentieth Century Fund, New York, 1963), ch. 3. Another historical survey is Tom Davis, 'Eight Decades of Inflation in Chile, 1879–1959: A Political Interpretation', in *Journal of Political Economy* (Aug 1963).

Eprime Eshag and Rosemary Thorp have published a useful analysis of postwar anti-inflation policy in Argentina: 'The Economic and Social Consequences of Orthodox Policies in Argentina in the Postwar Years', in *Bulletin of the Oxford University Institute of Economics and Statistics* (Feb 1965). The Harvard Development Advisory Service had a team in Argentina working for the government. The view of two members of the team are published as G. Maynard and W. Van Rijckeghem, 'Stabilization Policy in an Inflationary Economy: Argentina', in G. Papanek (ed.), *Development Policy: Theory and Practice* (Harvard University Press, Cambridge, 1968). The essay is a good example of the technologist's approach to inflation, but the authors never come to grips with the basic social and political problems which lie behind the phenomenon of rising prices.

Monetarists often cite Peru as an example of a successful orthodox stabilisation programme. For a contrary opinion, see Rosemary Thorp, 'Inflation and Orthodox Economic Policy in Peru', in *Bulletin of the Oxford University Institute of Economics and Statistics* (Aug 1967). Relatively little is available in English about the Bolivian inflation. There is, however, one lengthy account written by an American who was largely responsible for designing the stabilisation programme: George Jackson Eder, *Inflation and Development in Latin America: A Case Study of Inflation and Stabilization in Bolivia* (Michigan University Press, Ann Arbor, 1968).

Most of the writing in English on the Brazilian inflation has been by Celso Furtado and Werner Baer, and both of these men have been influenced by the structuralist tradition. See Celso Furtado, *The Economic Growth of Brazil* (University of California Press, Berkeley, 1963) ch. 35; also by the same author are *Development and Underdevelopment* (University of California Press, Berkeley, 1964), ch. 6, and *Diagnosis of the Brazilian Crisis* (University of California Press, Berkeley, 1965), ch. 8. Furtado's views are criticised by D. Huddle, 'Furtado on Exchange Control and Economic Development: An Evaluation and Reinterpretation of the Brazilian Case', in *Economic Development and Cultural Change* (April 1967). Werner Baer, like Furtado, believes that inflation redistributed income in favour of savings, promoted industrialisation and accelerated growth. See W. Baer, *Industrialization and Economic Development in Brazil* (Irwin, Homewood, Ill., 1965). This book is criticised at length by D. Huddle, 'The Brazilian Industrialization – Sources, Patterns and Policy Mix', in *Economic Development and Cultural Change* (July 1967). Also see two articles by Baer: 'Inflation and Economic Growth: An Interpretation of the Brazilian Case', in *Economic Development and Cultural Change* (Oct 1962), and 'Brazil: Inflation and Economic Efficiency', in *Economic Development and Cultural Change* (July 1963). A. P. Ruderman and Baer exchange brief comments in the April 1964 issue of the same journal. Recent anti-inflation policy is discussed by A. Kafka, 'The Brazilian Stabilization Program, 1964–66', in *Journal of Political Economy* (Aug 1967). E. S. Shaw has a 'Comment' on this article in the same issue, in which he stresses the importance of maintaining control over the supply of money. The best non-structuralist study of Brazil, however, is by R. Kahil, *Inflation and Economic Development in Brazil* (Oxford University Press, forthcoming 1971).

Foreign aid is the object of considerable discussion and controversy. There are many reasons for this. Recipient countries hope that massive foreign assistance will enable development to proceed swiftly and painlessly. Taxpayers in donor countries wish to reduce the fiscal burden and insist that aid be justified in terms of national interest. Critics on the left claim that aid is merely another tool of neocolonialism which tends to retard social and economic progress. The conventional view in favour of aid is ably presented in Lester B. Pearson, *Partners in Development, Report of the Commission on International Development* (Pall Mall Press, London, 1969). Pearson was chairman of a commission set up by the World Bank which was asked to study the effects of foreign aid in the last twenty years and make recommendations for the future. The report mentions everything in passing and makes no original contributions, but it does represent liberal opinion in capitalist countries.

The intellectual origins of the views expressed in the Pearson report go back to an article by Paul Rosenstein-Rodan: 'International Aid for Underdeveloped Countries', in *Review of Economics and Statistics* (May 1961). Since that article appeared a large number of models have been constructed which attempt to illustrate the role of capital imports in economic development. A simple model is that of R. J. Ball, 'Capital Imports and Economic Development: Paradoxy or Orthodoxy?', in *Kyklos* (1962). A series of arithmetical examples is provided in Sir Roy Harrod, 'Desirable International Movements of Capital in Relation to Growth of Borrowers and Lenders and Growth of Markets', in R. F. Harrod and D. Hague (eds), *International Trade Theory in a Developing World* (Macmillan, London, 1964). Professor Chenery's 'two-gap' model is, perhaps, the most frequently cited. See H. B. Chenery and A. M. Strout, 'Foreign Assistance and Economic Development', in *American Economic Review* (Sept 1966), and additional references to Professor Chenery's work in the bibliography to this article. Some writers stress the foreign exchange bottleneck. See for example R. Mackinnon, 'Foreign Exchange Constraints in Economic Development and Efficient Aid Allocation', in *Economic Journal* (June 1964). The best textbook is R. F. Mikesell, *The Economics of Foreign Aid* (Weidenfeld & Nicolson,

London, 1968). In addition, J. H. Adler (ed.), *Capital Movements and Economic Development* (Macmillan, London, 1967) is quite useful.

There are, of course, critics of foreign aid. Mahbub ul Haq has called attention to the high cost of tied aid: 'Tied Credits: A Quantitative Analysis', in J. H. Alder (ed.), *Capital Movements and Economic Development* (Macmillan, London, 1967). Several writers have become concerned about the problem of servicing foreign loans. See in particular G. Ohlin, *Aid and Indebtedness* (O.E.C.D., Paris, 1966); P. Lieftinck, *External Debt and Debt-Bearing Capacity of Developing Countries* (Essays in International Finance, Princeton, March 1966); D. Avramovic *et al.*, *Economic Growth and External Debt* (I.B.R.D., 1964).

K. Berrill has argued that historically foreign capital has contributed very little towards helping a country 'take off': 'Foreign Capital and Take-Off', in W. W. Rostow (ed.), *The Economics of Take-Off into Sustained Growth* (Macmillan, London, 1964). Hans Singer, 'The Distribution of Gains between Investing and Borrowing Countries', in *American Economic Review* (May 1950), argues that most of the benefits of international capital movements accrue to the lender, not the borrower. Griffin and Enos claim that in general there is no association between the amount of aid a country receives and its rate of growth: Keith Griffin and John Enos, 'Foreign Assistance: Objectives and Consequences', in *Economic Development and Cultural Change* (April 1970). In Latin America, moreover, capital imports appear to have had the effect of lowering domestic savings and perhaps raising the incremental capital–output ratio. See Keith Griffin, *Underdevelopment in Spanish America* (Allen & Unwin, London, 1969), ch. iii; and, by the same author, 'Foreign Capital, Domestic Savings and Economic Development', in *Bulletin of the Oxford University Institute of Economics and Statistics* (May 1970).

Most economists still believe that private foreign investment can make a substantial contribution to development. The majority opinion is well presented in C. P. Kindleberger, *American Business Abroad* (Yale University Press, New Haven, 1969). Others see many disadvantages to direct private investment but believe that on balance it is necessary. See for example V. Urquidi, 'Some Implications of Foreign Investment for Latin America', in C. Veliz (ed.), *Obstacles to Change in Latin America* (Oxford University Press, 1965). Mrs Penrose, in a detailed study of the petroleum industry, has shown how large, vertically integrated corporations can manipulate internal transfer prices so as to reduce the amount of taxes they must pay to the government of the producing country. Her book deserves careful study: Edith T. Penrose, *The Large International Firm in Developing Countries* (Allen & Unwin, London, 1968). Some critics of private overseas investment favour reforms which would increase the bargaining power of the small underdeveloped countries: Dudley Seers, 'Big Companies and Small Countries: A Practical Proposal', in *Kyklos* (1963). Others may favour nationalisation or confiscation. See for example M. Bronfenbrenner, 'The Appeal of Confiscation in Economic Development', in *Economic Development and Cultural Change* (April 1955), and discussion in the same journal in July 1963 and July 1964; A. O. Hirschman, *How to Divest in Latin America, and Why* (Essays in International Finance no. 76, Princeton, Nov 1969); A. G. Frank, *Capitalism and Underdevelopment in Latin America*, 2nd ed. (Monthly Review Press, New York, 1969), ch. v. An interesting presentation of many of the issues is contained in L. Whitehead, 'Aid to Latin America', to be published by Columbia University Press as part of the papers and proceedings of the February 1970 conference on the Pearson report.

Index

Aaron, H., 251
Abraham, W. I., 166, 180 n
Adler, J. H., 243 n, 247, 253
Agriculture, 33–4, 63, 113–14, 186, 187, 189, 192, 197, 200, 208, 209, 210, 213; development strategy in, 114–16; in colonial period, 2; priorities, 116–19; resource requirements for development, 122–8; significance of, 117–19; taxation of, 18, 40–3, 46, 113, 125, 130–42, 147–8. *See also* Food; Land
Aizenstat, A. J., 138 t
Alejandro, Carlos Diaz, 80 t, 174, 181 n, 202, 220 n, 233 n
Aranda, Sergio, 118
Argentina, 5, 6, 9, 13, 18, 21, 31, 61, 65 67, 75, 87, 94, 95, 103, 121, 122, 139, 140, 141, 142, 157, 158, 183, 197, 201, 202, 204, 205, 215, 217; savings in, 168–9, 174, 214; stabilisation programmes, 205–6
Armed forces, 13, 29, 36–7, 59, 62, 63, 121
Arrate, Jorge, 51, 245
Arriola, J. I., 135 t
Australia, 42
Avramovic, D., 253

Baer, W., 200, 209, 216, 217, 219 n, 220 n, 233 n, 224 n, 250, 215, 252
Baerrensen, D., 135 t
Balance of payments, 30–1, 38–9, 215, 217–18; and inflation, 213
Ball, R. J., 252
Balogh, T., 200, 219 n
Baraona, Rafael, 23 n
Barraclough, Solon, 116, 117, 148 n, 149 n, 219 n, 223 n

Becker, Arthur, 151 n
Benham, F., 246
Bergan, A., 250
Bergsman, J., 219 n, 224 n
Berrill, K., 253
Bertini, Jorge, 71 n
Bettleheim, Charles, 71 n
Bird, R. M., 150 n, 247, 249
Blair, Calvin, 105 t, 106, 112 n, 248
Bolivia, 13, 14, 15, 31, 61, 75, 79, 87, 120, 122, 127, 133, 134, 135, 136, 183, 203, 218; stabilisation programme, 206–7
Boskey, S., 248
Boulding, Kenneth E., 15, 24 n
Braun, Juan, 111 n, 248
Bray, J. O., 202, 219 n
Brazil, 6, 13, 21, 37, 65, 67, 75, 79, 85, 86, 87, 94, 103, 120, 137, 138, 161, 201, 203, 207, 214, 215, 216, 217, 232; B.N.D.E., 104–8; foreign aid, 233–4; inflation in, 191, 198, 199, 200, 209–10; public enterprises in, 79–84; savings in, 10, 164, 229; slavery in, 2; surplus in, 8
Brodersohn, M., 220 n, 223 n
Bronfenbrenner, M., 253
Brothers, D. S., 248
Brumberg, R. E., 171, 172, 180 n
Bruton, Henry, 6, 23 n
Bureaucracy, 60
Burma, 9

Campos, R. de Olivera, 219 n, 250, 251
Canada, 42
Carrasco, G., 150 n, 151 n
Carroll, T. F., 149 n
Carvalho, E. P. de, 220 n
Castro, J. de, 148 n

Savings, 2, 4, 30, 47, 54, 70, 84, 126, 129, 189, 209, 214, 218, 228; and dependency ratio, 172–3; and exports, 163–4; and income, 9–10, 159–61, 161–4, 166–7, 179; and income distribution, 10–12, 153, 168, 179; and interest rates, 160, 169, 170, 171, 211–12, 214–15; and investment incentives, 176–9; and rate of growth, 171–2; from social security funds, 91–100; measurement of, 155–61; of households, 159, 166, 167–73; private savings, 66, 152–79, 230; propensity, 162, 168, 169, 174, 195, 201; public savings, 18–19, 158, 230; transfer abroad, 242–3

Schatan, Jacobo, 148 n

Schlesinger, E. R., 247

Schultz, T. W., 202, 221 n

Schwartzman, D., 23 n

Seers, D., 187, 200, 203, 204, 221 n, 223 n, 250, 253

Shaalan, A. S., 212, 216, 217, 222 n

Shaw, E. S., 252

Shoup, Carl S., 25 n, 241 t, 246

Siegel, B. N., 222 n, 224 n

Sierra, E., 202, 211, 218, 222 n, 223 n, 224 n

Simonsen, M., 191, 216, 222 n, 224 n

Singer, H. W., 223 n, 253

Slavery, 2

Slawinsky, Sigmundt, 71 n

Smith, S., 150 n

Smitter, Philippe, 148 n

Social security, 60, 63, 70, 109; and private savings, 102; and public savings, 91–100; beneficiaries of, 96, 97, 100–1; investments financed, 101–4

Solis, M. L., 208, 209, 222 n, 223 n, 224 n, 248

Sommerfeld, R. M., 247

Southworth, H. M., 149 n, 150 n, 249

Spain, 2

State enterprise, 16, 18, 53, 86–91, 234; in Brazil, 79–84; in Mexico, 84–6; pricing policy of, 73, 75–7, 88 ff, 108–9, 192, 193, 213; profitability of, 75–7, 88 ff; role in development, 73–8

Sternberg, Marvin, 11, 24 n, 149 n, 175, 181 n, 250

Strasma, John, 148 n, 150 n, 151 n, 249

Streeten, P. P., 24 n, 244 n

Strout, A. M., 150 n, 252

Sturmthal, A., 11, 24 n, 177, 181 n, 250

Sunkel, O., 185, 188, 189, 190, 202, 218, 222 n, 223 n, 250, 251

Surplus, 2, 3, 4, 5, 12, 19, 52, 53, 54, 55, 56, 58, 63, 64, 65, 68, 69, 70, 82, 129; definition of, 52–3; uses of, 8, 53

Taiwan, 42

Tanzi, V., 247

Tariffs, 18, 66, 67, 70, 131, 192

Taubman, P., 168, 180 n

Tavares, Maria C., 71 n

Taxation, 2, 15, 23, 30, 37, 43–7, 51 f, 52, 55, 56, 62, 65, 66, 67, 68, 71, 74, 188, 190, 192, 193, 197, 198, 200, 209; and development strategy, 40–3, 131–2; burden of, 16–17, 21–2, 132–3; collection of, 58; direct taxation, 15, 17, 45–6, 65, 70, 159; elasticity of, 16, 18, 189; foreign trade taxes, 43, 44, 185; indirect taxation, 16–17, 46, 66, 67, 157; limitations of, 69; progressiveness of, 15–18; tax policy, 63, 64, 66, 70. *See also* Agriculture, taxation; Tariffs

Taylor, L. D., 169, 170, 179 n, 180 n

Technical progress, 43, 202, 213, 216–17; and capital flows, 239

Teran, J. M., 247

Ternent, J., 199, 200, 214, 222 n

Thorn, Richard, 71 n, 247

Thornbecke, E., 135 t